Metro CHICAGO POLITICAL Atlas '97-'98

James H. Lewis, PhD
Chicago Urban League

D. Garth Taylor, PhD
Metro Chicago Information Center

Paul Kleppner, PhD
Northern Illinois University

THE INSTITUTE FOR PUBLIC AFFAIRS

University of Illinois at Springfield
Springfield, Illinois

Library of Congress Catalog-in-Publication Data

Lewis, James H., 1956-
    Metro Chicago political atlas: '97-'98 / James H. Lewis, D. Garth
Taylor, Paul Kleppner.
        p.   cm.
    Shows ethinic/racial voting patterns and registration, from 1983
through 1996, including statistics, analysis, and redistricting.
    Rev. ed. of: Metro Chicago political atlas—1994. c1994.
    ISBN 0-938943-13-8 (pbk)
    1. Elections—Illinois—Chicago Region—Maps. 2. Elections—
Illinois—Chicago Region—Statistics. 3. Election districts—
Illinois—Chicago Region —Maps. I. Taylor, D. Garth.
II. Kleppner, Paul. III. Metro Chicago political atlas—1994.
IV. Title.
G1409.C6F9 M4   1997 <G&M>
324.7'8'0977311022—DC21   97-19199
                                     CIP
                                    MAPS

ISBN: 0-938943-13-8
ISSN: 1092-0870

Text and Cover Designer: Michelle Sutphin
Illustrators: Jason R. Pestine and Michelle Sutphin
Printer: United Graphics

Printed in the United States of America

10 9 8 7 6 5 4 3 2 1

The Institute for Public Affairs
Publication Unit
University of Illinois at Springfield
Springfield, IL 62794-9243

Phone: 217-786-6502
Fax: 217-786-6246

e-mail: whelpley.rodd@uis.edu
Web site: http://www.uis.edu/~ipapu/ipapu.html

CONTENTS

LIST OF MAPS

Acknowledgments

The authors would like to thank a number of individuals without whose outstanding efforts this book would not have been completed.

Jason Pestine of MCIC produced maps included in this volume. Kenneth Hahn and Madhusudan Karody of Northern Illinois University provided analysis of voting data. Cynthia Jordon-Hubbard of the Chicago Urban League assisted with data collection.

At the Institute for Public Affairs, Michelle Sutphin designed the volume, Jackie Wright and Kim Allen assisted with project management and Rodd Whelpley provided invaluable assistance as general editor and manager of the project.

Introduction

Introduction

Despite having world renowned art collections, symphony, and opera, Chicago has never pretended to be a genteel, sophisticated city. It has never contested Boston's reputation as the "Athens of America," the country's center of high culture and quiet refinement. Instead, it has been content to be described in Carl Sandburg's pithy but unglamorous phrases as the "hog butcher to the world," the city of the "big shoulders."

For most of its past, Chicago was a place where the foul odors of manufacturing plants and slaughterhouses mixed together and polluted the air. Its lakefront was always stunningly attractive, but otherwise the city was ugly and depressing, a motley mix of overcrowded and aging neighborhoods interspersed with industrial sites. Its civic image matched this physical appearance. Chicago was reputed to be a town inhabited by a tough, brawling people, a place where public corruption outstripped civic virtue. While Boston, New York, and Philadelphia could tout the humanitarian and civic accomplishments of their prominent residents, Alphonse Capone personified Chicago's civic image, and the St. Valentine's Day Massacre became its best-remembered event. In the popular mind, criminal violence became an integral part of Chicago's general reputation for toughness and corruption, a reputation to which the city's politics made its own distinctive contribution.

"Sure, politics aint bean-bags," Mr. Dooley concluded, explaining how one Billy O'Brien had held his own all these years in Chicago's 6th Ward. "He done dumb-bell exercises with a beer kag in wan hand an' a German polisman in the' other....The people up here like spirit," the loquacious Irish barkeep went on, summing up the essence of turn-of-the-century Chicago politics.[1] Mr. Dooley's remark, including its use of ethnic stereotypes, said a great deal about Chicago's politics. Election contests were bruising, no-holds-barred events because they pitted rival sets of ethnic groups and neighborhoods against each other. In Mr. Dooley's day, and only slightly less so in ours, politics focused on ethnicity and ethnic rivalries, with elections involving the mobilization of whole neighborhoods.

As in other American cities that recruited their labor forces from Europe during the late-nineteenth century, newcomers to Chicago established their own ethnic neighborhoods and networks of social relations. Subsequent involvement in the ethnically exclusive infrastructure of secondary institutions that inevitably grew up in these areas (e.g., churches, church societies, parochial schools, ethnic clubs, and benevolent societies) then worked to reinforce the individual's identity both with the group and the neighborhood. Through such a process, Chicago became a "city of neighborhoods," a place distinguished by identifiable concentrations of ethnic and racial groups.[2]

Introduction

Most Chicagoans, including its public officeholders, have proudly proclaimed that heritage. In 1976 the Chicago Department of Development and Planning published *Historic City—The Settlement of Chicago.* This volume, the city's own overview of its history, gave graphic testimony to the importance of its ethnic groups and their links to particular neighborhoods by depicting the pattern of their settlement over time. A series of large foldout maps show the pattern of ethnic group settlement in 1840, 1860, 1870, 1900, 1920, and 1950. As Andrew Greeley, a native Chicagoan and eminent sociologist, observed in the publication's foreward: "The neighborhoods *are* Chicago....Chicagoan or visitor, local or cosmopolitan—if you don't know the neighborhoods, you don't know the city." [3]

That sentiment holds today: Unless you know the neighborhoods, you can't understand Chicago politics. The city's long-standing ward-based system for electing aldermen and delivering city services has cemented the link between neighborhoods and political representation. As a result, election contests, especially for local offices, have frequently taken on the character of all-or-nothing battles to preserve the neighborhood. In recent decades, these battles have been fought along racial lines, as whites especially have resisted integrating their neighborhoods, their schools, or their workplaces.

The drama and occasional humor associated with Chicago's political battles have long made them interesting to political pundits. The underlying social dimension reflected in the city's election battles—the way racial and ethnic identities still resonate to mobilize whole neighborhoods—gives them much larger significance. The maps and statistics contained in this edition of the *Metro Chicago Political Atlas* show you that side of the city's politics. They also reflect the shape of political contests in the suburbs of Cook County and in the collar counties—DuPage, Kane, Lake, McHenry, and Will. Earlier in this century, analysts could pretty much explain politics in Illinois by noticing what was happening in Chicago, where most of the state's voting age population resided. But demographic trends since the end of World War II have reduced Chicago's "clout" both within the state and the metropolitan region. For that reason alone, it is important to see how the suburbs respond politically, especially since many of them are now undergoing the sorts of demographic transitions that Chicago experienced in the 1950s and 1960s.

The Political Atlas: What's in it for You?

This edition of the *Metro Chicago Political Atlas* explores the area's neighborhoods, racial/ethnic groups, and politics in several ways.

- **Chapter 1 The Political Environment** provides summary data describing the context in which elections take place. It offers a historical view of how the voting age population has been distributed between Chicago and its suburbs, the racial and ethnic composition of the city's voting age population, the numbers of people registered to vote, and the turnout rates for various elections. This chapter also looks at the significance of the most recent change in the "rules of the game"—i.e., the elimination of one-punch, straight-ticket voting in Illinois.

- **Chapter 2 Results from Recent Elections** reports the outcomes of the major 1994, 1995, and 1996 elections not covered in earlier editions of the *Metro Chicago Political Atlas*. In addition to racial and ethnic rates of turnout and breakdowns of the votes for candidates, chapter 2 includes maps showing the areas of candidate support and analyses of the factors that worked to produce election outcomes. For some offices, the results from the previous election are reported for comparative purposes, and for mayor of Chicago the results are mapped and analyzed since 1983.

- **Chapter 3 Republicans in Chicago** looks at Republican identifiers: where Republicans are in the city, who they are socially, and what positions they have on a range of issues. It also examines a number of elections, showing the races in which Republicans typically fare best and from which parts of the city their votes come. The results suggest ways that Chicago Republicans might rebuild to become competitive in the city.

- **Chapter 4 White Ethnicity in Chicago Politics** looks at the voting behavior of predominantly Irish and Polish communities. It shows the staying power of these ethnic identifications and their continuing relevance to understanding Chicago politics.

- **Chapter 5 Chicago's Registration Numbers: Facts or Fantasies?** offers a detailed examination of registration patterns in the city. It analyzes the registration numbers before and after the Chicago Board of Elections Commissioners' much-heralded 1995 canvass designed to eliminate duplicate and spurious registrations. Despite that effort, the current numbers remain inflated, especially in African-American wards that lack strong ward organizations.

- **Chapter 6 Financing Chicago Elections** shows where the money came from for the 1995 city council and mayoral elections. It uses zip code maps to show the sources of individual and business contributions to these election efforts.

Introduction

Chicago's Ward Groups

- **Chapter 7 Partisan Alignments in the Illinois State Legislature** examines the stunning Republican victory in state legislative contests in 1994 and the 1996 rebound that enabled Democrats to take control of the lower house of the Illinois legislature.

Chicago's Ward Groups

Before turning to these chapters, it is helpful to notice how this edition of the *Metro Chicago Political Atlas* organizes and presents voting information for Chicago. The 1992 and 1994 editions presented Chicago's election returns for each of eight "political areas" of the city. Each of these political areas consisted of a group of *precincts* that shared a common racial or ethnic composition as indicated by 1990 census figures. These precinct groups, or political areas, often cut across ward lines and conventional neighborhood definitions. Since the analysis indicated that the city's politics continued to pivot around race and ethnicity, grouping the precincts to overlay these fault lines seemed to be an informative way to present and map voting returns.

But some users of those previous editions found the "political areas" to be less useful and informative than we intended them to be. They suggested that the '97-'98 edition revert to the practice of the first edition in 1990— i.e., that it use groups of *wards* as the primary units for reporting and mapping Chicago voting returns. We were happy to comply. After all, Chicago prides itself on remaining a "city of neighborhoods," and most of its residents are more likely to be able to name their alderman than their congressional representative or U.S. senator. Therefore, in keeping with the culture of the city, nearly all the illustrative maps and tables in this text use eight groups of wards as the primary units for reporting and mapping Chicago voting returns.

To construct the eight ward groups for this edition, we took into account each ward's traditional voting patterns, its geographic location within the city, and the racial/ethnic mix of its population. Thus, because there have been historical differences in their voting responses, we distinguished the white wards in the Northwest Side of the city from those on its South Side, as well as the "Black West Side" wards from those on the "Black South Side." One group consists of the seven predominantly Latino wards, some of which are on the city's North Side and others on its South Side. We kept the "North Lakeshore" wards separate, both because they have a reputation for having been politically independent in the past and because they are the most racially and ethnically diverse wards in the city. We tagged another group of wards as "Other White North," which reflects its geographic location and dominant population but distinguishes it both from the Northwest and Lakeshore ward groups whose historic patterns of voting support were different. Finally, two wards simply did not fit into any of the other groups, and these we combined under the label "Mixed." Using these categories, we are able to track a manageable eight groups of wards rather than the scattered 50 wards that constitute the Chicago political landscape.

Table 1 shows the ethnic and racial characteristics of the voting age population within each of these ward groups. Figures 1 - 4 map the geographic locations of the eight ward groupings.

Introduction

Chicago's Ward Groups

Table 1

Voting Age Population by Ward Groups

Ward Group Name (Wards within the Group)	Percent White	Percent Black	Percent Latino	Percent Asian	Percent Other
White Northwest Side (Wards 30, 36, 38, 39, 41, 45)	88.5	1.2	6.8	3.4	.2
White South Side (Wards 11, 13, 14, 19, 23)	83.8	5.2	9.4	1.4	.2
Black South Side (Wards 2, 3, 4, 5, 6, 7, 8, 9, 15, 16, 17, 20, 21, 34)	7.4	88.8	3.1	.5	.2
Black West Side (Wards 24, 27, 28, 29, 37)	10.5	83.9	4.9	.5	.2
Latino (Wards 1, 12, 22, 25, 26, 31, 35)	30.8	11.7	53.9	3.1	.5
North Lakeshore (Wards 43, 44, 46, 48, 49)	74.8	14.9	6.1	3.7	.5
Other White North Side (Wards 32, 33, 40, 42, 47, 50)	75.6	5.0	13.1	5.9	.4
Mixed (Wards 10, 18)	49.4	35.6	14.6	.2	.2
Total	46.0	40.3	11.3	2.2	.3

Introduction

Chicago's Ward Groups

**Figure 1
The White Northwest
Side and the White
South Side**

Notes

[1]Finley Peter Dunne, *The World of Mr. Dooley* (New York: Crowell-Collier Publishing Company, 1962), 55-56.

[2]Dominic A. Pacyga and Ellen Skerrett, *Chicago: City of Neighborhoods* (Chicago: Loyola University Press, 1986).

[3]Chicago Department of Development and Planning, *Historic City—The Settlement of Chicago* (Chicago: City of Chicago, 1976), and for Greeley's comment, see p. v. A companion publication provided detailed data on the city's ethnic groups; see Chicago Department of Development and Planning, *The People of Chicago: Census Data on Foreign Born, Foreign Stock and Race, 1837-1970* (Chicago: City of Chicago, 1976).

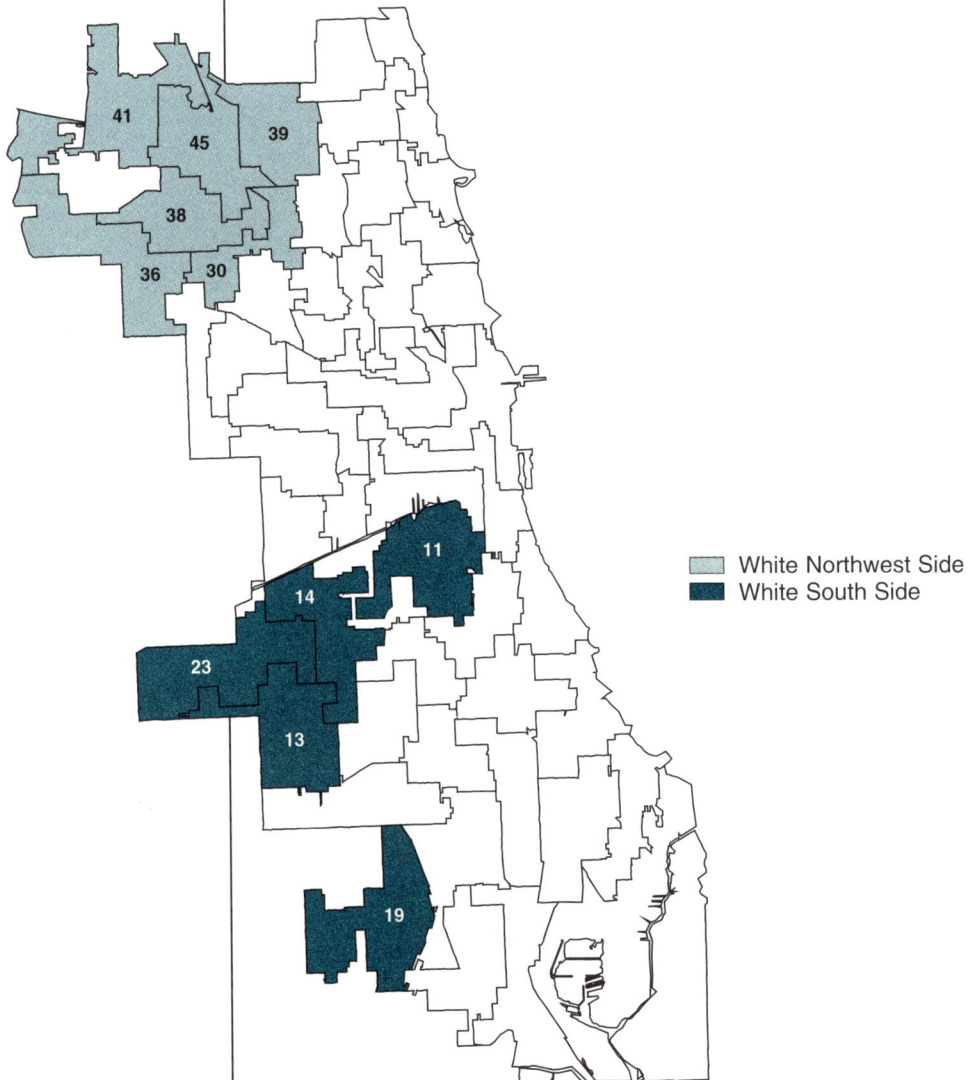

White Northwest Side
White South Side

Figure 2
The Black South Side and
the Black West Side

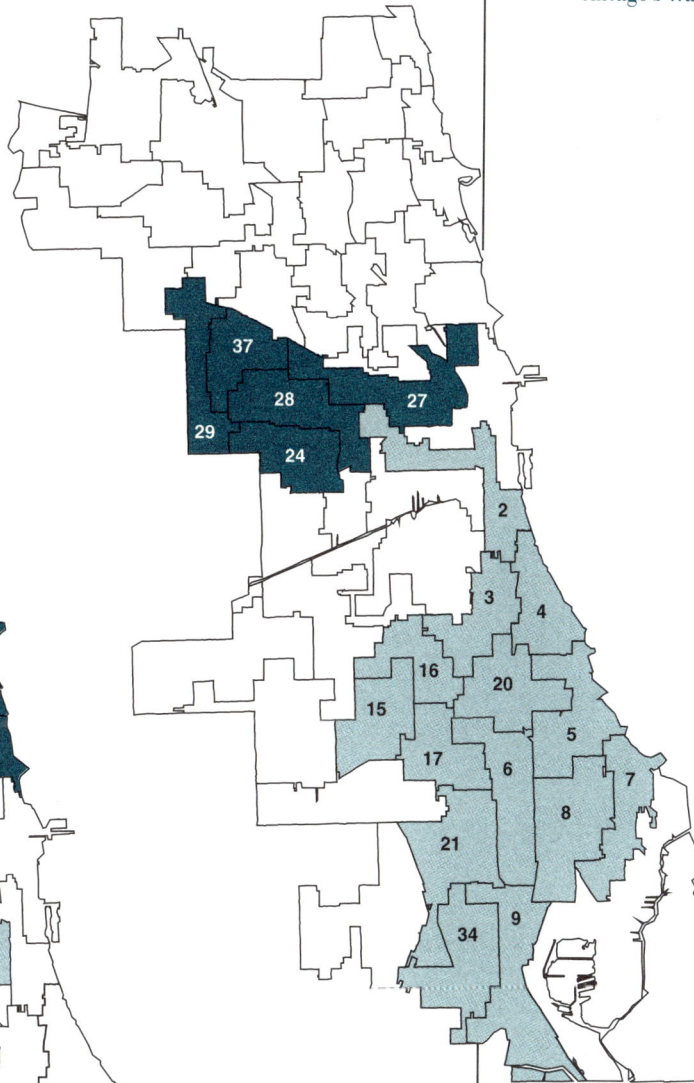

Introduction

Chicago's Ward Groups

Figure 3
The Latino and the
North Lakeshore Wards

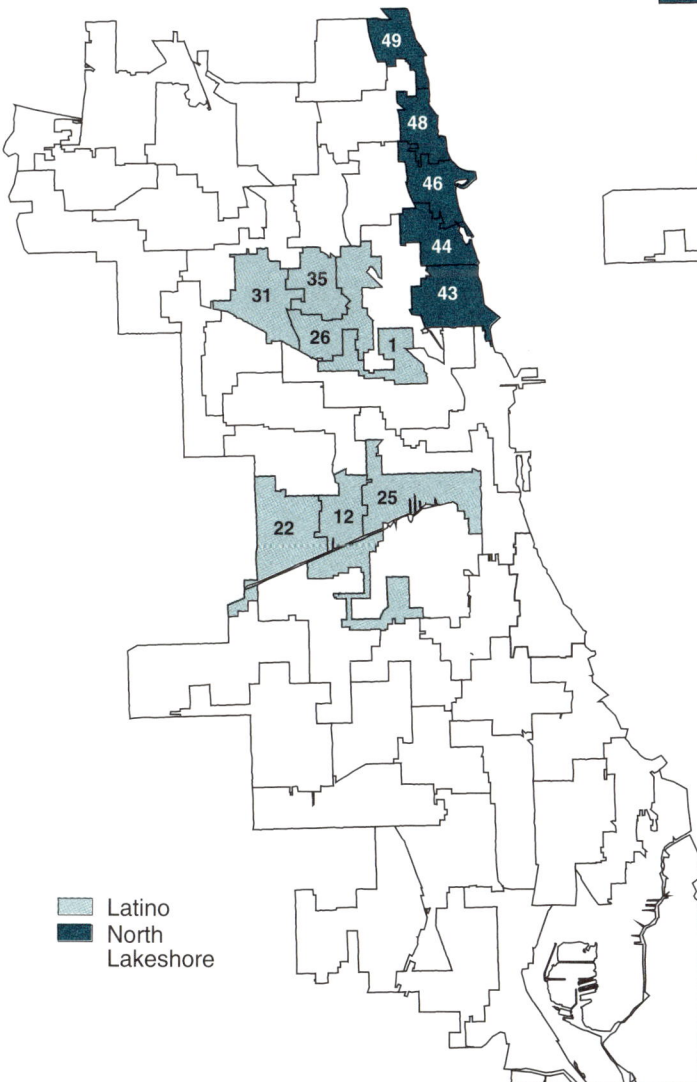

Black South Side
Black West Side

Latino
North
Lakeshore

Introduction

Chicago's Ward Groups

Figure 4
The Other White
North Side and
the Mixed Wards

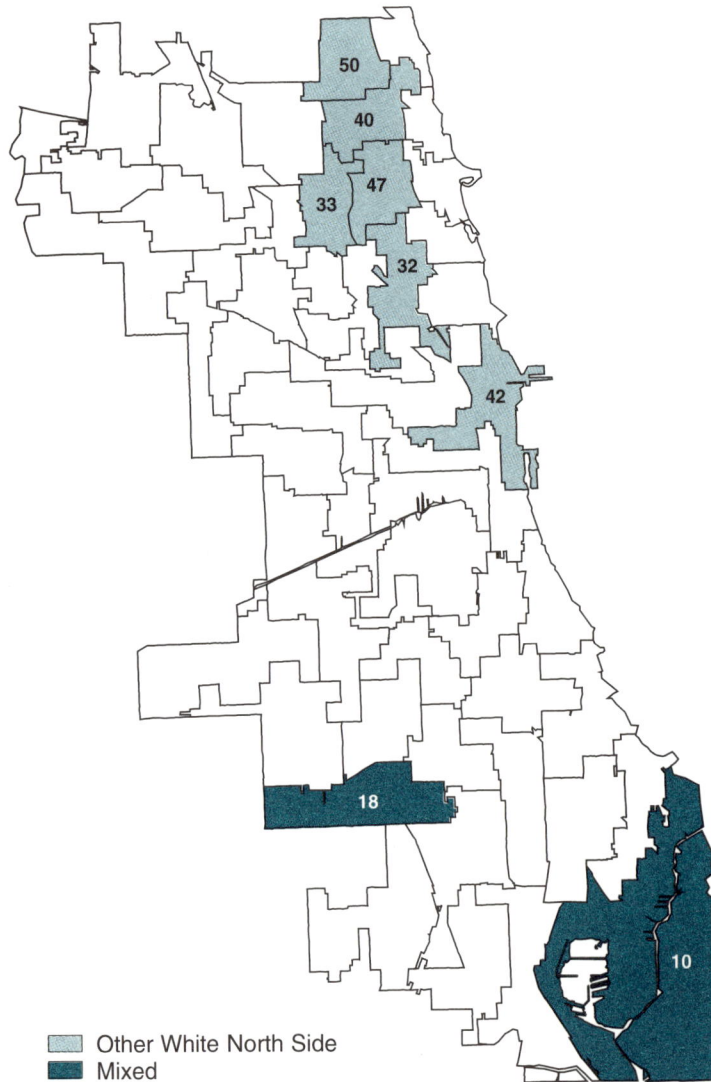

Legend:
- Other White North Side
- Mixed

Chapter 1: The Political Environment

Voters shape the political environment of the metro Chicago area. In this chapter we'll examine the shifts over time in the demographic makeup of the Chicago electorate. We'll first take a look at the distribution of the voting age population. Then we'll discuss the evolving patterns of voter registration in the metro area, with a particular emphasis on minority registration rates. Next, we'll examine voter turnout by again comparing turnouts of Chicago's ethnic communities. Finally, we'll examine the ramifications of the recent prohibition on straight-ticket voting. Arguably one of the most voter-unfriendly pieces of legislation to pass the General Assembly in years, the bill outlawing straight-ticket voting may encourage marginal candidacies and hinder Republican candidates in the collar counties.

Voting Age Population

Politics is a game of territories. Candidates as well as policy analysts make their livelihoods, in part, by knowing the political terrain, which shifts and flows as segments of the population move in and out of the city. Voters' concerns are often closely tied to their wallets and the issues they confront in their own back yard. Thus, historically, the public policy priorities of the people of DuPage County have seldom matched those of the people in the Austin, Bridgeport, or Pilsen neighborhoods.

What good are policy initiatives designed to benefit Chicago blacks if the trend is that black voters are finding homes in the suburbs? Ignorance of the shifting demographic patterns in the metro Chicago area cripples candidates for public office and makes for ill-informed public policy.

Let's examine the distribution of the voting age population (VAP) across the metro area and then break it down in terms of ethnicity.

Distribution of the Voting Age Population

As table 1.1 shows, in 1950 more than 7 of every 10 persons of voting age in the metropolitan area lived in the city of Chicago. Under these conditions, it was no wonder that Chicago dominated the politics of Cook County, the metropolitan area, and even the state of Illinois. But the demographic changes that have occurred since 1950 have dramatically rearranged the political landscape.

While the metropolitan area's total VAP has increased since 1950—from 3.6 to nearly 5.3 million—Chicago's has declined—from 2.5 to 1.8 million.

The Political Environment

At the same time, the VAPs of suburban Cook County and of the collar counties have grown consistently. As a result, Chicago's share of the metropolitan area's eligible voters is now only slightly larger than those of the suburbs in Cook County and the collar counties.

This demographic change underpins important political shifts. First, representation in the state legislature has shifted to reflect Chicago's decline and suburban growth. Chicago still sends the largest single delegation to Springfield, but the city's interests must now compete for a hearing with those of the growing suburbs. Second, candidates for statewide office have to come to terms with this new demography. Republicans can win statewide while losing Chicago by a fairly wide margin, and Democrats can no longer count on piling up majorities in the city to offset losses in the suburbs and downstate. Both parties now have to compete vigorously for support in the suburbs, with Republicans trying to win 70 percent or more as the springboard to statewide victory and Democrats trying to attract 40 percent or so and cut into the Republican margin. Both in the legislature and in statewide campaigns, this heightened sensitivity to suburban voters and their concerns often results in ignoring the interests of Chicago's voters, especially its minority groups.

Table 1.1

Distribution of the Voting Age Population: Chicago, Suburban Cook, and the Collar Counties, 1950-1996

Year	Chicago	Suburban Cook County	Collar Counties
1950	71.2%	16.5%	12.2%
1960	59.4%	24.2%	16.2%
1970	50.1%	29.9%	19.8%
1980	42.3%	32.2%	25.3%
1990	38.3%	32.8%	28.8%
1996[1]	34.9%	33.2%	31.9%

[1]Estimates developed from data and analysis provided by the Metro Chicago Information Center

Table 1.2

Voting Age Population: Chicago by Race/Ethnicity, 1950-1996

Year	White	African American	Latino	Other
1950	86.5%	13.4%[1]	NA	NA
1960	79.7%	20.2%[1]	NA	NA
1970	67.2%	27.1%	5.6%	NA
1980	53.5%	37.5%	7.5%	1.3%
1990	43.5%	35.7%	16.8%	4.0%
1996[2]	40.3%	34.6%	20.6%	4.4%

[1]Before the 1970 census, there were only two categories: "white" and "non-white." Most Latinos were counted only as "white."
[2]Estimates developed from data and analysis provided by the Metro Chicago Information Center.

Voting Age Population by Ethnicity

The Census Bureau's shifting definitions and labels complicate attempts to describe how Chicago's VAP has changed over time. But in 1950 and 1960, African Americans made up the vast majority of the city's "non-whites," with most Latinos counted only as "whites" (see table 1.2).

Despite the labeling difficulties, the change in Chicago's VAP since 1950 is very clear and easy to describe. Whites were the city's preponderant majority in 1950, with nearly 9 out of every 10 persons of voting age being white. But the white share of the city's VAP has shrunk consistently since then—in 1996 whites were only a plurality of Chicago's VAP. This change was particularly pronounced during the 1960s and 1970s, and it played a central role in shaping the substance and tenor of political battles in the city. The groups that were growing in numbers, African Americans and Latinos especially, sought political recognition, new resources, and an end to discriminatory practices in housing, education, and city hiring. The entrenched whites dug in, mobilized politically, and resisted any change in those public policies and practices that had for generations given them preferential treatment over the city's minorities.

Voter Registration

In recent years, voter registration grew to be a contentious topic in Illinois, as the state mired itself in a two-tier voter registration system before it finally complied with the federal "motor-voter" law just prior to the 1996 general election. Regardless of the registration process, Illinoisans in general (and Chicagoans in particular) have a nearly infamous reputation for registering to vote.

Voter Registration in the Metro Chicago Area vs. the Rest of the State

As table 1.3 illustrates, over 60 percent of Illinois' registered voters are concentrated in the Chicago area and the collar counties. If this bloc were homogeneous, candidates for statewide and federal elections could concentrate their election resources in six counties and turn their backs on the rest of the state. As we shall see, however, the ethnic diversity and socioeconomic inequities all but preclude Cook County and the collar counties from ever behaving as a reliable voting bloc.

Table 1.3

Location of Registered Voters in Illinois	
Area	Percentage of Illinois Total
Chicago	21.4%
Suburban Cook	19.9%
Collar Counties	19.0%
Downstate Counties	39.5%

Registered Voters in Chicago

As we've hinted at (and as we'll demonstrate throughout this atlas), Chicago voters often align themselves on the basis of their ethnicity. Therefore, the potential political clout of any given ethnic group rises in proportion to the increase of the registration rate of that group. Table 1.4 traces the rise and fall of the registration rates of Chicago's ethnic communities from 1980 to 1996.

The Political Environment

The Political Environment

Table 1.4

Registration by Race/Ethnicity:
Chicago General Elections, 1980-1996

Year/Office	White	African American	Latino	Other	Total
1980 President	82.8%	75.0%	49.7%	17.8%	75.5%
1982 Governor	78.6%	82.5%	53.7%	21.1%	77.1%
1983 Mayor	83.0%	84.5%	51.3%	21.4%	79.9%
1984 President	85.2%	81.3%	46.2%	23.1%	78.9%
1986 Governor	77.5%	73.2%	39.5%	23.3%	70.8%
1987 Mayor	83.5%	78.0%	43.2%	24.2%	75.8%
1988 President	84.4%	75.5%	42.2%	18.5%	74.4%
1989 Mayor	86.1%	73.8%	35.2%	22.1%	73.6%
1990 Governor	86.6%	82.5%	45.0%	17.9%	78.5%
1991 Mayor	83.2%	88.4%	60.7%	23.4%	81.2%
1992 President	83.3%	93.4%	68.0%	39.0%	84.2%
1994 Governor	72.5%	88.5%	41.6%	22.4%	75.0%
1995 Mayor	77.7%	90.5%	46.9%	20.5%	81.1%
1996 President	80.6%	86.4%	68.5%	35.8%	78.9%

An extraordinary voter registration drive in the summer and fall of 1982 boosted the African-American registration rate ahead of the white rate. The black registration rate went even higher during the hotly contested 1983 mayoral contest, which saw the election of the city's first African-American mayor, Harold Washington. While the black registration rate sagged somewhat thereafter, it remained reasonably close to the white rate through the rest of the 1980s.

Compared with the 1980s, the white registration rate in the 1990s didn't exhibit much change. And it varies in the ways that we would expect: typically lower for gubernatorial elections than for presidential and mayoral contests. But the African-American registration rate in the 1990s appears to be anomalous, showing a sharp increase in 1990 and reaching the 90 percent level for the 1992 and 1995 elections. Yet all other indicators, including election-day turnout, point to lower levels of political activity in the black community during the 1990s than in the 1980s. The seemingly high registration rate likely reflects the combination of an undercount of African Americans of voting age in the 1990 census and inadequately cleaned registration rolls.

Latino registration reached the 50 percent mark in 1982 and 1983, dropped back to a low of 35.2 percent in 1989, and then turned upward again. It reached the 60 percent mark for the first time in 1991 and in 1996 reached a new peak, 68.5 percent.

Other voters, mainly Asians, still show very low registration rates with only slightly more than a third of their eligible population enrolled.

Making demographic mapping interesting is the fact that ethnic voters to some extent remain geographically segregated within the metro Chicago area (see table 1.5).

Within Chicago, the two African-American ward groups show the highest registration rates. The registration rates in these areas are simply extraordinary, far surpassing the comparatively modest 71.1 percent rate in the city's most affluent area, the North Lakeshore wards. Typically, we expect high registration rates to be associated with high levels of income and education. But Chicago's most highly registered areas, the African-American ward groups, contain large numbers of inhabitants with low levels of education and income. In other words, the social characteristics of these wards

The Political Environment

Table 1.5

Registered Voters: November 1996

Ward Group[1]	Percent Registered	Number Registered
White Northwest Side	75.1%	175,325
White South Side	76.7%	144,063
Black South Side	85.2%	457,055
Black West Side	84.7%	153,084
Latino	72.9%	126,331
North Lakeshore	71.1%	146,341
Other White North Side	74.4%	162,506
Mixed	84.2%	64,090
Chicago Total	78.9%	**1,428,795**
Suburban Cook	75.3%	1,328,808
Collar Counties	81.7%	1,270,162
Metro Area Total	78.5%	**4,027,765**
Downstate Counties	84.8%	2,635,536
Illinois Total	80.9%	**6,663,301**

[1]See pages 4-8 for a detailed explanation and depiction of these ward groupings.

The Political Environment

would predict low registration rates, but instead they have the highest rates in the city.

As we'll discuss in greater detail in Chapter 5, the registration rates in the African-American areas are literally unbelievable. They reflect two sources of error. The 1990 census undercounted African-Americans and the registration rolls still remain inflated despite an unusual effort by the Chicago Board of Election Commissioners to clean them up. The result is a serious overestimate both of the number of registered voters in African-American precincts and of the proportionate share of the age-eligible population in these precincts that is registered.

Registration in the Latino wards continues to grow. It jumped 2.8 percentage points since March 1994, reaching a new peak of 72.9 percent in 1996.

Even with an overcount of registered voters boosting Chicago's registration rate, the city fell behind the rates of the collar and downstate counties in 1996. And Chicago's share of the state's registered electorate continued its 40-year decline, dropping by another .8 percentage point between 1994 and 1996. Suburban Cook's share also declined by .7 percentage point over the two-year period. The downstate counties grew by .4 percentage point, while the collar counties showed an even larger gain, jumping by 1 percentage point since 1994. These small changes are part of the longer-term trend that has seen Chicago lose its dominant political position in the state while the suburbs attained new political prominence and clout.

Turnout Rate

Chicago has a national reputation as a city where both the quick and the dead vote as many times as possible on election day. Tables 1.6 and 1.7 take a few swipes at that myth and show the voter turnout trends of Chicago's racial and ethnic communities since 1980.

When considering a turnout rate, it's important to understand how the rate is calculated. There are two options. The turnout rate can be measured as the percentage of voting age population that cast ballots in an election (see table 1.6) or the percentage of registered voters who cast ballots (see table 1.7).

Table 1.6

Turnout Rate by Race/Ethnicity: Chicago General Elections, 1980-1996

(Measured as percentage of the VAP that cast ballots)

Year/Office	White	African American	Latino	Other	Total
1980 President	67.0%	53.2%	36.9%	14.8%	58.8%
1982 Governor	53.8%	49.4%	30.7%	27.0%	49.7%
1983 Mayor	66.6%	67.7%	31.1%	22.4%	63.2%
1984 President	68.6%	54.7%	30.1%	22.1%	58.7%
1986 Governor	47.9%	33.4%	12.0%	23.1%	37.9%
1987 Mayor	58.7%	58.5%	23.1%	25.0%	54.1%
1988 President	65.3%	45.8%	18.2%	18.9%	50.9%
1989 Mayor	62.6%	43.7%	16.0%	21.8%	48.3%
1990 Governor	53.7%	26.7%	10.9%	14.7%	37.3%
1991 Mayor	46.7%	26.9%	18.5%	15.3%	30.9%
1992 President	71.9%	64.0%	33.7%	23.2%	62.8%
1994 Governor	44.2%	32.7%	8.0%	7.5%	35.0%
1995 Mayor	42.9%	35.8%	11.4%	15.0%	34.2%
1996 President	60.2%	52.9%	32.0%	20.5%	49.8%

The Political Environment

African-American turnout hit its recent peak in the 1983 mayoral contest, when Harold Washington was elected mayor in a bitterly fought battle. In that election, African-American turnout was even higher than white turnout. Since then, black participation has declined and, except for Washington's reelection effort in 1987, it has fallen well below white turnout. The roughly 20-percentage-point differences between white and African-American turnout rates in the 1989 and 1991 mayoral contests doomed the efforts of black candidates. The turnout difference was smaller in the 1995 mayoral contest, but it was still large enough to help shape the outcome.

Latino turnout declined sharply after the elections of the early 1980s but then rebounded somewhat in the early 1990s. In the 1992 and 1996 presidential election years, about a third of the city's Latinos of voting age cast ballots.

Turnout among Chicago's other voters, mainly Asians, is still extremely low. Typically, under a quarter of the voting age population casts ballots, even in presidential election years.

The Political Environment

As table 1.7 shows, measuring turnout as a percentage of registered voters has the effect of artificially "boosting" the turnout rates. It does this because it excludes from consideration that segment of each group's voting age population that hadn't registered for the election. Literally, in this way of calculating turnout, people who don't register don't count. The pattern exhibited by Chicago's "Other" voters illustrates the point. Measured as a percentage of the voting age population (table 1.6), this group's turnout has been consistently quite low, never even reaching as much as a third of its VAP. But this category also shows a very low registration rate: the recent peak was a mere 39 percent in 1992. So, if its turnout is calculated as a percentage of its registered voters, the participation rate for this category looks nearly phenomenal, often going well above 90 percent. Looked at in this way, the group would appear to be highly mobilized and engaged politically. Of course, the opposite is the case: this voting category is woefully undermobilized, as its very low registration rate attests.

Table 1.7

Turnout Rate by Race/Ethnicity:
Chicago General Elections, 1980-1996

(Measured as percentage of the registered voters who cast ballots)

Year/Office	White	African American	Latino	Other	Total
1980 President	80.9%	70.9%	74.2%	83.1%	76.8%
1982 Governor	68.4%	59.8%	57.1%	99.9%	64.4%
1983 Mayor	80.2%	80.1%	60.6%	99.9%	79.3%
1984 President	80.5%	67.2%	64.9%	95.6%	74.3%
1986 Governor	61.8%	45.6%	30.3%	99.1%	53.5%
1987 Mayor	70.2%	75.0%	53.4%	99.9%	71.3%
1988 President	77.3%	60.6%	43.1%	99.9%	68.4%
1989 Mayor	72.7%	59.2%	45.4%	98.6%	65.6%
1990 Governor	62.0%	32.3%	24.2%	82.1%	47.5%
1991 Mayor	56.1%	30.6%	30.4%	98.3%	43.3%
1992 President	86.3%	68.5%	49.5%	66.9%	85.1%
1994 Governor	60.9%	36.9%	19.2%	33.4%	46.7%
1995 Mayor	55.2%	39.5%	24.3%	73.1%	42.2%
1996 President	74.6%	61.2%	46.7%	57.2%	63.1%

The Republican Response to "Punch 10": Punch Minorities

The "rules of the game," i.e., those governing behavior at the polling place, are also part of the political environment. In Illinois, one long-standing rule has allowed citizens to vote for all of the candidates of one party by making a single mark on the ballot. The 1996 effort by Democrats in Cook County to encourage this type of straight-ticket voting—the so-called "Punch 10" campaign—was reputed to be very successful, especially among Chicago's minority voters. Responding to this effort after the election, irate Republican legislators in the Illinois General Assembly simply changed the rules by eliminating one-mark, straight-ticket voting. This legal knockout punch was aimed at reducing the impact of Chicago's minorities in future elections. Further, this punch signified a complete break with tradition. Political parties have always encouraged their supporters to vote for all of the candidates the party has endorsed. In the nineteenth century, when there were no official ballots, each party printed ballots listing only its own nominees. As voters came to the polling places, they selected a ballot from a party worker and then deposited it in the ballot box to cast their vote. By the end of the nineteenth century, governments had taken the administration of elections away from political parties and official ballots had come into general use. These listed the candidates nominated by all the parties, thus requiring the voter to mark the ballot to signal the choice for each office. To facilitate the process, most states allowed the voter to indicate a preference for all of the candidates of the same party by making a single mark after that party's designation at the beginning of the ballot. This allowed the voter to cast a straight ticket with a single mark, rather than having to make separate marks indicating the choices for each office. Coincidentally, this also cut the time required for voting and both the time and costs involved in tabulating the results.

Since it first adopted official ballots, Illinois has allowed voters to cast a straight ticket by making a single mark on the ballot. Since ballots are now processed and tabulated by machines, the recent version allowed an Illinois voter to designate a straight-party ticket with a single punch. But the voter can also punch the party designation and still vote for candidates of another party by simply punching the appropriate spot after their names. For instance, a voter wanting to vote for Republicans for all offices except one could punch the Republican party designation and then punch the appropriate spot to vote for another party's candidate for a particular office.

During the fall 1996 election season, Cook County Democrats mounted a highly visible campaign to encourage voters to cast straight tickets by punching the party's designation. Their motto was "Punch 10"—the ballot-line number assigned to the party's designation. This effort was so visible—and ostensibly successful—that Republicans used the waning hours of the

The Political Environment

The Political Environment

post-election legislative session to enact a measure—subsequently signed by the governor—that eliminated one-punch, straight-ticket voting in future elections.

How much this will change the political environment is hard to say. But inferences can be drawn from the history of straight-party voting in recent elections. In 1992, over 1.5 million voters in the state cast straight tickets. In the 1994 off-year election, the number dropped to 998,525; but it rose again in 1996 to over 1.7 million, or 210,369 more straight tickets than had been cast in the 1992 presidential year. However, measured as a percentage of the total ballots cast, the frequency of straight-ticket voting has not been disproportionately associated with Chicago or with Cook County in these recent elections, as table 1.8 shows.

In all three elections shown in table 1.8, Chicago had a lower rate of straight-ticket voting than suburban Cook. And Cook County as a whole had a slightly higher rate of straight ticketing than the collar counties in both 1992 and 1996, but not by as much as a full percentage point in either year. However, the rate of straight-ticket voting in the collar counties in 1994 was 6.4 percentage points higher than in Cook County. Finally, while all the major subareas of the state showed a gain in straight-ticket voting between 1992 and 1996, the collar counties led the parade with a 10.7 percentage-point increase. And among the collars, DuPage County did better yet, jumping from a straight-ticket rate of 30.4 percent in 1992 to 43.7 percent in 1996, a gain of 13.3 percentage points. By eliminating straight-ticket voting, Republican legislators may have inadvertently undercut a major prop of the DuPage County Republican Machine's hegemony: high rates of straight-ticket voting among well-educated, affluent citizens who otherwise might be expected to be ticket splitters.

Before acting to eradicate straight-ticket voting, however, Republican legislators likely did not look at patterns across time. Neither did they take into account the long-term implications—and possible unanticipated consequences—of their action on their own bailiwicks. They were irked at having lost control of the lower house of the legislature and impressed with the fact that there were so many more straight Democratic tickets cast in the state than straight Republican ones—202,767 more, to be exact. Since they associated these two developments and blamed the "Punch 10" campaign for both, they moved with unseemly haste to eliminate one-punch, straight-ticket voting.

Table 1.8

Straight Tickets as a Percentage of Total Ballots, 1992-1996

Area	1992	1994	1996
Chicago	29.8%	31.4%	40.4%
Suburban Cook	31.3%	31.8%	41.0%
Total Cook County	30.5%	31.6%	41.0%
Collar Counties	29.7%	38.0%	40.4%
Metro Area Total	30.2%	33.7%	40.8%
Downstate Counties	27.1%	27.2%	35.6%
Illinois Total	29.1%	31.0%	38.7%

But comparing the geographic distribution of straight-ticket ballots over time shows that more was involved than the effort by Cook County's Democratic Machine. Compared to 1992, the number of straight Democratic ballots in 1996 increased in all the major subareas of the state. In the downstate counties, the number of straight Democratic ballots increased by 8,011, and there were 17,051 more straight Democratic ballots cast than straight Republican ones. And there were even 29,739 more straight Democratic ballots in 1996 than in 1992 in the solidly Republican collar counties, where Republicans still had a better than two-to-one advantage over Democrats in straight-ticket voting. These developments cannot plausibly be attributed to the Cook County "Punch 10" campaign, but they probably were related to a lack of popularity on the part of some of the Republican nominees. Weak candidates, especially for president and U.S. Senate, simply discouraged straight-ticket voting by Republicans, allowing Democrats to enjoy a fairly healthy statewide advantage.

When the Republican ticket has not been burdened by unappealing candidates, the party has either matched or surpassed Democrats in attracting straight-ticket votes. In 1988, for example, 839,467 voters in the state cast straight Republican tickets, only 15,935 below the number of straight Democratic voters. And in 1994 the Republicans swept the state elections, carrying all the statewide offices and the lower house of the legislature, in no small part because there were 179,812 more straight Republican tickets cast than Democratic ones. Moreover, in the off-year election, Republicans enjoyed a better than two-to-one edge over Democrats in straight tickets in suburban Cook County; but in 1996, with weak candidates at the top of the Republican ticket, Democrats polled 24,935 more straight ballots there. Rather than seeing the elimination of one-punch voting as their route to future success, Republican leaders might try to exert closer control over their own primary and thus prevent the nomination of candidates who are out of the mainstream.

Nevertheless, Republican claims about the 1996 results were correct on at least one count. The "Punch 10" campaign did have a clear impact on the outcome of the race for Cook County state's attorney. Richard Devine upset the incumbent Republican mainly because of the high levels of voting support he received from minorities—and especially African Americans—in Chicago. And straight-ticket voting was the key factor in producing that support. Table 1.9 shows this by presenting a measure of the importance of straight Democratic tickets to the size of the total vote polled by the Democratic nominees for state's attorney in 1992 and 1996.

In 1992, the 406,269 straight Democratic ballots cast in Cook County accounted for only about half of the total vote received by Patrick O'Connor, the party's candidate for state's attorney. But in 1996 there were 510,066 straight Democratic ballots, and they accounted for 63.4 percent of Devine's

The Political Environment

total vote. Moreover, more than 7 of every 10 votes that Devine received in minority areas resulted from straight-ticket voting. The "Punch 10" effort apparently worked effectively among African Americans to counter the appeal of the two African-American candidates who were running for state's attorney. Without one-punch voting, more votes in the African-American areas would likely have been cast—as they have in past elections—for these minor candidates. Seen in this context, the action by Republican legislators in eliminating one-punch voting may have been aimed at the voting practices of Chicago's minority communities. Whether or not this was its expressed intent, the action is likely to encourage marginal candidacies because it outlaws a mechanism that has proven effective in countering attempts to splinter the vote of minority communities.

Table 1.9

Straight Democratic Ballots as a Percentage of the Total Votes for Democratic Candidates for State's Attorney, 1992 and 1996

Area[1]	Percentage of Total Democratic Ballots Coming from Straight-Ticket Voting	
	1992	1996
White Northwest Side	39.2%	55.7%
White South Side	47.6%	65.9%
Black South Side	56.6%	74.3%
Black West Side	64.1%	77.0%
Latino	57.4%	70.5%
North Lakeshore	48.6%	57.2%
Other White North Side	48.0%	59.0%
Mixed	50.5%	67.2%
Chicago Total	**53.7%**	**67.1%**
Suburban Cook	44.3%	57.9%
Cook County Total	**50.6%**	**63.4%**

[1]See pages 4-8 for a detailed explanation and depiction of these ward groupings.

Chapter 2: Results from Recent Elections

Results from Recent Elections

As we said in chapter 1, the metro Chicago area rarely behaves as a reliable voting bloc. How do we know this to be true? Because we've been able to track the results of recent elections and have found that different sets of ward groupings from areas across the city follow unique patterns. In the introduction to this atlas (pages 4-8) we explained that these ward groupings are distinct from one another not only in their location but also in the racial/ethnic heritage of their constituencies. Specifically the eight ward groupings we've identified are:

- White Northwest Side (wards 30, 36, 38, 39, 41, 45),

- White South Side (wards 11, 13, 14, 19, 23),

- Black South Side (wards 2, 3, 4, 5, 6, 7, 8, 9, 15, 16, 17, 20, 21, 34),

- Black West Side (wards 24, 27, 28, 29, 37),

- Latino (wards 1, 12, 22, 25, 26, 31, 35),

- North Lakeshore (wards 43, 44, 46, 48, 49),

- Other White North Side (wards 32, 33, 40, 42, 47, 50), and

- Mixed (wards 10, 18).

In this chapter we'll track the voting patterns of each of these groups through 23 races for political office, ranging from the 1983 Chicago mayoral race to the 1996 presidential race. The tables in this chapter present the voting returns for groups of wards, and the maps show the boundaries of each ward but then shade the precincts within it to show any variations in voting support that occurred.

Results from Recent Elections

U.S. President, November 1992

U.S. President, November 1992

Illinois was one of Clinton's strongest states in 1992. He polled 48.5 percent of the state's total vote, beating Bush by 719,254 votes, a 14.2 percentage-point lead. Bush won the collar counties by 107,407 votes, but Clinton carried all the other major political areas in the state. He carried Chicago by 593,300 votes, a lead of 54 percentage points. He held a narrow 50,933 vote edge in suburban Cook County, while carrying the downstate counties by 182,428 votes.

Clinton piled up his large Chicago lead by trouncing Bush in the African-American and Latino areas. He polled 97 percent of the African-American vote citywide, and 79.3 percent of the Latino vote. Clinton's support was less strong and decisive among white voters. While he garnered 49.3 percent of the white vote citywide, he failed to muster a majority in the Northwest Side wards and polled only 51.1 percent in the White South Side wards. Both of these white ethnic bastions typically give much higher levels of support to local Democratic candidates. Among whites, Clinton ran best in the North Lakeshore and North Side wards .

Table 2.1

The 1992 Presidential Race

Ward Group[1]/Area	% Bill Clinton (D)	%George Bush (R)	%Ross Perot (I)	% Others	Total Votes
White Northwest Side	45.1	37.1	17.4	.4	144,478
White South Side	51.1	31.6	16.9	.4	129,158
Black South Side	93.4	3.4	2.7	.5	336,130
Black West Side	91.3	5.0	3.2	.5	104,404
Latino	69.8	19.7	9.8	.7	77,220
North Lakeshore	66.4	22.8	10.2	.6	122,280
Other White North Side	61.5	25.5	12.4	.6	132,558
Mixed	66.0	21.7	11.9	.4	50,087
Chicago Total	72.1	18.1	9.3	.5	**1,096,315**
Suburban Cook County	43.6	38.7	17.2	.3	1,045,631
Collar Counties	33.7	44.9	20.8	.4	963,329
Metro Area Total	50.6	33.3	15.5	.4	**3,105,275**
Illinois Total	48.5	34.3	16.6	.4	**5,050,157**

Note: D=Democrat, R=Republican, I=Independent

[1]For a detailed explanation of these ward groupings, see pages 4-8 in the introduction to this atlas.

Clinton coasted to an easy win in Illinois in 1992, with Bush conceding the battle by pulling his television advertising early in September. Yet Clinton's final percentage was actually below the 48.6 percent that Michael Dukakis had polled statewide in 1988. The difference, of course, was that the vote not cast for the Democratic candidate was divided in 1992 between Bush and Perot. That division made Clinton's victory easy and made it appear to be more decisive than it actually was.

Results from Recent Elections

U.S. President, November 1992

The Race in the City: How Voters of Different Races/Ethnicities Supported the Candidates

Race/Ethnicity	Clinton	Bush	Perot	Turnout[1]
White	49.3%	33.8%	16.3%	71.9%
Black	97.0%	1.0%	1.4%	64.0%
Latino	79.3%	14.6%	5.0%	33.7%
Total				62.8%

[1]Turnout is the percentage of the voting age population who cast ballots for a candidate for this office in this election.

Results from Recent Elections

U.S. President, November 1992

Figure 2.1a
Chicago Support for Clinton

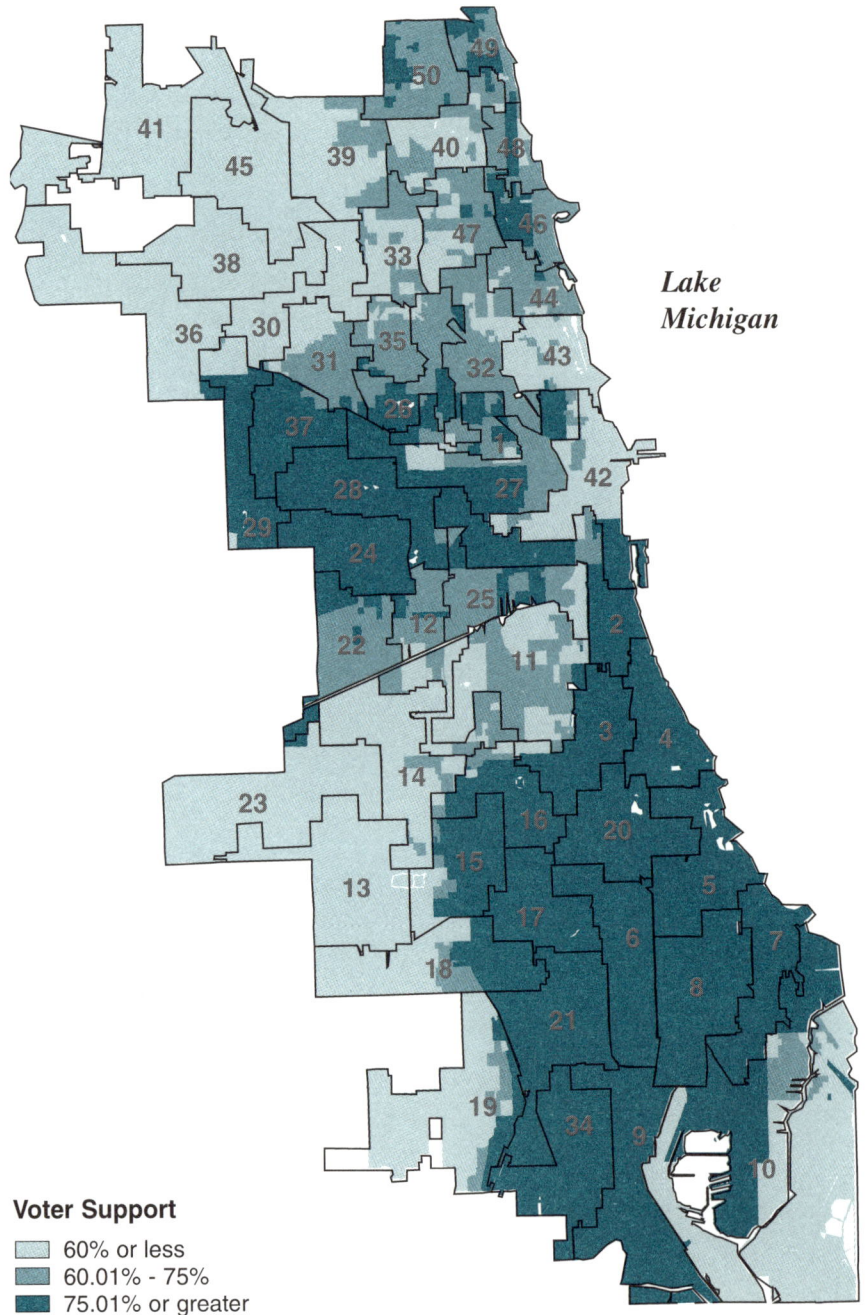

Lake Michigan

Voter Support
- 60% or less
- 60.01% - 75%
- 75.01% or greater

Figure 2.1b
Cook County Township
Support for Clinton

Results from Recent Elections

U.S. President, November 1992

Townships

1. Barrington	12. Leyden	23. Proviso
2. Berwyn	13. Lyons	24. Rich
3. Bloom	14. Maine	25. River Forest
4. Bremen	15. New Trier	26. Riverside
5. Calumet	16. Niles	27. Schaumburg
6. See figure a	17. Northfield	28. Stickney
7. Cicero	18. Norwood Park	29. Thornton
8. Elk Grove	19. Oak Park	30. Wheeling
9. Evanston	20. Orland Park	31. Worth
10. Hanover	21. Palatine	
11. Lemont	22. Palos	

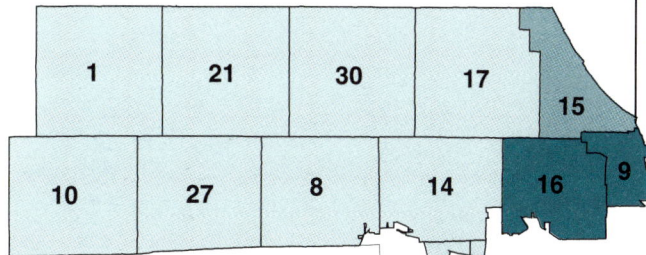

Voter Support

☐	0% - 40%
☐	40.01% - 50%
☐	50.01% - 100%

Figure 2.1c
Collar County Support for Clinton

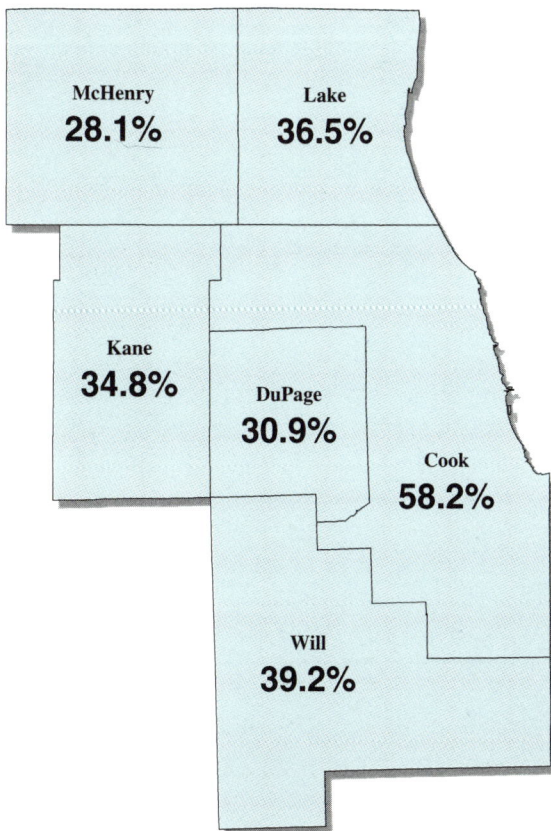

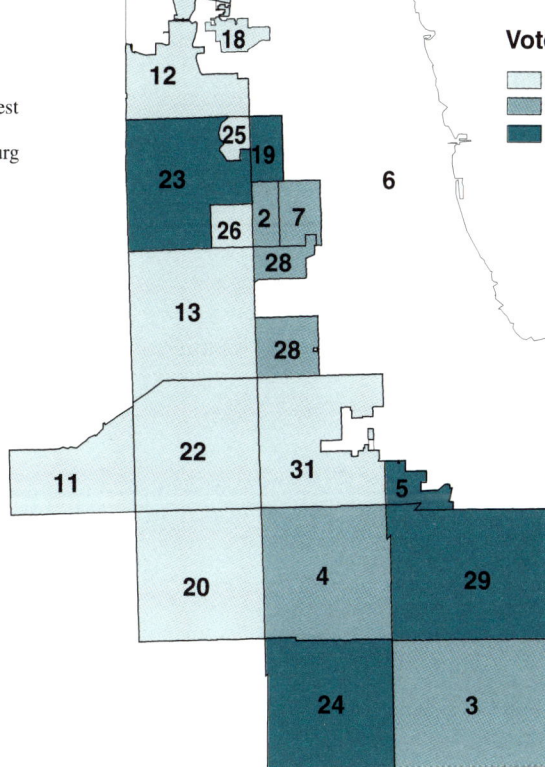

McHenry
28.1%

Lake
36.5%

Kane
34.8%

DuPage
30.9%

Cook
58.2%

Will
39.2%

U.S. President, November 1996

As it had been four years earlier, Illinois was one of the states in which Clinton ran best in 1996. He polled 54.3 percent of the state's vote, beating Dole by 754,723 votes statewide. Clinton's percentage-point margin over Dole—17.5—was 3.3 percentage points better than his 1992 lead over Bush.

Dole carried only the collar counties and these by a mere 44,276 votes. This was less than half the size of Bush's lead in these counties four years earlier and well below the margin Republicans need from them to carry the state. Clinton carried all the other major political areas of the state. He beat Dole by 64.4 percentage points in Chicago and by 15.4 in suburban Cook County. These large leads more than offset Clinton's narrow 5 percentage-point loss in the collar counties and enabled him to carry the metro area by 645,957 votes, a margin of 24.8 percentage points. Clinton also carried the downstate counties by 6.4 percentage points.

Table 2.2

The 1996 Presidential Race

Ward Group[1]/ Area	%Bill Clinton (D)	%Bob Dole (R)	% Minor Candidates	Total Votes
White Northwest Side	59.8	31.9	8.3	117,491
White South Side	67.2	24.8	8.0	106,215
Black South Side	95.2	2.5	2.3	263,867
Black West Side	93.5	3.9	2.6	79,234
Latino	84.1	10.8	5.1	62,781
North Lakeshore	72.1	23.0	4.9	92,396
Other White North Side	70.2	23.7	6.1	104,515
Mixed	78.0	16.1	5.9	39,664
Chicago Total	79.7	15.3	4.9	**866,163**
Suburban Cook	53.7	38.3	7.9	856,839
Collar Counties	42.4	47.4	10.0	875,503
Metro Area Total	58.5	33.7	7.6	**2,598,505**
Illinois Total	54.3	36.8	8.8	**4,311,391**

Note: D=Democrat, R=Republican

[1] For a detailed explanation of these ward groupings, see pages 4-8 in the introduction to this atlas.

Compared to 1992, Clinton gained proportionate strength in Chicago, suburban Cook County, and the collar counties, while losing .7 percentage point in the downstate counties. Dole ran better than Bush had by 2.5 percentage points in the collar counties and by 5.6 percentage points in the downstate counties.

Clinton piled up his huge lead over Dole in Chicago by polling strong majorities from all three of the city's largest voting groups. African Americans gave him 97 percent of their vote, the same level they had delivered four years earlier. Latinos boosted their support by over 15 percentage points, giving the president 94.5 percent. Chicago's white voters had given Clinton only a plurality in 1992, but nearly two-thirds of them voted for him in 1996. However, Clinton still polled his strongest percentages among whites in the North Lakeshore and North Side wards, while lagging slightly behind these marks in the white ethnic redoubts on the city's Northwest and South Sides.

Chicago's voter participation in the presidential contest dropped by 14.9 percentage points from its 1992 level. Each of the city's largest voting groups contributed to that decline: white turnout dropped 13 percentage points; African-American turnout by 13.5 percentage points; and Latino participation by 4 percentage points.

The Race in the City: How Voters of Different Races/Ethnicities Supported the Candidates

Race/ Ethnicity	Clinton	Dole	Minor Candidates	Turnout[1]
White	61.6%	30.6%	7.6%	58.9%
Black	97.0%	.9%	1.9%	50.5%
Latino	94.5%	2.0%	3.3%	29.7%
Total				47.9%

[1]Turnout is the percentage of the voting age population who cast ballots for a candidate for this office in this election.

Results from Recent Elections

U.S. President, November 1996

Figure 2.2a
Chicago Support for Clinton

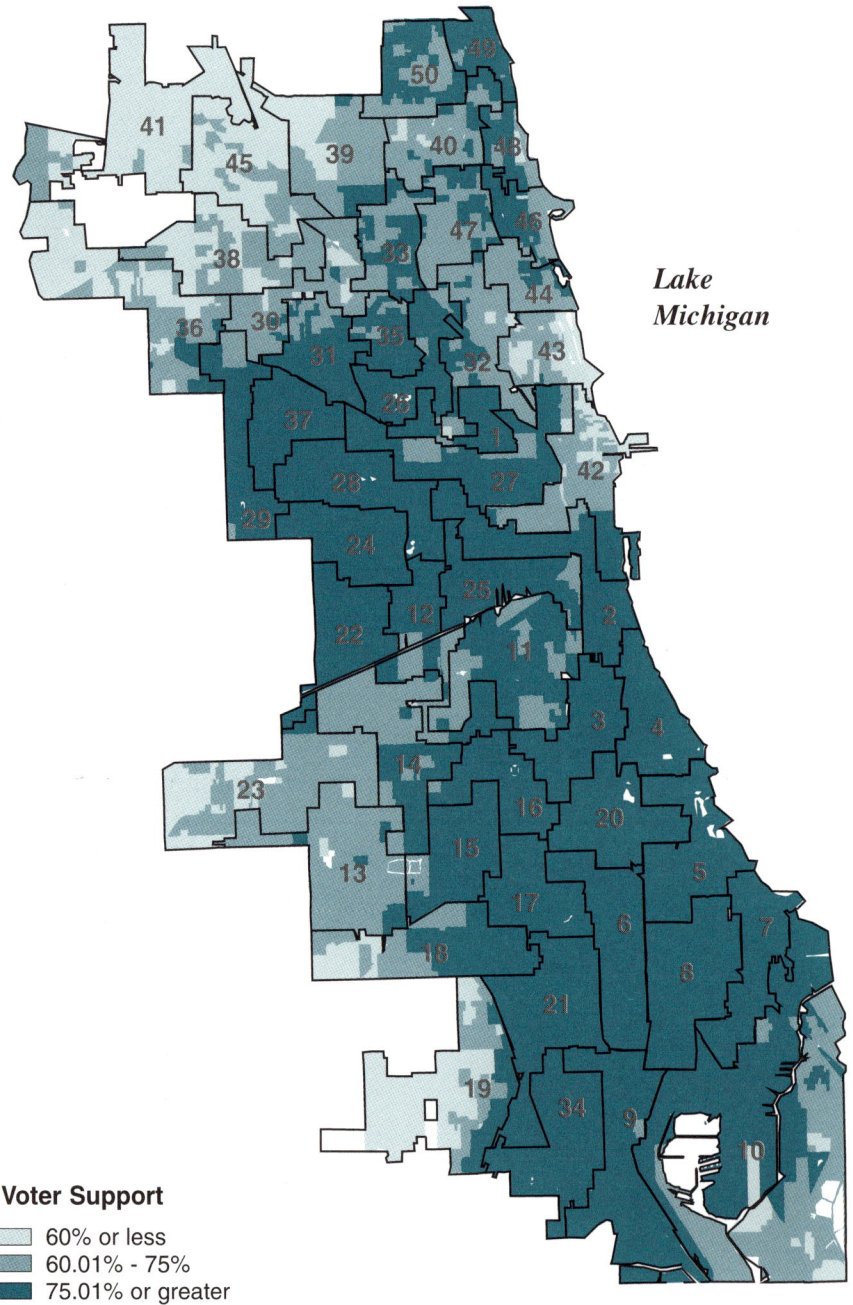

Lake Michigan

Voter Support
- 60% or less
- 60.01% - 75%
- 75.01% or greater

Figure 2.2b
Cook County Township
Support for Clinton

Results from Recent Elections

U.S. President, November 1996

Townships

1. Barrington
2. Berwyn
3. Bloom
4. Bremen
5. Calumet
6. See figure a
7. Cicero
8. Elk Grove
9. Evanston
10. Hanover
11. Lemont
12. Leyden
13. Lyons
14. Maine
15. New Trier
16. Niles
17. Northfield
18. Norwood Park
19. Oak Park
20. Orland Park
21. Palatine
22. Palos
23. Proviso
24. Rich
25. River Forest
26. Riverside
27. Schaumburg
28. Stickney
29. Thornton
30. Wheeling
31. Worth

Voter Support
- 0% - 40%
- 40.01% - 50%
- 50.01% - 100%

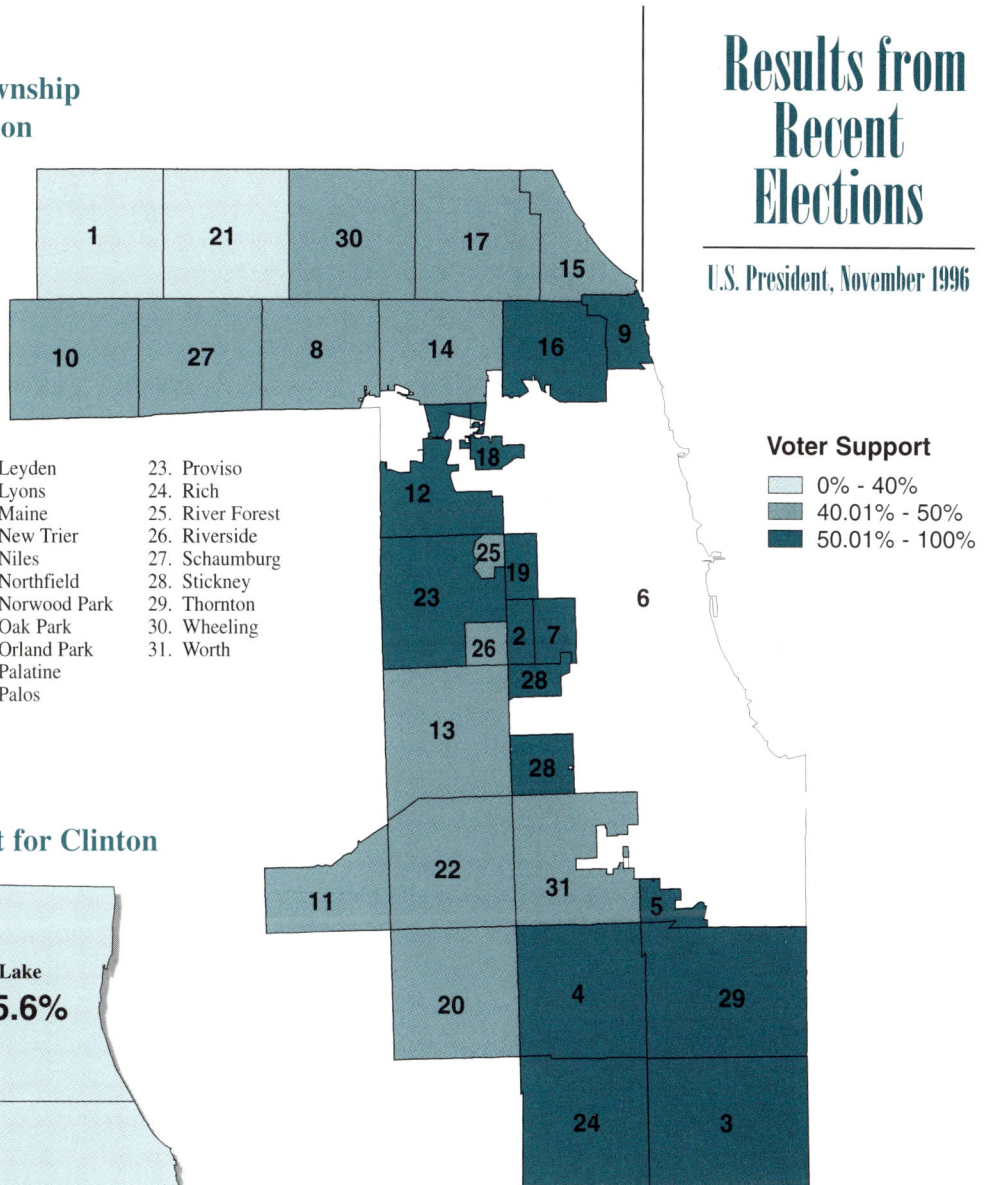

Figure 2.2c
Collar County Support for Clinton

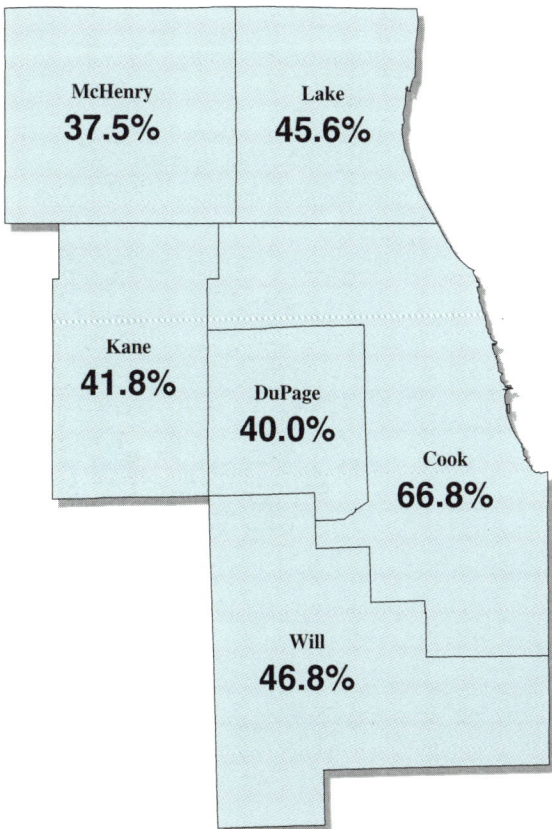

McHenry **37.5%**
Lake **45.6%**
Kane **41.8%**
DuPage **40.0%**
Cook **66.8%**
Will **46.8%**

29

Results from
Recent
Elections

U.S. Senator, November 1992

U.S. Senator, November 1992

Senator Carol Moseley-Braun defeated Rich Williamson by 504,396 votes statewide. She owed her win mainly to the enormous margin she piled up in Chicago, 558,218 votes, a 51.7 percentage-point lead. Although he carried both, Williamson ran poorly for a Republican in suburban Cook and the collar counties. His margin over Moseley-Braun in these two areas combined was only 148,977 votes, not nearly enough to balance her Chicago lead. As a result, Moseley-Braun carried the metro Chicago area by 409,241 votes, a 13.5 percentage-point edge.

Moseley-Braun's huge lead in Chicago owed mainly to her support in the African-American community. African-American voters gave her nearly unanimous and enthusiastic support: they voted 99.5 percent for her and their turnout soared to 63.7 percent, lagging behind white turnout by only 6.1 percentage points. Moseley-Braun also captured nearly three-quarters of the Latino vote. The division was closer among whites, however, with Moseley-Braun barely eking out a majority at 50.5 percent. Her strength

Table 2.3

The 1992 U.S. Senate Race

Ward Group[1]/ Area	%Carol Moseley-Braun (D)	%Rich Williamson (R)	%Minor Candidates	Total Votes
White Northwest Side	46.0	50.9	3.2	140,138
White South Side	51.0	46.1	2.9	125,770
Black South Side	96.4	2.9	.7	334,617
Black West Side	94.1	5.0	1.0	103,453
Latino	74.8	22.3	2.9	75,201
North Lakeshore	71.7	26.0	2.3	119,557
Other White North Side	64.6	32.8	2.7	129,093
Mixed	66.1	31.9	2.0	49,300
Chicago Total	74.9	23.2	1.9	**1,077,129**
Suburban Cook County	47.3	49.1	3.4	1,023,570
Collar Counties	40.8	54.7	4.3	943,287
Metro Area Total	55.1	41.6	3.1	**3,043,986**
Illinois Total	53.2	43.0	3.6	**4,939,559**

Note: D=Democrat, R=Republican

[1]For a detailed explanation of these ward groupings, see pages 4-8 in the introduction to this atlas.

among whites was mainly concentrated in the Lakeshore and North Side wards. She fared less well in the white ethnic strongholds on the Northwest Side and South Side, losing the former and reaching just 51 percent in the latter.

Results from Recent Elections

U.S. Senator, November 1992

The Race in the City: How Voters of Different Races/Ethnicities Supported the Candidates

Race/ Ethnicity	Moseley-Braun	Williamson	Turnout[1]
White	50.5%	46.8%	69.8%
Black	99.5%	0.0%	63.7%
Latino	87.8%	9.6%	32.5%
Total			59.4%

[1]Turnout is the percentage of the voting age population who cast ballots for a candidate for this office in this election.

Results from Recent Elections

U.S. Senator, November 1992

Figure 2.3a
Chicago Support for Moseley-Braun

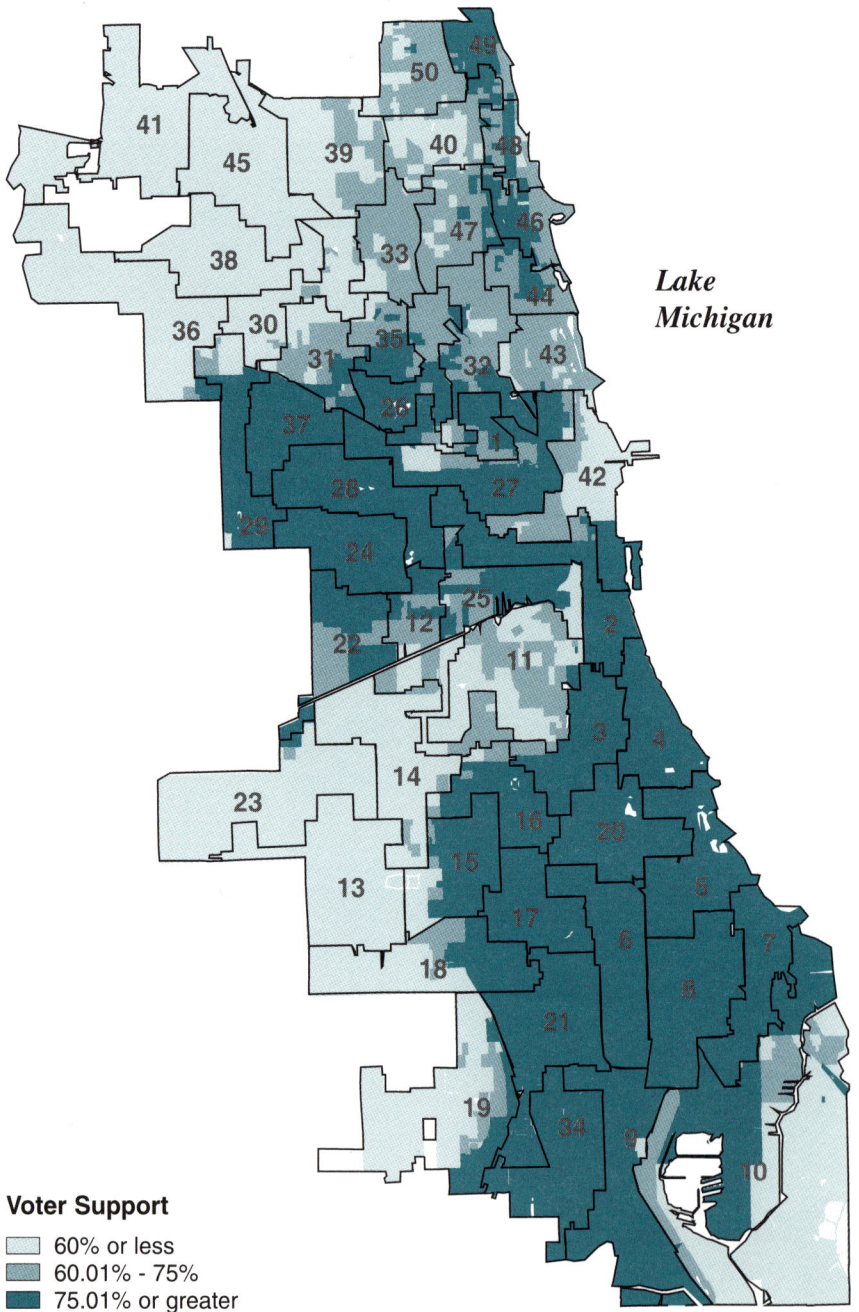

Lake Michigan

Voter Support

- 60% or less
- 60.01% - 75%
- 75.01% or greater

Figure 2.3b
Cook County Township
Support for Moseley-Braun

Results from Recent Elections

U.S. Senator, November 1992

Townships

1. Barrington
2. Berwyn
3. Bloom
4. Bremen
5. Calumet
6. See figure a
7. Cicero
8. Elk Grove
9. Evanston
10. Hanover
11. Lemont
12. Leyden
13. Lyons
14. Maine
15. New Trier
16. Niles
17. Northfield
18. Norwood Park
19. Oak Park
20. Orland Park
21. Palatine
22. Palos
23. Proviso
24. Rich
25. River Forest
26. Riverside
27. Schaumburg
28. Stickney
29. Thornton
30. Wheeling
31. Worth

Voter Support
- 0% - 40%
- 40.01% - 50%
- 50.01% - 100%

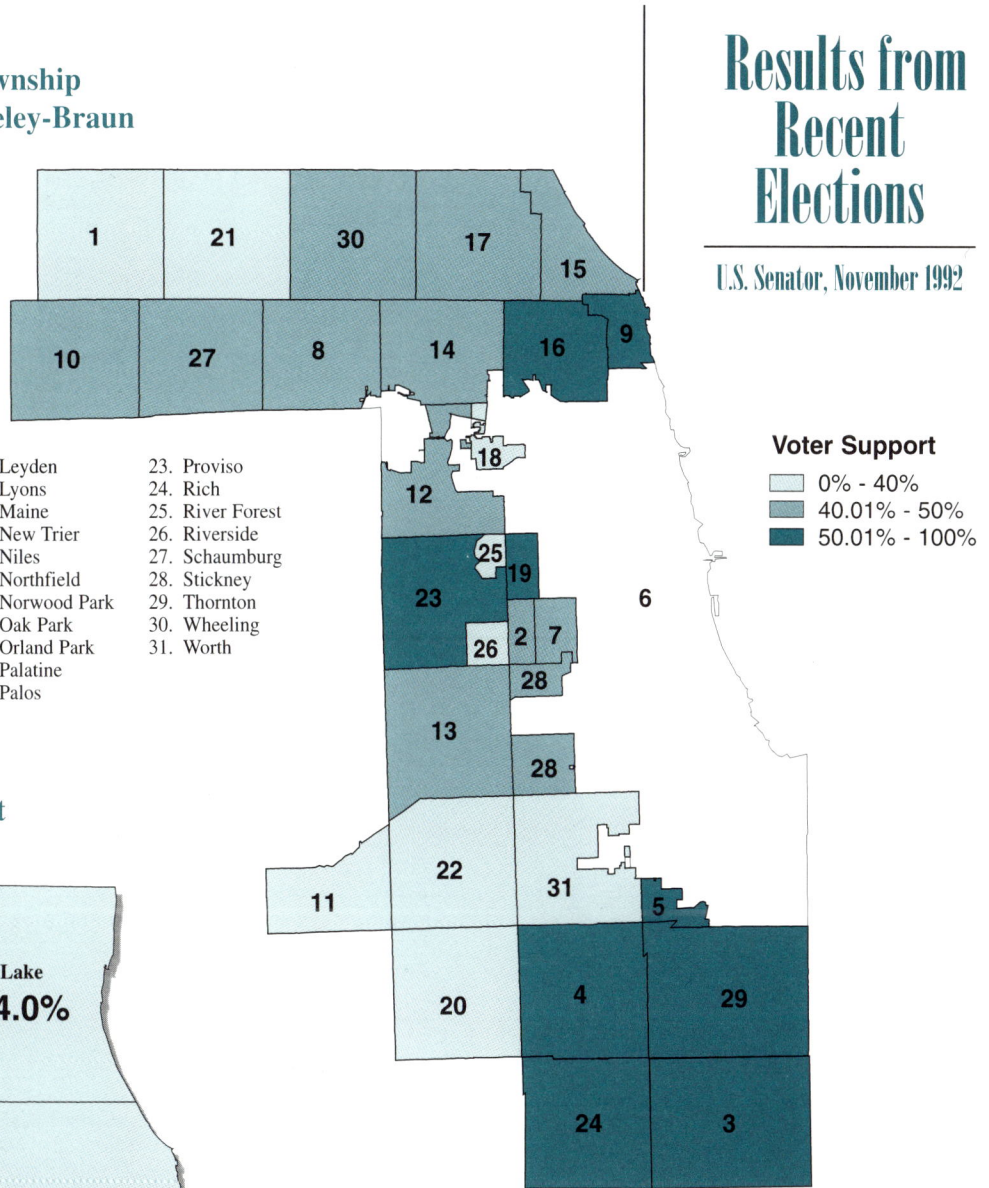

Figure 2.3c
Collar County Support
for Moseley-Braun

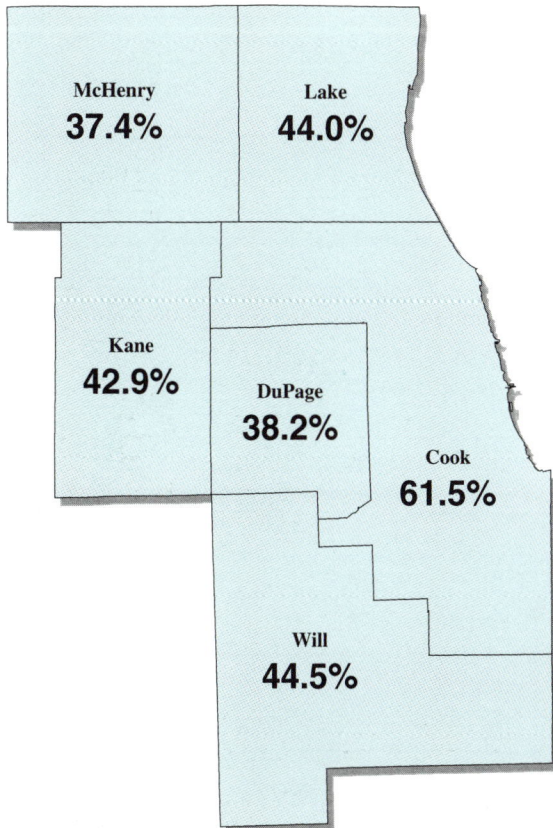

McHenry **37.4%**
Lake **44.0%**
Kane **42.9%**
DuPage **38.2%**
Cook **61.5%**
Will **44.5%**

Results from Recent Elections

U.S. Senator, November 1996

U.S. Senator, November 1996

It was hard to imagine that anyone could run a weaker race for a U.S. Senate seat than the underfunded and stolid Rich Williamson had in losing decisively in 1992. But for all his energy, media savvy, and money, Al Salvi accomplished the unimaginable in 1996.

The voting results showed Salvi to be a remarkably weak candidate. Salvi carried only the collar counties, and these by just 57,642 votes, while Williamson had carried them by over twice that margin. Durbin carried all the other major political areas of the state. Durbin won Chicago by 537,252 votes, a 62.9 percentage-point lead; he carried suburban Cook County—which had gone for Williamson in 1992—by 125,746 votes, a 14.9 percentage-point lead; and he edged out Salvi by 49,848 votes in the downstate counties, a 3 percentage-point lead. Except in the downstate counties, Salvi managed to run well behind Williamson's miserable showing four years earlier.

Table 2.4

The 1992 U.S. Senate Race

Ward Group[1]/ Area	%Dick Durbin (D)	%Al Salvi (R)	%Minor Candidates	Total Votes
White Northwest Side	62.1	35.5	2.5	115,353
White South Side	69.9	27.9	2.3	104,848
Black South Side	93.2	4.5	2.4	259,622
Black West Side	91.9	5.7	2.3	78,001
Latino	82.7	14.4	2.9	61,721
North Lakeshore	75.7	21.9	2.4	91,623
Other White North Side	73.5	24.0	2.6	103,312
Mixed	77.6	20.1	2.3	39,096
Chicago Totals	80.3	17.3	2.4	**853,576**
Suburban Cook	56.0	41.1	2.7	844,508
Collar Counties	44.4	51.1	4.3	862,716
Metro Area Total	60.2	36.5	3.2	**2,560,800**
Illinois Total	56.0	40.6	3.2	**4,250,722**

Note: D=Democrat, R=Republican

[1]For a detailed explanation of these ward grouping, see pages 4-8 in the introduction to this atlas.

Durbin's huge Chicago lead reflected strong support from all three of the city's largest voting groups. African Americans gave over 90 percent of their vote to Durbin, while Latinos fell just below that level. And the city's white voters, who had given Moseley-Braun a bare majority in 1992, delivered nearly two-thirds of their vote to Durbin in 1996. Durbin ran weakest in the White Northwest Side wards, where he polled "only" 62.1 percent of the vote. But this had been the only area of the city that Williamson had carried in 1992, polling 50.9 percent.

Results from Recent Elections

U.S. Senator, November 1996

The Race in the City: How Voters of Different Races/Ethnicities Supported the Candidates

Race/ Ethnicity	Durbin	Salvi	Minor Candidates	Turnout[1]
White	65.4%	32.4%	2.0%	58.1%
Black	94.5%	3.2%	2.2%	49.7%
Latino	89.9%	7.2%	2.7%	28.9%
Total				47.2%

[1]Turnout is the percentage of the voting age population who cast ballots for a candidate for this office in this election.

Results from Recent Elections

U.S. Senator, November 1996

Figure 2.4a
Chicago Support for Durbin

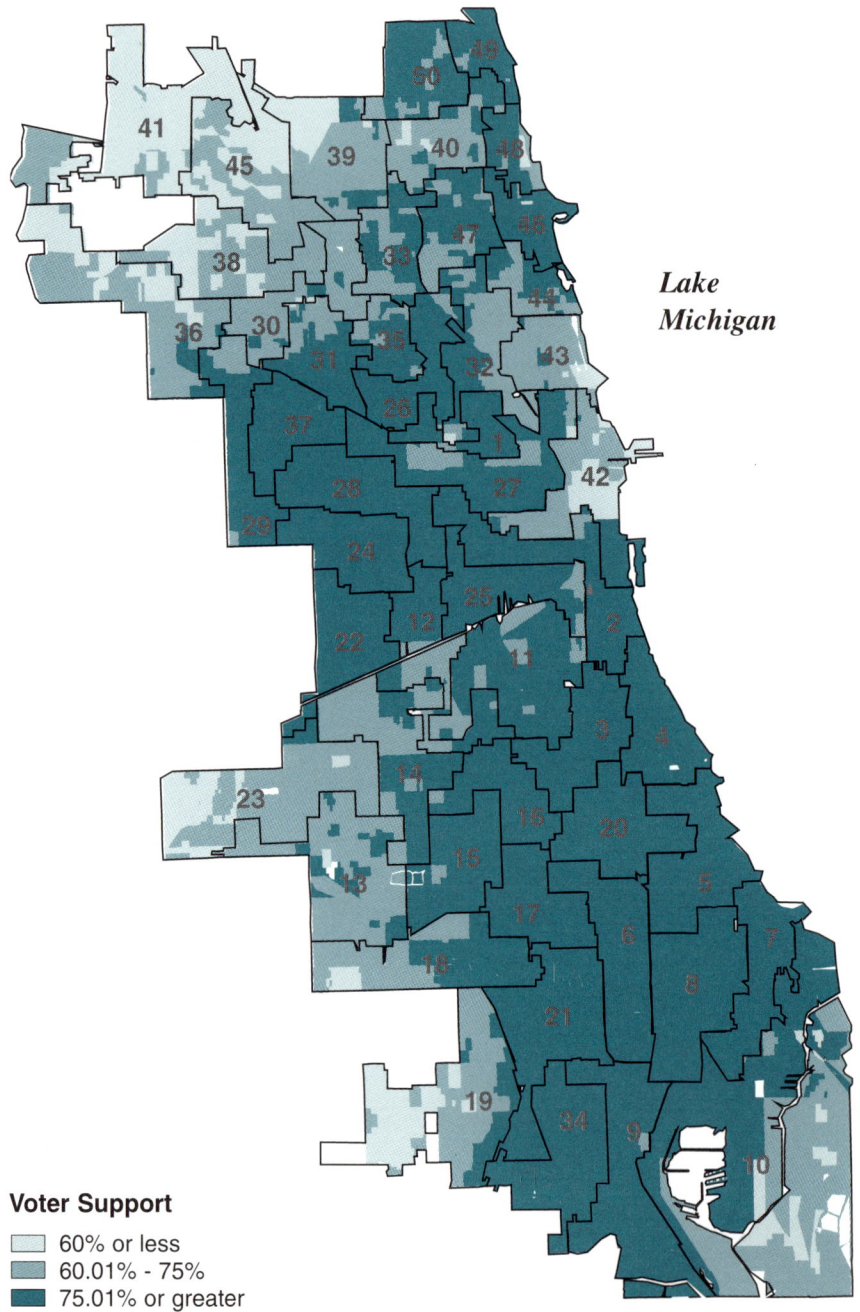

Lake Michigan

Voter Support

- 60% or less
- 60.01% - 75%
- 75.01% or greater

Figure 2.4b
Cook County Township
Support for Durbin

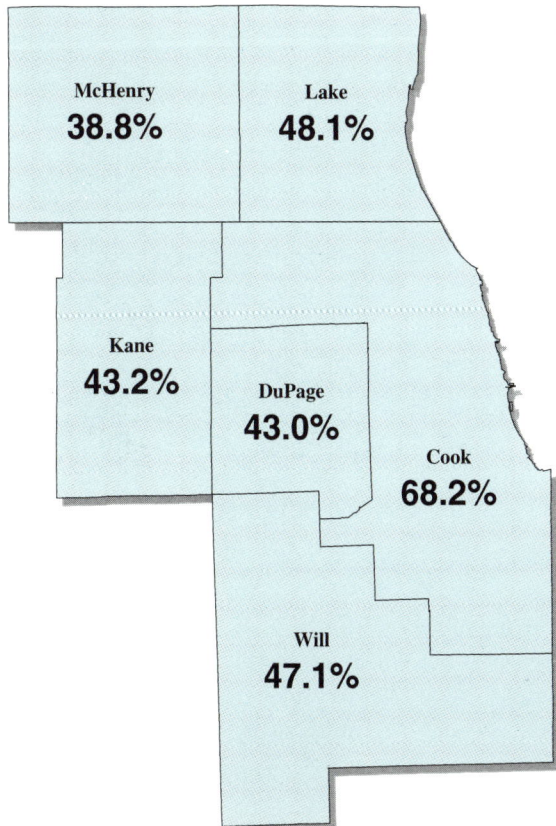

Results from Recent Elections

U.S. Senator, November 1996

Townships

1. Barrington	12. Leyden	23. Proviso
2. Berwyn	13. Lyons	24. Rich
3. Bloom	14. Maine	25. River Forest
4. Bremen	15. New Trier	26. Riverside
5. Calumet	16. Niles	27. Schaumburg
6. See figure a	17. Northfield	28. Stickney
7. Cicero	18. Norwood Park	29. Thornton
8. Elk Grove	19. Oak Park	30. Wheeling
9. Evanston	20. Orland Park	31. Worth
10. Hanover	21. Palatine	
11. Lemont	22. Palos	

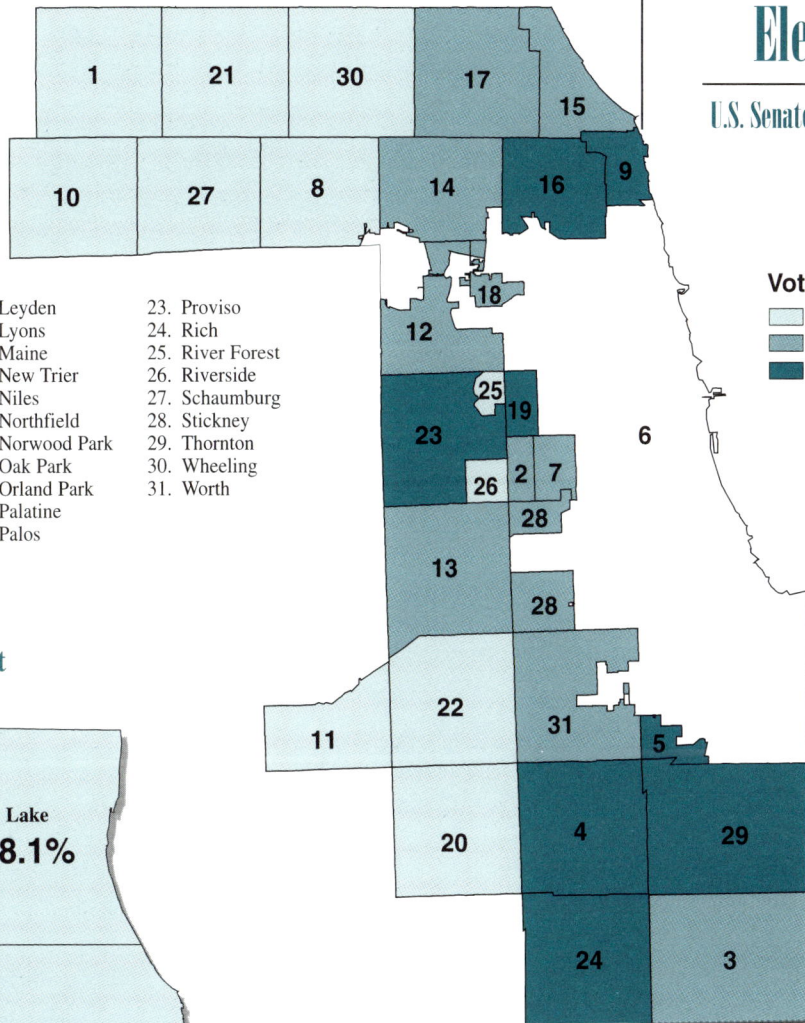

Voter Support

- 0% - 50%
- 50.01% - 60%
- 60.01% - 100%

Figure 2.4c

Collar County Support for Durbin

McHenry
38.8%

Lake
48.1%

Kane
43.2%

DuPage
43.0%

Cook
68.2%

Will
47.1%

Results from Recent Elections

Illinois Governor, November 1994

Illinois Governor, November 1994

As Neil Hartigan had four years earlier, Dawn Clark Netsch carried Chicago against Jim Edgar in 1994. But her margin of victory was much smaller than Hartigan's had been—only 155,559 votes compared to Hartigan's 220,752-vote edge. However, neither of these margins was large enough to offset Edgar's strength in the suburbs and downstate.

In 1990 Edgar lost the white ethnic strongholds on the city's Northwest and South Sides, although polling a respectable 42.4 percent of the white vote citywide. Four years later, Edgar won both of these areas, and he carried the Northwest Side by a nearly two-to-one margin. While these two areas combined encompass only 11 of the city's 50 wards, in 1994 they accounted for 46.6 percent of all of the votes that Edgar received in Chicago. Citywide, Edgar polled 56.0 percent of the white vote, a gain of 13.6 percentage points over his 1990 showing among Chicago's white voters.

In spite of Edgar's strength among white voters, Netsch won Chicago. She did so because white turnout was 5.7 percentage points lower than it had

Table 2.5

The 1994 Gubernatorial Race

Ward Group[1]/Area	%Dawn Clark Netsch (D)	%Jim Edgar (R)	%Minor Candidate	Total Votes
White Northwest Side	36.3	62.3	1.4	91,886
White South Side	49.2	49.6	1.2	90,529
Black South Side	83.9	15.0	1.1	173,659
Black West Side	81.6	17.1	1.3	46,679
Latino	59.8	38.8	1.4	36,711
North Lakeshore	60.3	38.3	1.4	59,232
Other White North Side	53.8	44.8	1.4	73,326
Mixed	54.2	44.6	1.2	29,262
Chicago Total	62.3	36.4	1.3	**601,284**
Suburban Cook County	31.4	67.2	1.3	617,660
Collar Counties	22.4	75.7	1.7	592,184
Metro Area Total	38.7	59.8	1.4	**1,811,128**
Illinois Total	34.4	63.8	1.6	**3,106,556**

Note: D=Democrat, R=Republican

[1]For a detailed explanation of these ward groupings, see pages 4-8 in the introduction to this atlas.

been four years earlier and because she enjoyed strong support among the city's minority voters, especially blacks who had given Edgar 16.4 percent of their votes four years earlier. In 1994, however, blacks voted 6.1 percentage points more strongly for Netsch than they had for Hartigan, and their turnout was 6.2 percentage points higher than it had been in 1990.

Netsch ran 14.0 percentage points behind Hartigan's strength among the white voters citywide. She showed significant strength in white areas of the city only in the North Lakeshore wards, where she ran at 60.3 percent, 3.5 percentage points above Hartigan's mark. Netsch's weakness in Chicago perhaps is best illustrated by noting that running at the top of the ticket as the gubernatorial candidate she polled 124,440 fewer votes than she had when running four years earlier as the candidate for comptroller.

The Race in the City: How Voters of Different Races/Ethnicities Supported the Candidates

Race/Ethnicity	Netsch	Edgar	Turnout [1]
White	42.8%	56.0%	44.2%
Black	86.1%	12.8%	32.7%
Latino	65.3%	33.7%	8.0%
Total			35.0%

[1]Turnout is the percentage of the voting age population who cast ballots for a candidate for this office in this election.

Results from Recent Elections

Illinois Governor, November 1994

Figure 2.5a
Chicago Support for Edgar

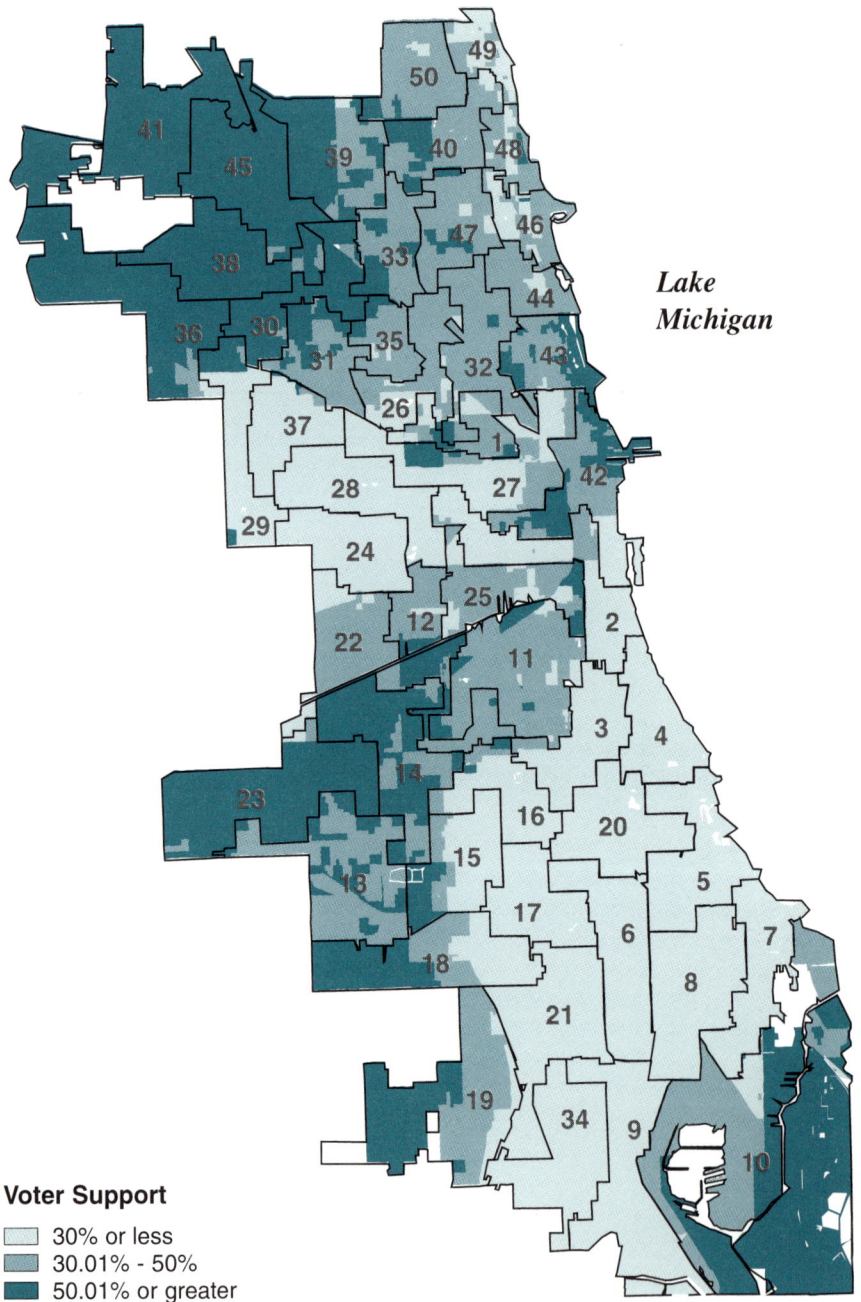

Lake Michigan

Voter Support

☐ 30% or less
☐ 30.01% - 50%
■ 50.01% or greater

Figure 2.5b
Cook County Township
Support for Edgar

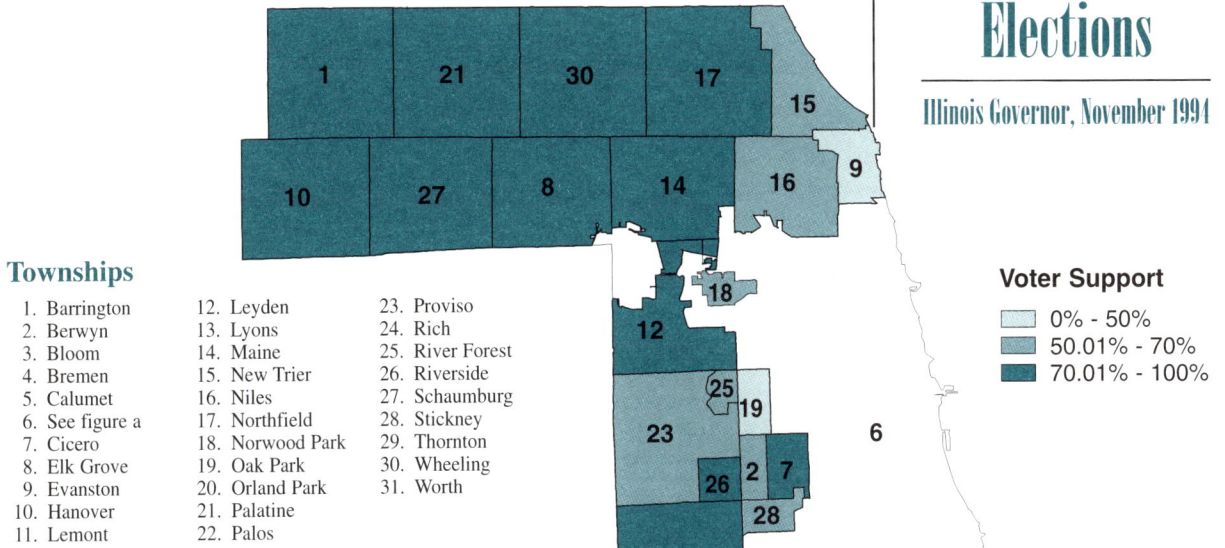

Townships

1. Barrington	12. Leyden	23. Proviso
2. Berwyn	13. Lyons	24. Rich
3. Bloom	14. Maine	25. River Forest
4. Bremen	15. New Trier	26. Riverside
5. Calumet	16. Niles	27. Schaumburg
6. See figure a	17. Northfield	28. Stickney
7. Cicero	18. Norwood Park	29. Thornton
8. Elk Grove	19. Oak Park	30. Wheeling
9. Evanston	20. Orland Park	31. Worth
10. Hanover	21. Palatine	
11. Lemont	22. Palos	

Voter Support

- 0% - 50%
- 50.01% - 70%
- 70.01% - 100%

Figure 2.5c
Collar County
Support for Edgar

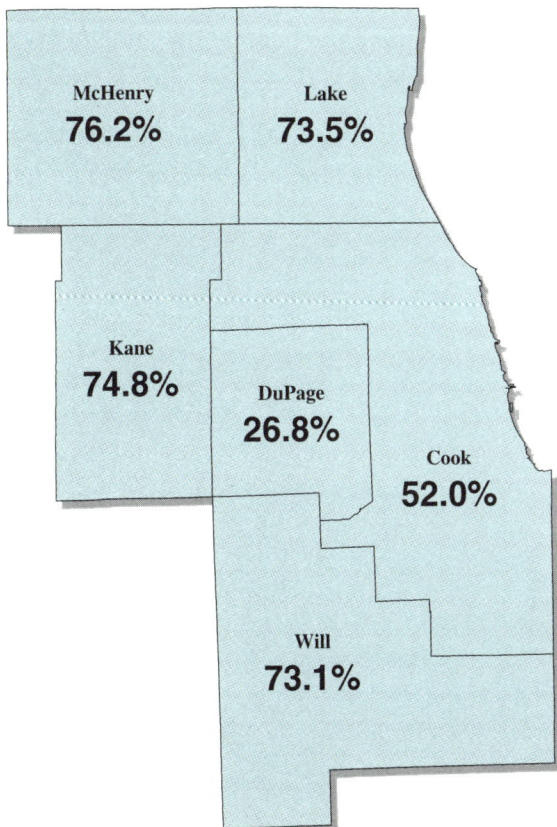

McHenry **76.2%**

Lake **73.5%**

Kane **74.8%**

DuPage **26.8%**

Cook **52.0%**

Will **73.1%**

Results from Recent Elections

Illinois Secretary of State, November 1994

Illinois Secretary of State, November 1994

The 1994 race for secretary of state was expected to be a closely contested one, with the populist Pat Quinn (the incumbent treasurer) challenging George Ryan, the incumbent secretary of state. Quinn, a colorful campaigner, was expected to have wide appeal, especially running against a professional politician and long-time officeholder. But Ryan easily turned back the challenge, defeating Quinn by 685,515 votes, a margin over three times the size of his 1990 edge against Jerry Cosentino.

Except for Chicago, Ryan carried all of the state's major political areas. And he ran 3 to 4 percentage points better in all of them than he had in 1990.

Even in Chicago, Ryan ran better than he had four years earlier against Jerry Cosentino. Ryan's Chicago deficit was 46,561 votes smaller than it had been in 1990, as he increased his strength among the city's three largest voter groups. Ryan carried 50.5 percent of the white vote, a 6 percentage-point jump over four years earlier. He also gained nearly 4 percentage points

Table 2.6

The 1994 Secretary of State Race

Ward Group[1]/ Area	%Pat Quinn (D)	%George Ryan (R)	% Minor Candidate	Total Votes
White Northwest Side	44.8	54.1	1.0	90,380
White South Side	57.1	42.1	.9	89,892
Black South Side	3.3	15.5	1.1	169,741
Black West Side	1.1	17.7	1.2	45,701
Latino	64.7	33.6	1.6	35,578
North Lakeshore	56.5	42.0	1.5	57,761
Other White North Side	54.2	44.3	1.4	71,821
Mixed	60.8	38.2	1.0	28,861
Chicago Total	64.9	34.0	1.2	**589,735**
Suburban Cook County	35.5	63.3	1.0	613,680
Collar Counties	27.2	71.3	1.3	589,527
Metro Area Total	42.4	56.3	1.2	**1,792,942**
Illinois Total	38.2	60.4	1.2	**3,088,847**

Note: D=Democrat, R=Republican

[1]For a detailed explanation of these ward groupings, see pages 4-8 in the introduction to this atlas.

among blacks and carried a quarter of the Latino vote, where he had gotten virtually no support four years earlier.

In contrast, Quinn's appeal proved remarkably shallow. He was weaker than Cosentino had been among whites, blacks, and Latinos, and he trailed Cosentino's percentages in every area of the city except the North Lakeshore wards, where he ran 2.4 percentage points ahead of Cosentino's 1990 mark. Even so, his 54.2 percent on the North Lakeshore was below that of any of his Democratic ticket mates in 1994, and even behind the 66.3 percent he had polled in those wards when running for treasurer in 1990.

Results from Recent Elections

Illinois Secretary of State, November 1994

The Race in the City: How Voters of Different Races/Ethnicities Supported the Candidates			
Race/ Ethnicity	Quinn	Ryan	Turnout[1]
White	48.5%	50.5%	43.6%
Black	85.2%	13.4%	32.0%
Latino	72.3%	25.0%	7.6%
Total			32.5%

[1]Turnout is the percentage of the voting age population who cast ballots for a candidate for this office in this election.

Results from Recent Elections

Illinois Secretary of State,
November 1994

Figure 2.6a
Chicago Support for Ryan

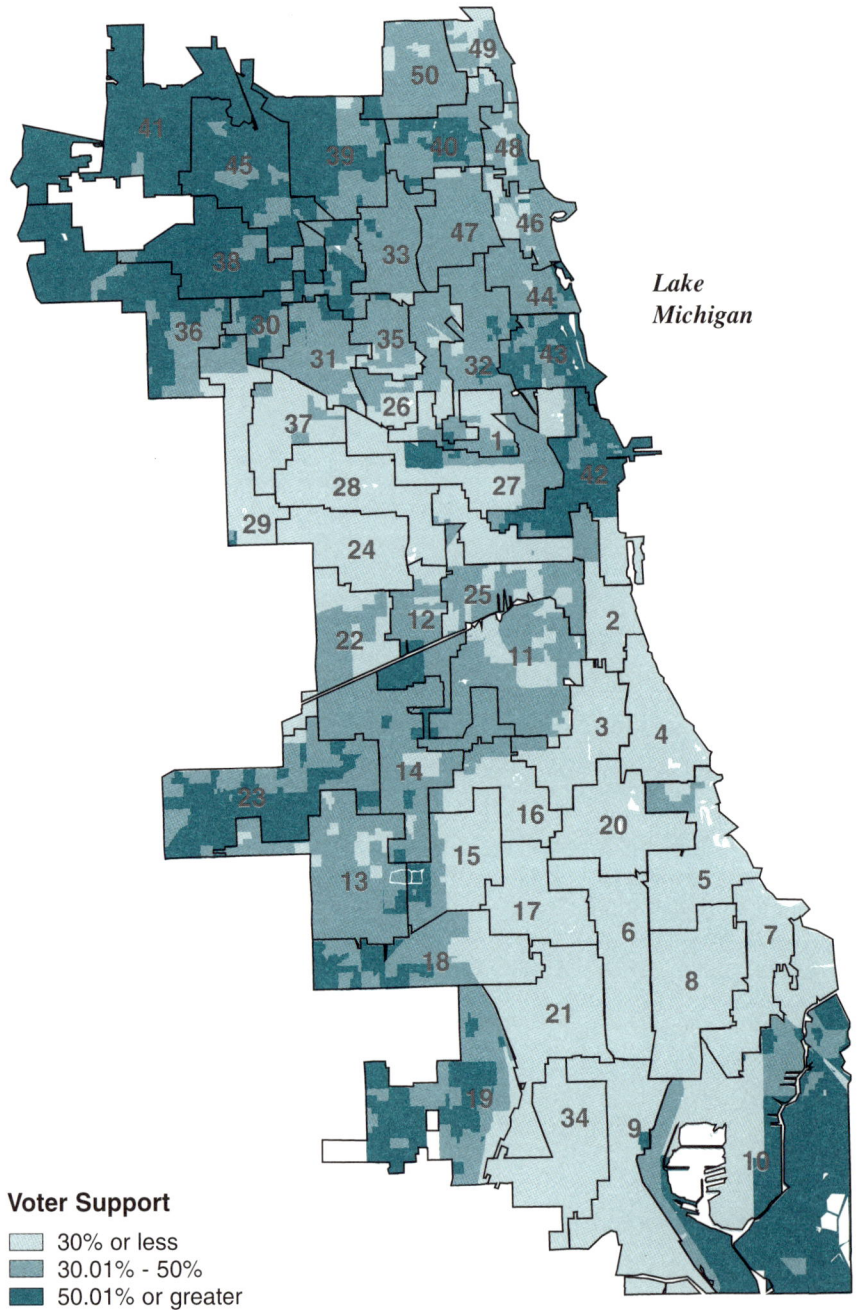

Lake Michigan

Voter Support

- 30% or less
- 30.01% - 50%
- 50.01% or greater

Figure 2.6b
Cook County Township
Support for Ryan

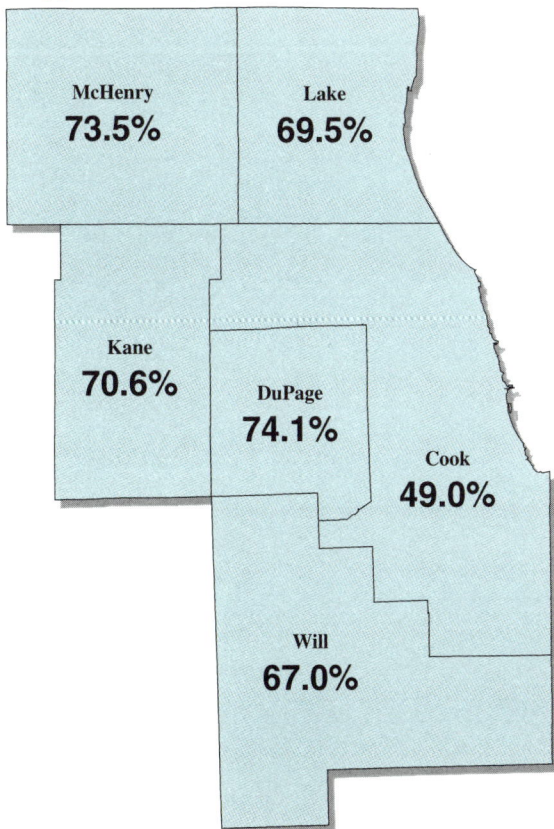

Results from Recent Elections

Illinois Secretary of State, November 1994

Townships

1. Barrington	12. Leyden	23. Proviso
2. Berwyn	13. Lyons	24. Rich
3. Bloom	14. Maine	25. River Forest
4. Bremen	15. New Trier	26. Riverside
5. Calumet	16. Niles	27. Schaumburg
6. See figure a	17. Northfield	28. Stickney
7. Cicero	18. Norwood Park	29. Thornton
8. Elk Grove	19. Oak Park	30. Wheeling
9. Evanston	20. Orland Park	31. Worth
10. Hanover	21. Palatine	
11. Lemont	22. Palos	

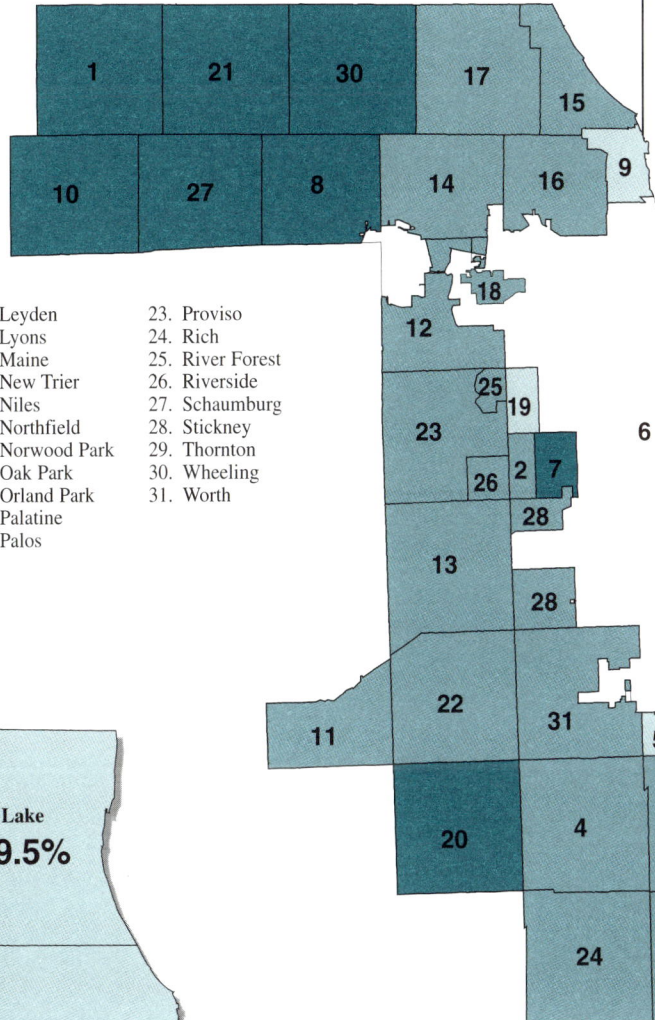

Voter Support

	0% - 50%
	50.01% - 70%
	70.01% - 100%

Figure 2.6c

Collar County
Support for Ryan

McHenry **73.5%**

Lake **69.5%**

Kane **70.6%**

DuPage **74.1%**

Cook **49.0%**

Will **67.0%**

Illinois Attorney General, November 1994

In 1994 Jim Ryan won the attorney general's office, a position he had unsuccessfully sought four years earlier. When he lost to Roland Burris in 1990, Ryan carried suburban Cook County and the collars, but was trounced in Chicago (by 45.6 percentage points). Burris's 305,176-vote margin in the city offset Ryan's successes in the suburbs and enabled Burris to carry the metro area by a scant 22,296 votes, a 1.3 percentage-point edge. Burris also carried the downstate counties—by 72,918 votes, a 5.3 percentage-point margin.

The 1994 voting patterns differed in two critical respects. First, while Ryan again lost Chicago, he did so by a smaller margin—only 243,988 votes. Second, Ryan carried the downstate counties, registering 58.7 percent of the vote there and outpolling his opponent by 250,651 votes, which more than offset his Chicago deficit.

Table 2.7

The 1994 Attorney General Race

Ward Group[1]/ Area	%Al Hofeld (D)	%Jim Ryan (R)	%Minor Candidate	Total Votes
White Northwest Side	49.4	49.1	1.5	90,295
White South Side	61.4	37.4	1.2	89,844
Black South Side	87.1	10.5	2.3	169,939
Black West Side	84.6	13.2	2.3	45,350
Latino	68.8	28.7	2.5	35,704
North Lakeshore	64.3	33.4	2.4	58,163
Other White North Side	62.1	36.0	2.0	72,124
Mixed	64.0	34.4	1.6	28,896
Chicago Total	69.7	28.3	2.0	**590,315**
Suburban Cook County	42.0	56.3	1.5	611,774
Collar Counties	33.2	64.9	1.7	589,665
Metro Area Total	48.2	49.9	1.7	**1,791,754**
Illinois Total	44.5	53.6	1.8	**3,080,375**

Note: D=Democrat, R=Republican

[1]For a detailed explanation of these ward groupings, see pages 4-8 in the introduction to this atlas.

In Chicago, Ryan garnered 14,648 more votes than he had in 1990, while the vote for his Democratic opponent was off by 75,836. Al Hofeld failed to match Burris's strength in any of the city's ward groups. Ryan gained 4 percentage points among whites citywide, 5 among blacks, and an enormous 23 among Latinos over his 1990 run. The city's overall turnout also dropped from its 1990 level, and by a larger amount than it dropped in suburban Cook County or the collar counties. All of these factors combined to produce Ryan's 1994 victory.

Results from Recent Elections

Illinois Attorney General, November 1994

The Race in the City: How Voters of Different Races/Ethnicities Supported the Candidates

Race/ Ethnicity	Hofeld	Ryan	Turnout[1]
White	54.3%	44.2%	43.6%
Black	88.9%	8.8%	31.9%
Latino	73.0%	23.0%	7.8%
Total			32.6%

[1]Turnout is the percentage of the voting age population who cast ballots for a candidate for this office in this election.

Results from Recent Elections

Illinois Attorney General,
November 1994

Figure 2.7a
Chicago Support for Ryan

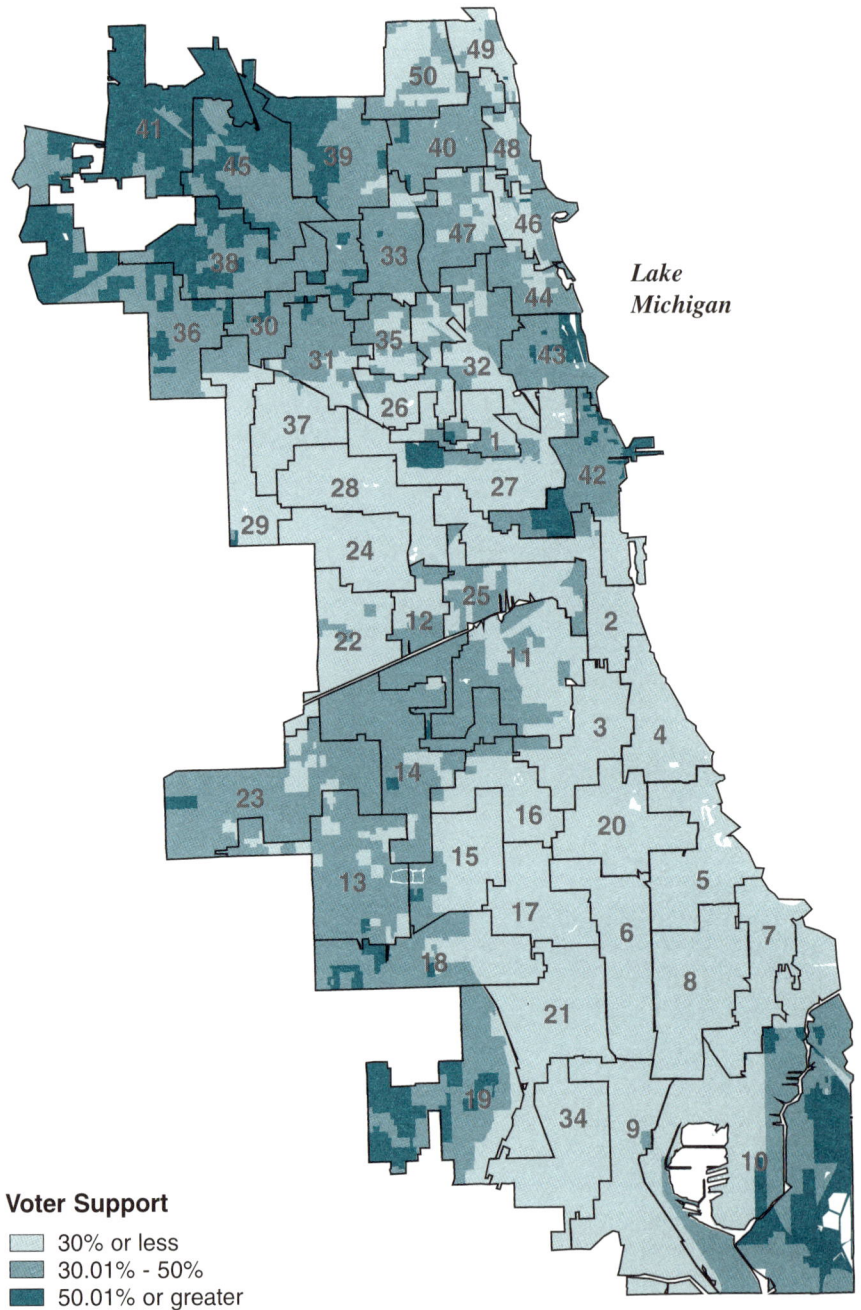

Lake Michigan

Voter Support
- 30% or less
- 30.01% - 50%
- 50.01% or greater

Figure 2.7b
Cook County Township
Support for Ryan

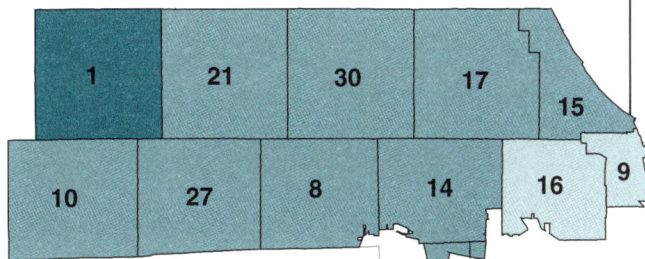

Results from Recent Elections

Illinois Attorney General,
November 1994

Townships

1. Barrington
2. Berwyn
3. Bloom
4. Bremen
5. Calumet
6. See figure a
7. Cicero
8. Elk Grove
9. Evanston
10. Hanover
11. Lemont

12. Leyden
13. Lyons
14. Maine
15. New Trier
16. Niles
17. Northfield
18. Norwood Park
19. Oak Park
20. Orland Park
21. Palatine
22. Palos

23. Proviso
24. Rich
25. River Forest
26. Riverside
27. Schaumburg
28. Stickney
29. Thornton
30. Wheeling
31. Worth

Voter Support

- 0% - 50%
- 50.01% - 70%
- 70.01% - 100%

Figure 2.7c
Collar County Support for Ryan

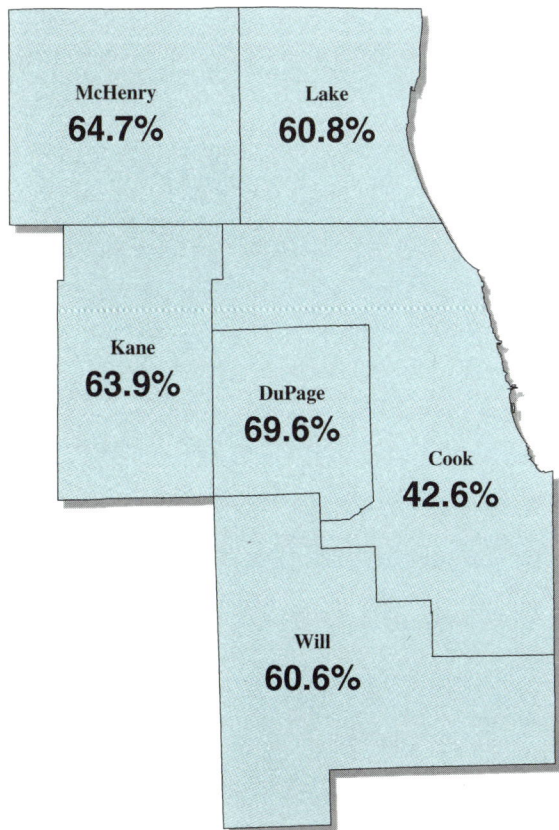

McHenry
64.7%

Lake
60.8%

Kane
63.9%

DuPage
69.6%

Cook
42.6%

Will
60.6%

49

Results from Recent Elections

Illinois State Treasurer, November 1994

Illinois Democrats have long been accustomed to winning the office of treasurer. In 1990, Pat Quinn defeated his Republican opponent statewide by 356,250 votes, a margin of 11.3 percentage points. Quinn carried Chicago, which was to be expected; but he also carried suburban Cook County and the downstate counties. Among the state's major political areas, he lost only the collar counties, and those by the comparatively slim margin of 79,223 votes.

The patterns of support were very different in 1994. The statewide result was close: Nancy Drew Sheehan, the Democratic candidate, polled 47.8 percent of the vote, losing by only 77,018 votes, or 2.6 percentage points. But among the state's major political areas, she carried only Chicago, losing suburban Cook County, the collar counties, and the downstate counties. However, her margin of victory in Chicago was large—302,396 votes—which offset her deficits in suburban Cook and the collar counties and allowed her to carry the Chicago metropolitan area by a razor-thin margin of

Table 2.8

The 1994 State Treasurer Race

Ward Group[1]/ Area	% Nancy Drew Sheehan (D)	%Judy Baar Topinka (R)	%Minor Candidate	Total Votes
White Northwest Side	56.0	42.6	1.4	87,999
White South Side	70.6	28.4	1.0	88,556
Black South Side	92.8	6.0	1.2	166,545
Black West Side	91.3	7.5	1.2	44,784
Latino	75.9	22.3	1.7	34,826
North Lakeshore	64.7	33.4	1.9	56,539
Other White North Side	64.3	33.9	1.8	70,163
Mixed	73.0	26.0	1.0	28,196
Chicago Total	75.5	23.1	1.4	**577,608**
Suburban Cook County	41.0	57.6	1.3	602,300
Collar Counties	31.6	66.3	2.0	570,366
Metro Area Total	49.3	49.0	1.5	**1,750,274**
Illinois Total	47.8	50.4	1.7	**2,984,760**

Note: D=Democrat, R=Republican

[1]For a detailed explanation of these ward groupings, see pages 4-8 in the introduction to this atlas.

4,664 votes. The Republican candidate, Judy Baar Topinka, offset this slim edge by outpolling Sheehan in the downstate counties by 81,682 votes.

In Chicago, African Americans and Latinos proved again that they are the Democratic party's most reliable voters. They delivered the bulk of their vote to Sheehan, and their turnout was also slightly higher than it had been four years earlier. Sheehan also ran well among the city's white voters, carrying all of the nonminority ward groups, including the White Northwest Side wards that gave majorities to the Republican candidates for governor, secretary of state, and comptroller. Citywide, Sheehan polled 60.4 percent of the white vote. But this was 9.5 percentage points below Quinn's 1990 margin among whites, and white turnout was also down by 5.1 percentage points. But even if Sheehan had matched Quinn's numbers among Chicago's white voters, she would have increased her margin over Topinka by 68,310 votes, still not enough to offset the Republican's downstate edge.

The Race in the City: How Voters of Different Races/Ethnicities Supported the Candidates

Race/Ethnicity	Sheehan	Topinka	Turnout[1]
White	60.4%	38.3%	42.6%
Black	94.8%	3.8%	31.4%
Latino	87.8%	10.8%	7.6%
Total			31.8%

[1]Turnout is the percentage of the voting age population who cast ballots for a candidate for this office in this election.

Results from Recent Elections

Illinois State Treasurer,
November 1994

Figure 2.8a
Chicago Support for Topinka

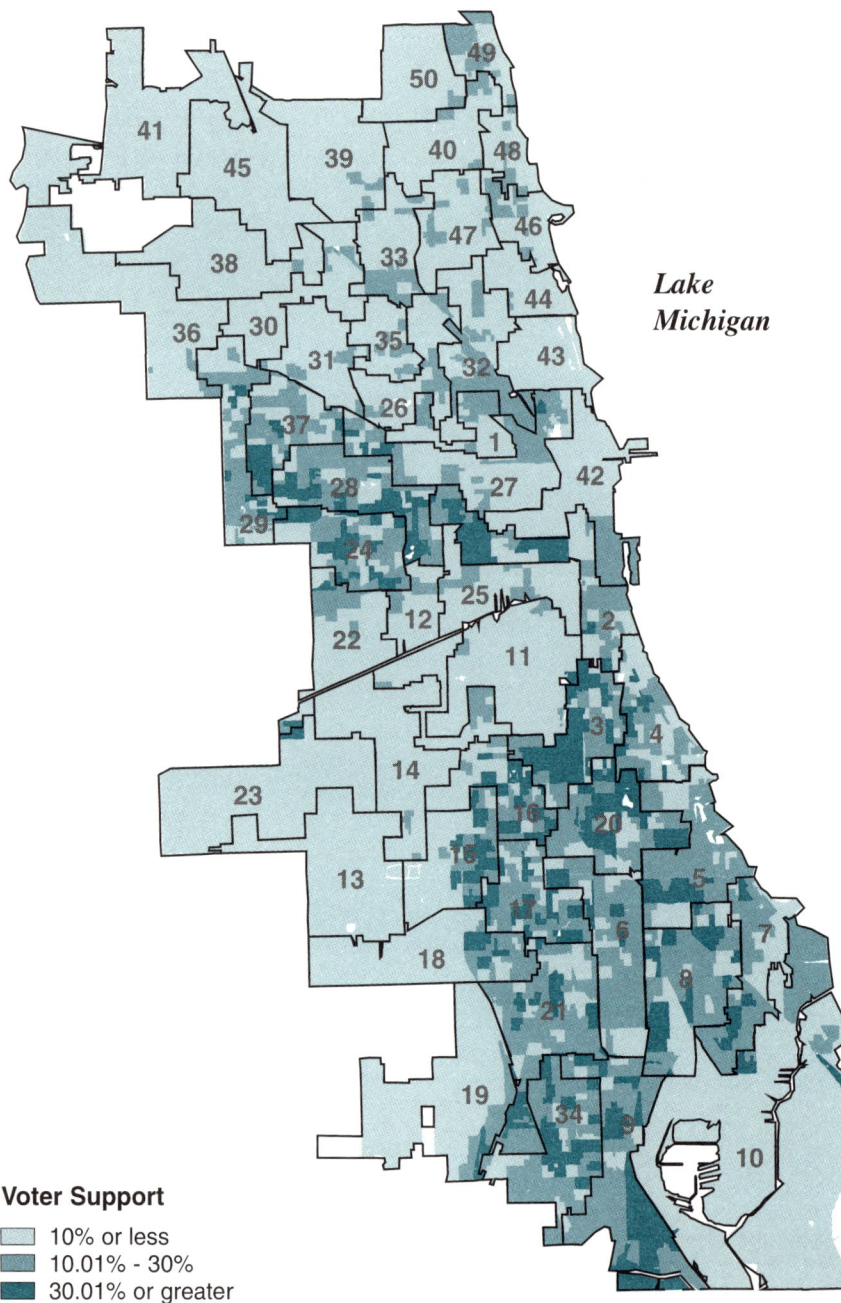

Lake Michigan

Voter Support

- 10% or less
- 10.01% - 30%
- 30.01% or greater

Figure 2.8b
Cook County Township
Support for Topinka

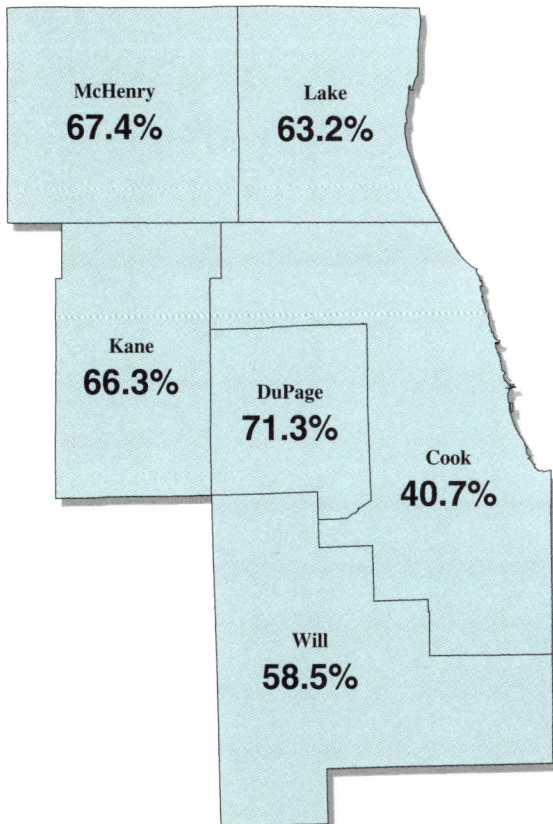

Results from Recent Elections

Illinois State Treasurer,
November 1994

Townships

1. Barrington	12. Leyden	23. Proviso
2. Berwyn	13. Lyons	24. Rich
3. Bloom	14. Maine	25. River Forest
4. Bremen	15. New Trier	26. Riverside
5. Calumet	16. Niles	27. Schaumburg
6. See figure a	17. Northfield	28. Stickney
7. Cicero	18. Norwood Park	29. Thornton
8. Elk Grove	19. Oak Park	30. Wheeling
9. Evanston	20. Orland Park	31. Worth
10. Hanover	21. Palatine	
11. Lemont	22. Palos	

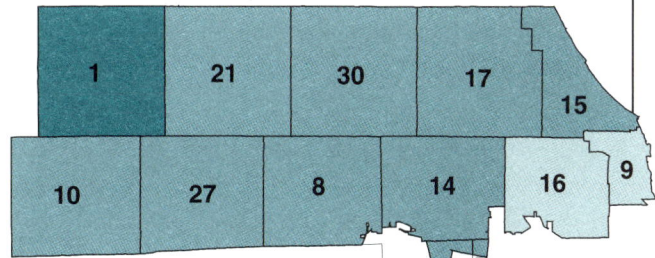

Voter Support
0% - 50%
50.01% - 70%
70.01% - 100%

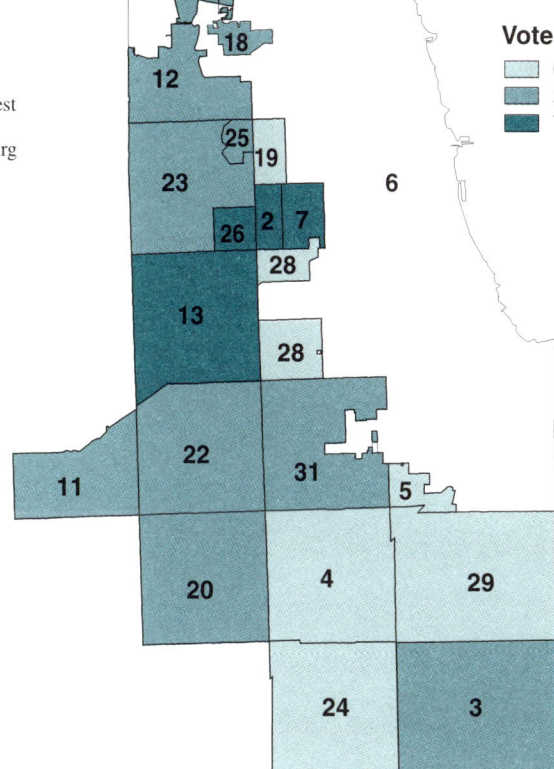

Figure 2.8c

Collar County
Support for Topinka

McHenry **67.4%**
Lake **63.2%**
Kane **66.3%**
DuPage **71.3%**
Cook **40.7%**
Will **58.5%**

Illinois State Comptroller, November 1994

In the early 1990s, Democratic candidates toward the bottom of the state ticket fared rather well. In 1990, for example, Dawn Clark Netsch handily defeated her Republican opponent for comptroller, winning by an 8.1 percentage-point edge. Netsch outpolled the Republican candidate in Chicago by 352,946 votes, a 54.8 percentage-point margin. She even carried suburban Cook County, although by a scant 14,128 votes. And, by holding her Republican opponent to a comparatively slim 87,703-vote edge in the collar counties, Netsch managed to carry the Chicago metro area by 275,371 votes, a 15.3 percentage-point bulge.

Four years later, the Democratic candidate for comptroller, Earlean Collins, did not run nearly as well in any of these areas. She carried Chicago, of course, but only by 250,426 votes—down by 102,520 from Netsch's 1990 margin in the city. Collins lost suburban Cook County by 169,551 votes allowing a 29.3 percentage-point edge for the Republican candidate, Loleta Didrickson. In the collar counties, Didrickson beat Collins by 46.5 percent-

Table 2.9

The 1994 Comptroller Race

Ward Group[1]/ Area	%Earlean Collins (D)	%Loleta Didrickson (R)	%Minor Candidate	Total Votes
White Northwest Side	44.4	51.1	4.5	83,431
White South Side	61.6	34.4	4.0	83,882
Black South Side	94.0	4.9	1.1	167,034
Black West Side	92.2	6.6	1.2	45,035
Latino	71.2	24.7	4.1	33,563
North Lakeshore	56.3	38.3	5.4	54,154
Other White North Side	55.4	39.0	5.6	67,177
Mixed	65.8	30.7	3.4	27,247
Chicago Total	70.7	26.1	3.3	**561,523**
Suburban Cook County	33.3	62.6	4.0	578,582
Collar Counties	24.7	71.2	4.0	566,880
Metro Area Total	42.7	53.4	3.7	**1,706,985**
Illinois Total	41.1	55.0	3.8	**2,936,321**

Note: D=Democrat, R=Republican

age points, or 263,938 votes. Thus, the metro area, which Netsch had carried by a wide margin in 1990, went almost as decisively to the Republican candidate in 1994—by 183,063 votes, a 10.7 percentage-point lead. Statewide, Didrickson won by 406,994 votes, or 13.9 percentage points, over Collins.

In Chicago, Collins, an African American, ran strongly only among the city's minority voters. She polled 96.5 percent of the African-American vote, beating Netsch's mark by 2.8 percentage points. African-American turnout for this contest was also higher than it had been in 1990, by 6.6 percentage points. Collins also did well among Latino voters, garnering 86.1 percent of their vote, although this was still 12.8 percentage points below Netsch's mark four years earlier. More tellingly, in 1990, Netsch had run at over 70 percent in all the other ward groups, except the White Northwest Side, where she received 61.8 percent. But Collins in 1994 was not able to reach 70 percent in any of the nonminority ward groups, and she actually lost the Northwest Side white wards to Didrickson. Citywide, Collins polled only a plurality of the white vote—49.0 percent, just 2.8 percentage points more than Didrickson. In contrast, Netsch had defeated her Republican opponent by 37.5 percentage points among Chicago's white voters. Finally, white turnout in 1994 was 7.6 percentage points lower than it had been in 1990.

The Race in the City: How Voters of Different Races/Ethnicities Supported the Candidates			
Race/ Ethnicity	Collins	Didrickson	Turnout[1]
White	49.0%	46.2%	40.3%
Black	96.5%	2.5%	31.6%
Latino	86.1%	11.1%	7.4%
Total			31.0%

[1]Turnout is the percentage of the voting age population who cast ballots for a candidate for this office in this election.

Results from Recent Elections

Illinois State Comptroller,
November 1994

Figure 2.9a
Chicago Support for Didrickson

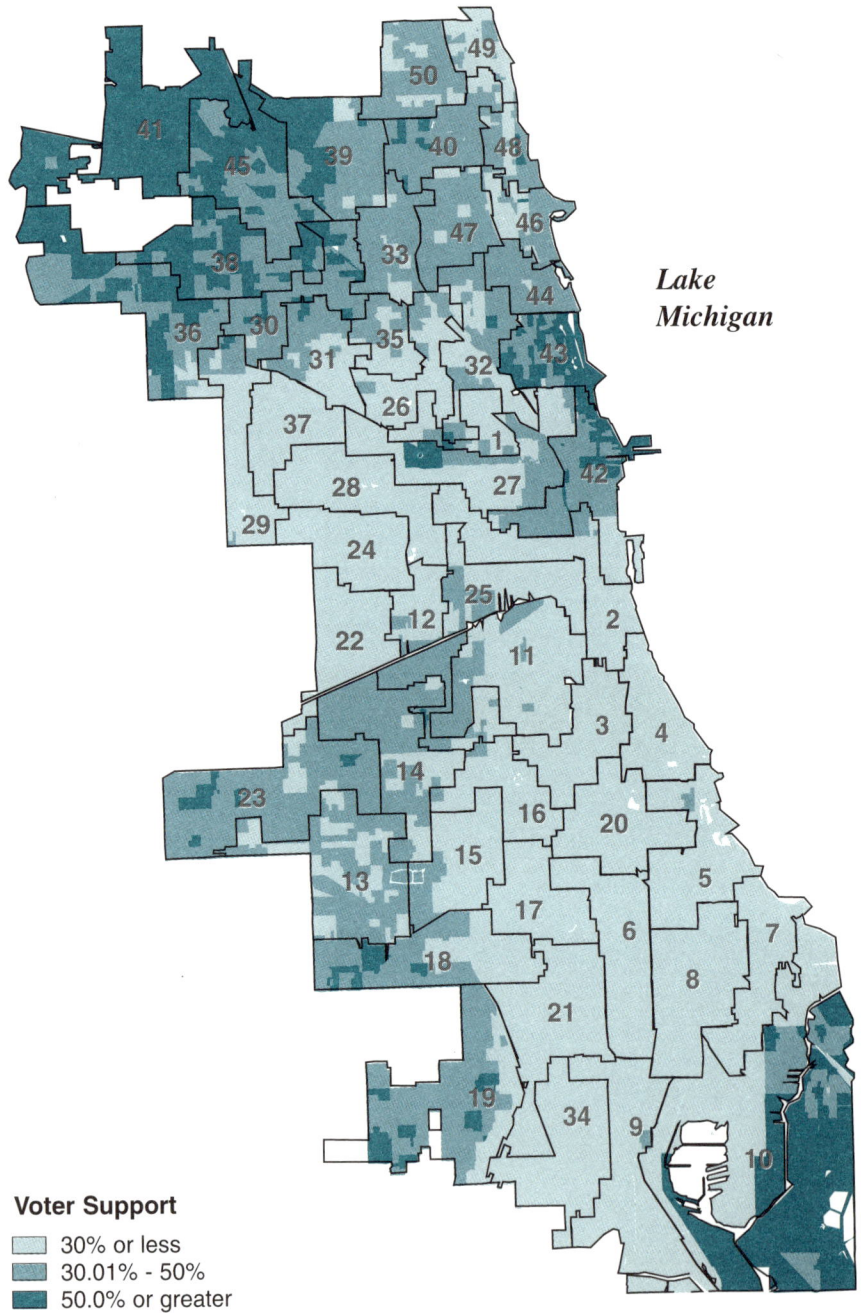

Lake Michigan

Voter Support

- 30% or less
- 30.01% - 50%
- 50.0% or greater

Figure 2.9b
Cook County Township
Support for Didrickson

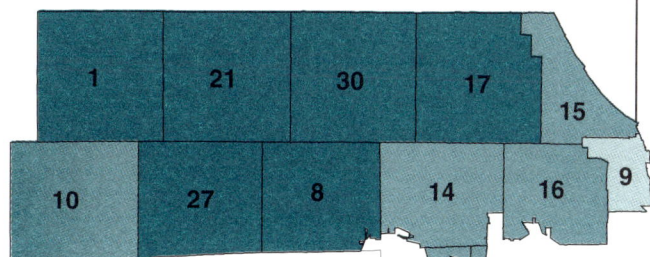

Results from Recent Elections

Illinois State Comptroller, November 1994

Townships

1. Barrington
2. Berwyn
3. Bloom
4. Bremen
5. Calumet
6. See figure a
7. Cicero
8. Elk Grove
9. Evanston
10. Hanover
11. Lemont
12. Leyden
13. Lyons
14. Maine
15. New Trier
16. Niles
17. Northfield
18. Norwood Park
19. Oak Park
20. Orland Park
21. Palatine
22. Palos
23. Proviso
24. Rich
25. River Forest
26. Riverside
27. Schaumburg
28. Stickney
29. Thornton
30. Wheeling
31. Worth

Voter Support

- 0% - 50%
- 50.01% - 70%
- 70.01% - 100%

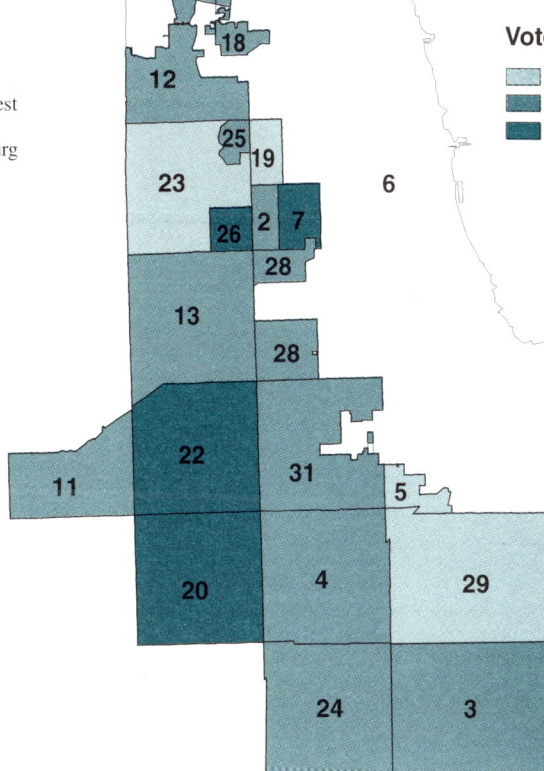

Figure 2.9c
Collar County
Support for Didrickson

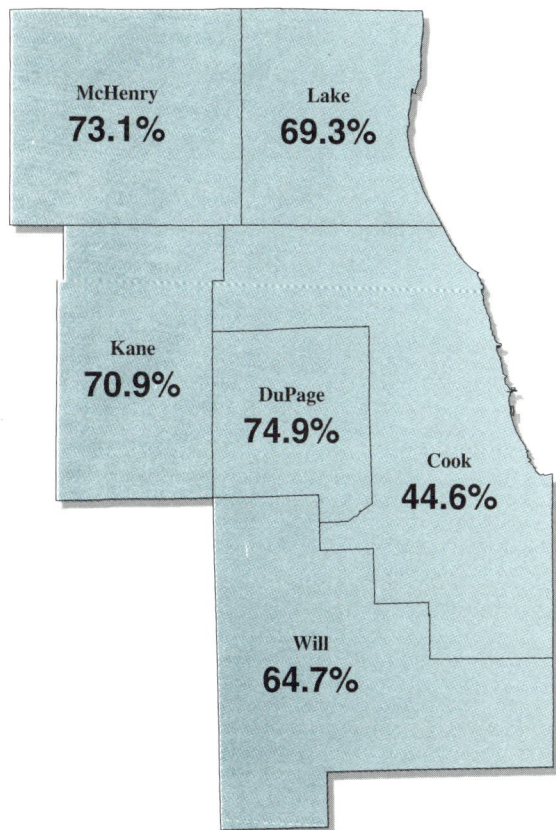

McHenry
73.1%

Lake
69.3%

Kane
70.9%

DuPage
74.9%

Cook
44.6%

Will
64.7%

57

Results from Recent Elections

Mayor of Chicago, April 1983

Mayor of Chicago, April 1983

This was the election that gave Chicago its first African-American mayor, Harold Washington. It was also an election marked by an extraordinary intensity and racial polarization. Blatantly racist literature, of the sort that had not been seen in decades except in some southern backwaters, was widely circulated. "Bye, Bye Blackbird," the racial anthem of Chicago politics in the 1920s, was resurrected and often played at Epton rallies. The mainstream media didn't report the details of the racist campaigning at the grassroots, but nevertheless managed to keep the focus on race by constantly referring to Washington as "the black candidate."

The intensity of the campaign carried over to election day: turnout was extremely high, even for a city that always takes local politics more seriously than state or national contests. Two-thirds of the city's white and black voters cast ballots on election day, as did just under a third of Latinos who were of voting age. The vote polarized along racial lines: almost 9 out of 10 whites voted for the Republican candidate, Bernard Epton, while over 9 out of 10 African Americans and 8 out of 10 Latinos cast their ballots for Washington.

Table 2.10

The 1983 Chicago Mayoral Race

Ward Group[1]	%Harold Washington (D)	%Bernard Epton (R)	%Minor Candidate	Total Votes
White Northwest Side	8.6	91.1	.3	207,469
White South Side	16.4	83.2	.3	212,145
Black South Side	94.0	5.8	.2	385,868
Black West Side	92.1	7.7	.3	113,766
Latino	51.9	47.6	.5	53,770
North Lakeshore	41.9	57.7	.4	151,597
Other White North Side	25.5	74.1	.5	111,760
Mixed	50.8	48.9	.3	54,917
Chicago Total	51.7	48.0	.3	**1,291,292**

Note: D=Democrat, R=Republican

[1]For a detailed explanation of these ward groupings, see pages 4-8 in the introduction to this atlas. Keep in mind, however, that figure 2.10 maps the city using the ward boundaries in effect at the time of the election.

When the votes were counted, Washington barely managed to win by the narrow margin of 48,321 votes. He did so by pulling together a coalition of African Americans, Latinos, and a small number of white voters. Figure 2.10 shows the ward-by-ward levels of support Washington earned. It reveals that 18 wards—the Latino, the Black South Side, and the Black West Side wards—gave Washington over 75 percent of their support.

Even so, in a city where Republicans had not won the mayoralty since 1927, a little-known Republican former legislator had nearly been victorious. Except for the fact that he was white, Epton brought no special qualifications to the contest. But his racial identity was the one qualification he needed, as 80 percent of the city's white Democrats cast their ballots for the white Republican candidate and against an African-American Democrat. Most of the city's prominent white Democratic "leaders" also deserted their party's nominee and either openly or covertly supported Epton.

Results from Recent Elections

Mayor of Chicago, April 1983

The Race in the City: How Voters of Different Races/Ethnicities Supported the Candidates			
Race/Ethnicity	**Washington**	**Epton**	**Turnout[1]**
White	12.3%	87.6%	66.6%
Black	99.7%	.2%	67.7%
Latino	82.3%	17.6%	31.1%
Total			63.2%

[1]Turnout is the percentage of the voting age population who cast ballots for a candidate for this office in this election.

Results from Recent Elections

Mayor of Chicago, April 1983

**Figure 2.10
Support for Washington**

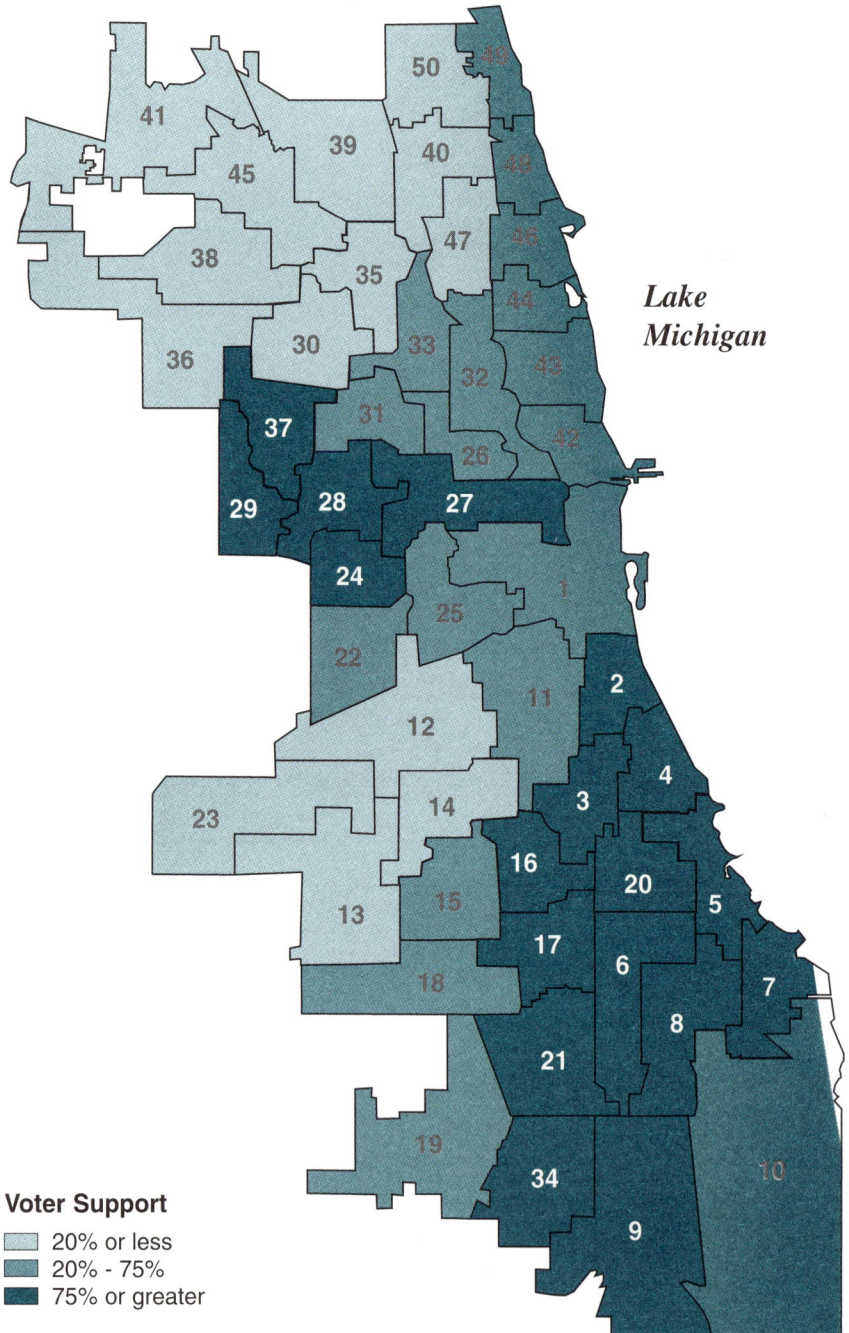

Lake Michigan

Voter Support

- 20% or less
- 20% - 75%
- 75% or greater

Mayor of Chicago, April 1987

Washington's reelection campaign lacked the intensity and fervor that marked the 1983 mayoral election. His opponents in the general election were Donald Haider, the Republican nominee, and Edward Vrdolyak, who ran as an independent. Vrdolyak was the 10th ward alderman, chair of the Democratic party of Cook County, and the principal leader of the anti-Washington majority in the city council.

Vrdolyak's entry into the contest created the possibility of an electoral showdown between him and the mayor. But the waters were muddied considerably when Cook County Assessor Thomas Hynes also decided to contest Washington's reelection. Hynes, who was also the 19th ward Democratic committeeman, was one of the Southwest Side white Democrats who play prominent and important roles in the Daley faction. It was clear that with Hynes and Vrdolyak both in the battle the white vote would be split. Washington benefitted from this situation, as his candidacy took on an

Results from Recent Elections

Mayor of Chicago, April 1987

Table 2.11

The 1987 Chicago Mayoral Race

Ward Group[1]	% Harold Washington (D)	% Donald Haider (R)	% Edward Vrdolyak (I)	Total Votes
White Northwest Side	9.7	6.7	3.6	173,454
White South Side	15.1	3.2	1.7	188,487
Black South Side	95.5	.8	3.7	344,356
Black West Side	96.0	.6	3.4	101,168
Latino	62.3	3.1	34.6	43,805
North Lakeshore	41.8	13.0	45.2	125,498
Other White North Side	24.4	8.5	67.1	86,651
Mixed	52.9	2.9	44.2	52,925
Chicago Total	53.8	4.3	42.0	**1,116,344**

Note: D=Democrat, R=Republican, I=Independent

[1]For a detailed explanation of these ward groupings, see pages 4-8 in the introduction to this atlas. Keep in mind, however, that figure 2.11 maps the city using the ward boundaries in effect at the time of the election.

Results from Recent Elections

Mayor of Chicago, April 1987

air of inevitability. Finally, about a week prior to the election, Hynes withdrew, declaring that he loved Chicago enough not to be its mayor.

The essentially one-on-one contest that Vrdolyak had hoped for did not have the outcome he expected. Washington defeated Vrdolyak by 131,808 votes, a margin nearly three times the size of his 1983 victory.

As he had four years earlier, Washington captured nearly all of the African-American vote and over 80 percent of the Latino vote. But he didn't run any better among whites than he had in 1983, polling only 11.7 percent of the white vote. Turnout also fell below its unusually high level of 1983, but white and black turnout remained essentially the same. The shape of Washington's coalition also remained about the same as it had been in 1983: a large African-American core augmented by much smaller segments of Latinos and whites.

The Race in the City: How Voters of Different Races/Ethnicities Supported the Candidates				
Race/ Ethnicity	**Washington**	**Haider**	**Vrdolyak**	**Turnout**[1]
White	11.7%	7.9%	80.3%	58.7%
Black	99.3%	.4%	.1%	58.5%
Latino	83.5%	.1%	16.3%	23.1%
Total				54.1%

[1]Turnout is the percentage of the voting age population who cast ballots for a candidate for this office in this election.

Figure 2.11
Support for Washington

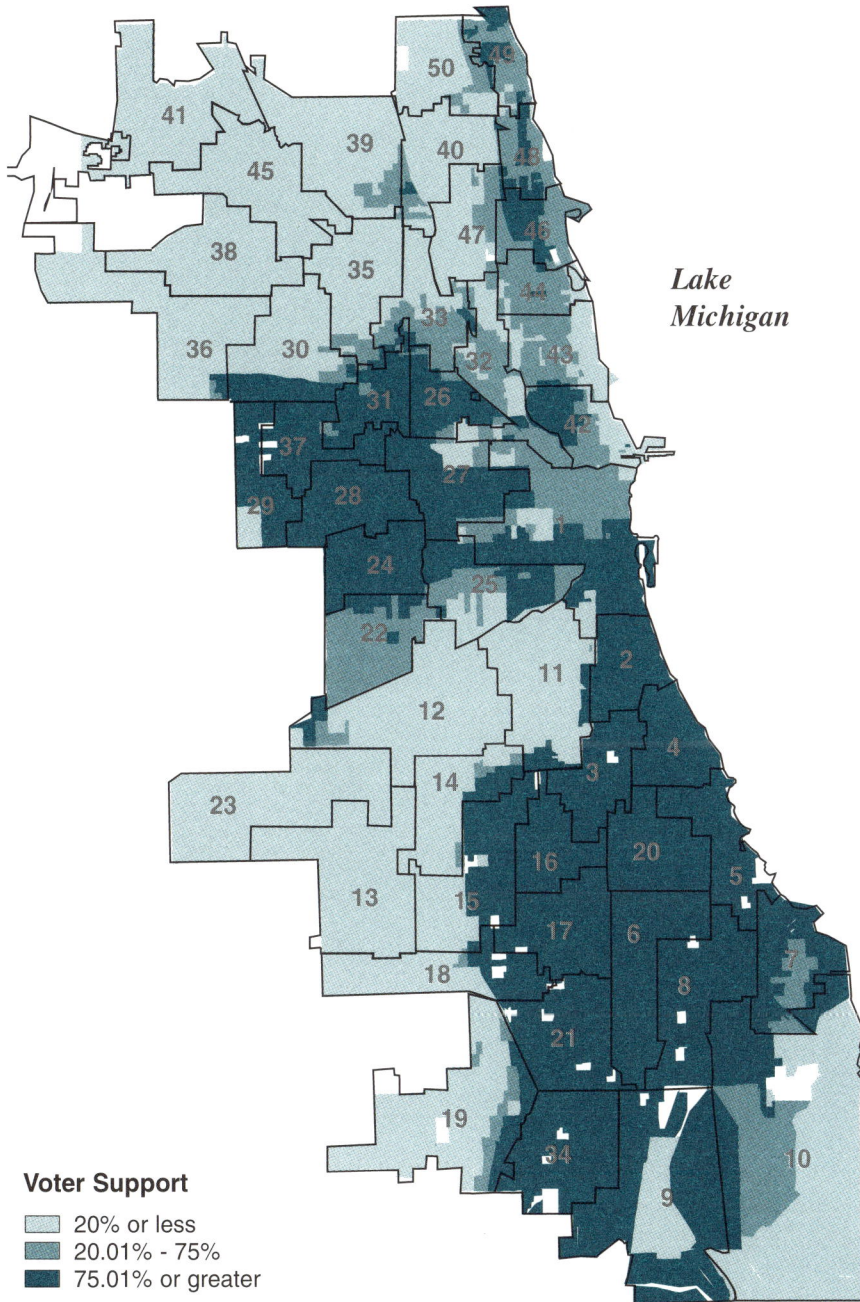

Lake Michigan

Voter Support

- 20% or less
- 20.01% - 75%
- 75.01% or greater

Results from Recent Elections

Mayor of Chicago, April 1989

Following Harold Washington's sudden death in November 1987, the African-American aldermen split over the selection of a successor as mayor. At a stormy 11-hour council session that began on the night of December 1 and broke up in the morning of December 2, Eugene Sawyer (6th ward) emerged as the acting mayor of Chicago. But Sawyer was the choice of only five African-American aldermen, including himself; 11 of the other 12 African-American aldermen voted for Timothy Evans (4th ward), who had been Washington's floor leader in the council. Sawyer won because 24 white aldermen, including several of the principal leaders of the opposition to Washington, supported him.

This Sawyer/Evans split carried over into the special election in early 1989. Sawyer ran in the Democratic primary; and Evans, not wanting to split the African-American vote in the primary, chose to contest the general election as the candidate of a newly formed Harold Washington Party. This fissure in the African-American community prevented the kind of community mobilization that had marked Washington's elections. Daley, of course, benefitted from the resulting decline in African-American enthusiasm and turnout on election day.

Table 2.12

The 1989 Chicago Mayoral Race

Ward Group[1]	%Richard M. Daley (D)	%Edward Vrdolyak (R)	%Timothy Evans (HW)	Total Votes
White Northwest Side	91.5	4.8	3.7	179,049
White South Side	83.6	6.4	10.0	187,818
Black South Side	8.8	1.2	90.0	289,576
Black West Side	8.2	.9	90.9	82,440
Latino	70.0	2.8	27.2	40,052
North Lakeshore	73.3	4.2	22.5	118,772
Other White North Side	87.6	3.9	8.6	93,437
Mixed	53.8	2.8	43.4	49,394
Chicago Total	55.4	3.5	41.1	**1,040,538**

Note: D=Democrat, R=Republican, HW=Harold Washington Party

[1]For a detailed explanation of these ward groupings, see pages 4-8 in the introduction to this atlas. Keep in mind, however, that figure 2.12 maps the city using the ward boundaries in effect at the time of the election.

Daley defeated Sawyer by 101,647 in the primary and Evans by 148,660 in the general election. The key to Daley's success was the solid support and high turnout he received from white voters, especially in the white ethnic enclaves. He also carried the North Lakeshore wards by a wider margin than Washington's opponents had in 1983 or 1987.

In the general election, Evans polled 95.3 percent of the African-American vote, only slightly lower than the 97.3 percent that Sawyer had received in the primary. But both Sawyer and Evans suffered from the decline in black turnout. In both 1983 and 1987, black and white turnout had been about the same, but in 1989 white turnout was 18.9 percentage points higher. As a result of lower black turnout, while Evans carried the two black ward groups, he received 131,887 fewer votes from them than Washington had in 1983. In the Lakeshore wards, Evans ran 36,820 votes behind Washington's 1983 total. Had black turnout been as high as it had been in 1983 and had the Lakeshore wards given him as much of the vote as it had Washington, Evans would have defeated Daley by about 20,047 votes in the 1989 general election.

Results from Recent Elections

Mayor of Chicago, April 1989

The Race in the City: How Voters of Different Races/Ethnicities Supported the Candidates				
Race/ Ethnicity	Daley	Vrdolyak	Evans	Turnout[1]
White	88.2%	5.3%	6.4%	62.6%
Black	3.6%	1.0%	95.3%	43.7%
Latino	52.4%	1.4%	46.0%	16.0%
Total				48.3%

[1]Turnout is the percentage of the voting age population who cast ballots for a candidate for this office in this election.

Results from Recent Elections

Mayor of Chicago, April 1989

Figure 2.12
Support for Daley

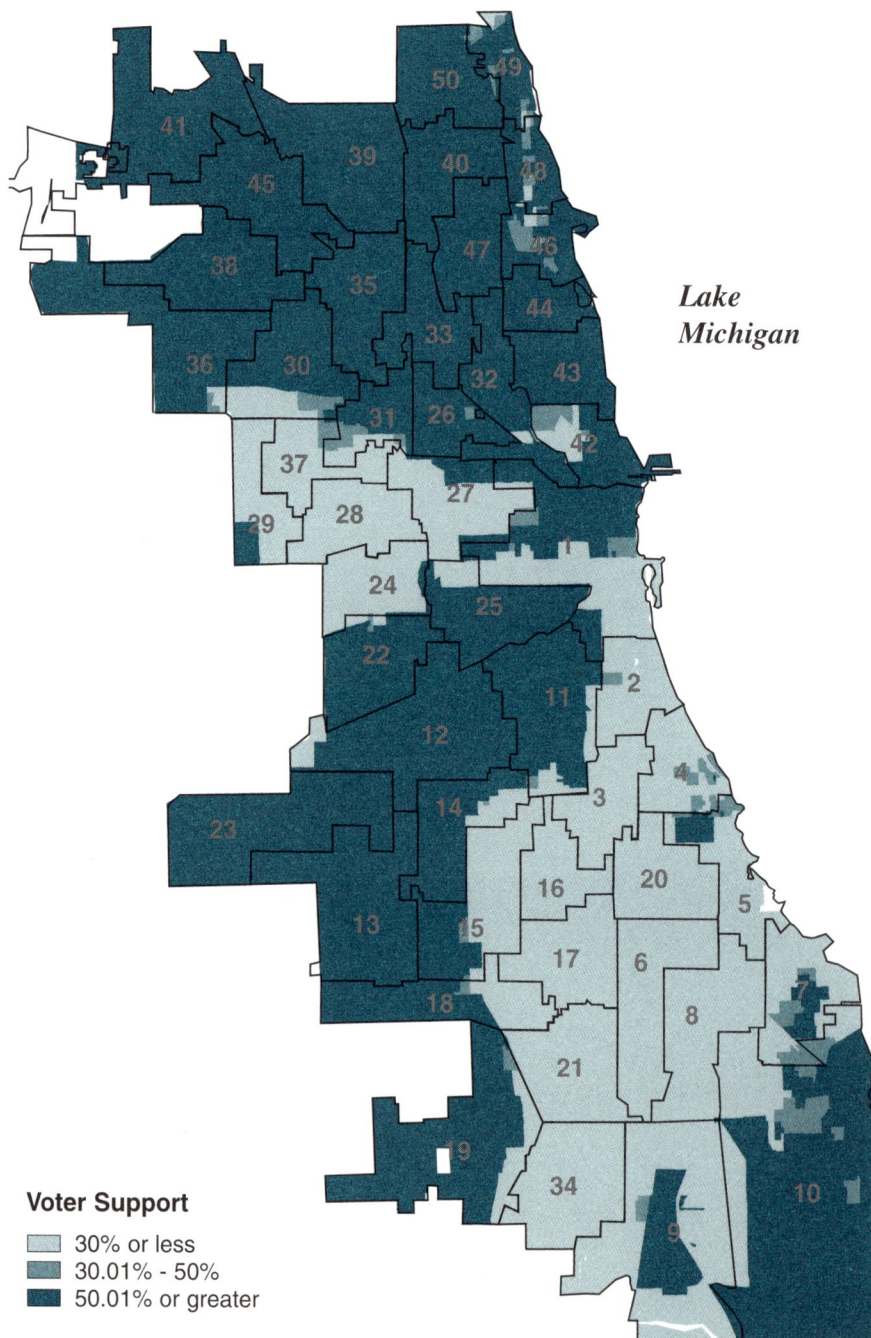

Lake Michigan

Voter Support

☐ 30% or less
☐ 30.01% - 50%
■ 50.01% or greater

Mayor of Chicago, April 1991

Daley's opponents in 1991 were unable to mount any challenge that seriously jeopardized his hold on the mayor's office. The mayor's two-year record was unremarkable, but the media treated his reelection as an inevitable and highly desirable event. Operating within this context, African-American leaders were simply unable to raise the funds necessary to offset the mayor's organizational advantage and wage a successful campaign against him.

Danny Davis, then a member of the Cook County Board but formerly the 29th ward alderman, challenged Daley in the primary. While Davis carried 83.6 percent of the African-American vote, turnout was only 29.7 percent—15.5 percentage points below white turnout. Daley polled 92.6 percent of the white vote and defeated Davis by 209,010 votes.

The general election was a repeat performance, as the mayor's extremely well-funded campaign steamrolled the opposition. R. Eugene Pincham, a distinguished trial lawyer and former judge, tried to mobilize the African-American community, but its turnout remained low at only 26.9 percent.

Results from Recent Elections

Mayor of Chicago, April 1991

Table 2.13

The 1991 Chicago Mayoral Race					
Ward Group[1]	%Richard M. Daley (D)	%George Gottlieb (R)	%R. Eugene Pincham (HW)	%James Warren (SWP)	Total Votes
White Northwest Side	91.8	5.8	2.1	.2	107,336
White South Side	90.1	4.0	5.7	.2	138,337
Black South Side	27.6	1.4	70.4	.6	140,561
Black West Side	27.1	1.3	70.8	.8	40,491
Latino	82.2	2.9	14.1	.9	25,328
North Lakeshore	82.0	5.1	11.5	1.5	73,113
Other White North Side	91.6	4.1	3.5	.8	60,704
Mixed	70.5	3.2	25.9	.4	31,503
Chicago Total	69.9	3.6	25.9	.6	**617,373**

Note: D=Democrat, R=Republican, HW=Harold Washington Party, SWP=Socialist Workers Party

[1]For a detailed explanation of these ward groupings, see pages 4-8 in the introduction to this atlas. Keep in mind, however, that figure 2.13 maps the city using the ward boundaries in effect at the time of the election.

Results from Recent Elections

Mayor of Chicago, April 1991

That was 19.8 percentage points below white turnout. Moreover, as it had been in the primary, but unlike 1989, the white vote was more cohesive than the African-American vote. More than 9 out of 10 voters cast their ballots for Daley, but less than 8 out of 10 voted for Pincham. Cohesive white support—in the 90 percent range in the white ethnic areas and in the mid-70s or better in the North Lakeshore wards—and low turnout among African-American voters was (and remains) the key to Daley's continued electoral success.

The Race in the City: How Voters of Different Races/Ethnicities Supported the Candidates				
Race/ Ethnicity	Daley	Gottlieb	Pincham	Turnout[1]
White	92.5%	5.2%	1.6%	46.7%
Black	22.0%	.8%	76.5%	26.9%
Latino	90.8%	2.2%	4.9%	18.5%
Total				30.9%

[1]Turnout is the percentage of the voting age population who cast ballots for a candidate for this office in this election.

Figure 2.13
Support for Daley

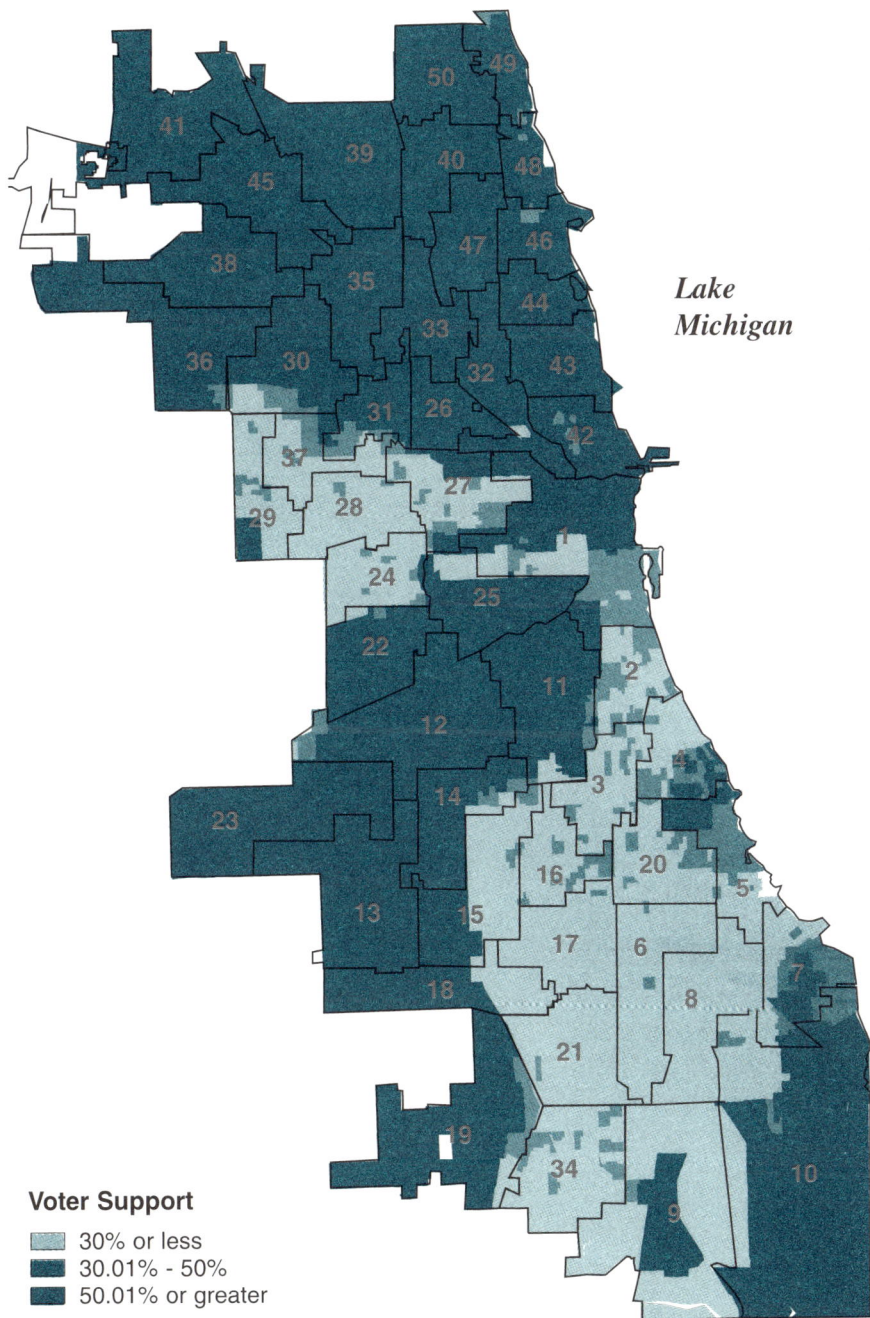

Lake Michigan

Voter Support

30% or less
30.01% - 50%
50.01% or greater

Mayor of Chicago: Democratic Primary, February 1995

Daley was challenged for the Democratic mayoral nomination in 1995 by Joseph Gardner, a commissioner of the Water Reclamation District. Gardner's effort was poorly funded and badly organized, and he had no realistic prospect of winning the nomination. In the final count, Daley ran 173,210 votes ahead of him.

Daley's formula for victory held up again—cohesive bloc voting by whites coupled with low black turnout. In rolling to his easy victory, Daley did not fall below 70 percent in any of the white areas of the city, and he polled over 90 percent in its white ethnic enclaves on the Northwest and South Sides. Whites voted even more cohesively for Daley in 1995 (94.0 percent) than they had for Bernard Epton (87.6 percent) in his contest against Washington in 1983. But Gardner's financial inability to mount a serious campaign and the inevitability of Daley's triumph worked to depress white turnout, although it still remained 7.8 percentage points higher than the African-American turnout rate.

Gardner faced a dual problem: a growing lack of cohesiveness in black voting and declining black turnout. Both of these were probably rooted in the same source—a perception that Daley couldn't be beaten. While African-American voters had given over 90 percent of their vote to African-

Table 2.14

The 1995 Chicago Mayoral Democratic Primary Race

Ward Group[1]	%Richard M. Daley	%Joseph Gardner	%Sheila Jones	Total Votes
White Northwest Side	93.2	6.0	.8	79,716
White South Side	93.3	6.1	.6	86,497
Black South Side	27.1	71.4	1.5	151,841
Black West Side	33.1	65.1	1.9	43,134
Latino	83.7	14.9	1.4	42,563
North Lakeshore	78.6	20.2	1.2	40,229
Other White North Side	89.0	10.1	.9	54,813
Mixed	71.5	27.6	.9	30,370
Chicago Total	65.8	33.1	1.1	**529,163**

[1]For a detailed explanation of these ward groupings, see pages 4-8 in the introduction to this atlas.

American candidates in the 1983, 1987, and 1989 mayoral contests, their cohesiveness fell to 83.6 percent in the 1991 primary and to 76.5 percent in the 1991 general election. Gardner polled an even lower percentage, 75.4 percent. And African-American turnout continued to lag far behind white turnout.

The outcome in the two black ward groups illustrates Gardner's problem. He carried both of them and by wide margins, of course. But turnout in these areas was low—only 27.2 percent—and he didn't benefit from as cohesive an African-American vote as Washington had. As a result, Gardner polled only 136,481 votes in the two areas that provided 78 percent of his citywide vote. This wasn't nearly enough to match Daley's vote total in the two white ethnic ward groups (155,026 votes).

Results from Recent Elections

Mayor of Chicago: Democratic Primary, February 1995

The Race in the City: How Voters of Different Races/Ethnicities Supported the Candidates			
Race/ Ethnicity	Daley	Gardner	Turnout[1]
White	94.0%	5.4%	39.8%
Black	23.1%	75.4%	32.0%
Latino	90.5%	7.8%	14.4%
Total			29.2%

[1]Turnout is the percentage of the voting age population who cast ballots for a candidate for this office in this election.

Results from Recent Elections

Mayor of Chicago: Democratic
Primary, February 1995

Figure 2.14
Support for Daley

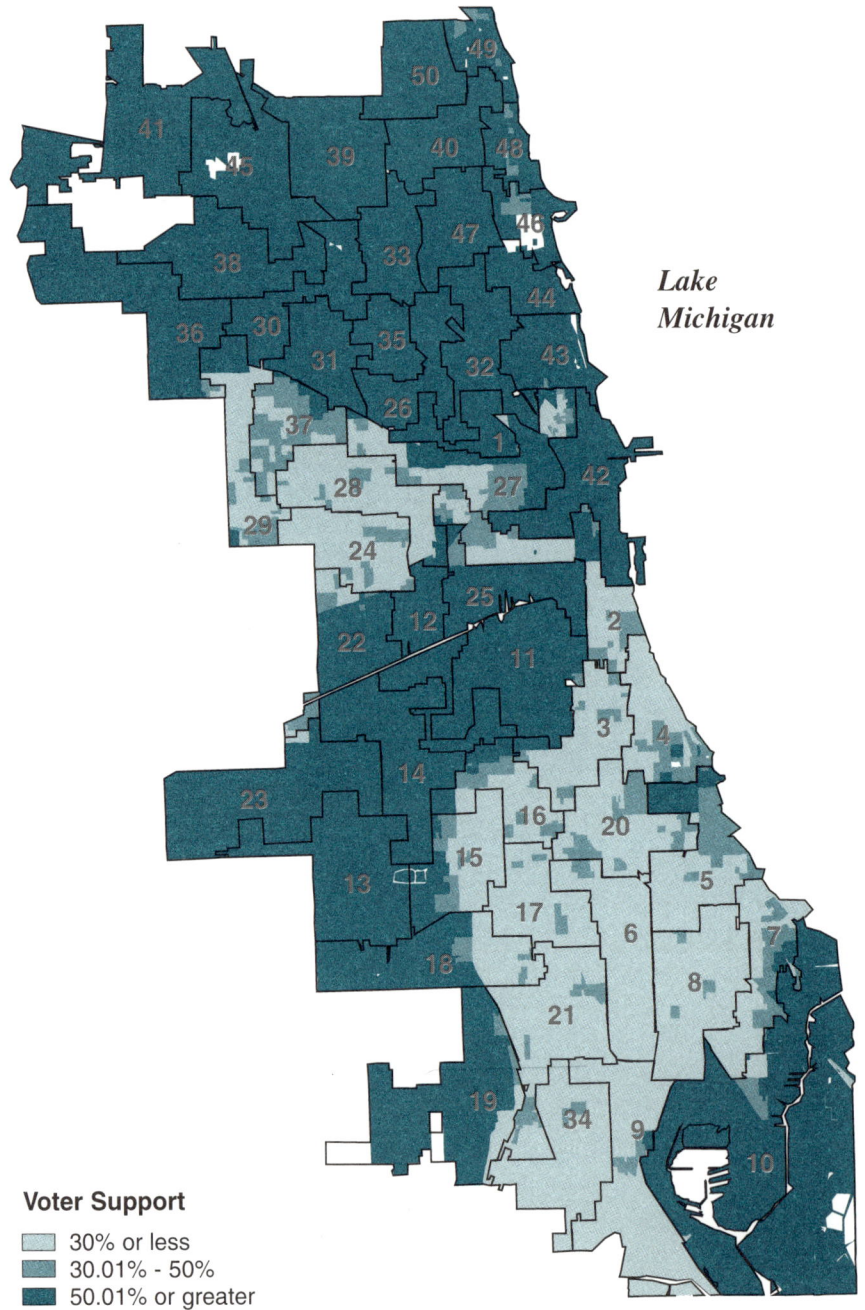

Lake Michigan

Voter Support
- 30% or less
- 30.01% - 50%
- 50.01% or greater

Mayor of Chicago, April 1995

When Gardner's primary challenge to Daley failed, African-American leaders recruited Roland Burris to run as an independent in the general election. Burris had been attorney general of Illinois, but in 1994 he lost his bid for the Democratic gubernatorial nomination and went into private law practice. However, he accepted the invitation of African-American community leaders and entered the lists against Daley in the 1995 general election.

Burris brought to the contest widespread name recognition and a reputation for good government. Unfortunately for his effort, he did not have deep pockets and was unable to raise the kind of money needed to mount a serious threat to the extremely well-funded Daley. Nevertheless, given the last-minute character of his effort, Burris made a respectable showing. He lost to Daley by 142,442 votes, but that was a smaller margin than Gardner's deficit.

Daley again attracted overwhelming white support, running at 89.3 percent among white voters citywide. And white turnout was 3.1 percentage points higher than it had been in the primary, although still well below the levels of the 1980s.

Table 2.15

The 1995 Chicago Mayoral Race

Ward Group[1]	%Richard M. Daley (D)	%Raymond Wardingly (R)	%Lawrence Redmond (HW)	%Roland Burris (I)	Total Votes
White Northwest Side	88.0	5.2	.3	6.5	93,653
White South Side	89.1	3.9	.2	6.8	95,169
Black South Side	20.3	.7	1.3	77.7	179,236
Black West Side	26.4	1.2	1.8	70.6	48,973
Latino	80.6	2.7	1.2	15.5	40,757
North Lakeshore	77.3	3.7	1.0	18.1	44,600
Other White North Side	86.3	3.9	.6	9.2	61,817
Mixed	65.4	3.3	6	30.7	34,013
Chicago Total	60.1	2.8	.9	6.3	**598,218**

Note: D=Democrat, R=Republican, HW=Harold Washington Party, I=Independent

* For a detailed explanation of these ward groupings, see pages 4-8 in the introduction to this atlas.

Results from Recent Elections

Mayor of Chicago, April 1995

Burris's candidacy worked to boost African-American turnout by 5.0 percentage points over its mark in the primary, although it too was still well below the highs of 1983 and 1987. Blacks also voted slightly more cohesively in the general election than they had in the primary, delivering 82.9 percent of their vote to Burris. As a result, Burris polled more votes in the city's two predominantly black ward groups than Gardner had—a total of 173,902 votes. But this total was still very far below the 467,407 votes that Washington had received from the same areas in 1983. Thus, even Burris's somewhat improved showing over Gardner's effort in the primary was not nearly enough to overcome Daley's funding and incumbency advantages.

The Race in the City: How Voters of Different Races/Ethnicities Supported the Candidates			
Race/ Ethnicity	Daley	Burris	Turnout[1]
White	89.3%	5.7%	42.9%
Black	15.2%	82.9%	35.8%
Latino	90.4%	7.6%	11.4%
Total			34.2%

[1]Turnout is the percentage of the voting age population who cast ballots for a candidate for this office in this election.

Figure 2.15
Support for Daley

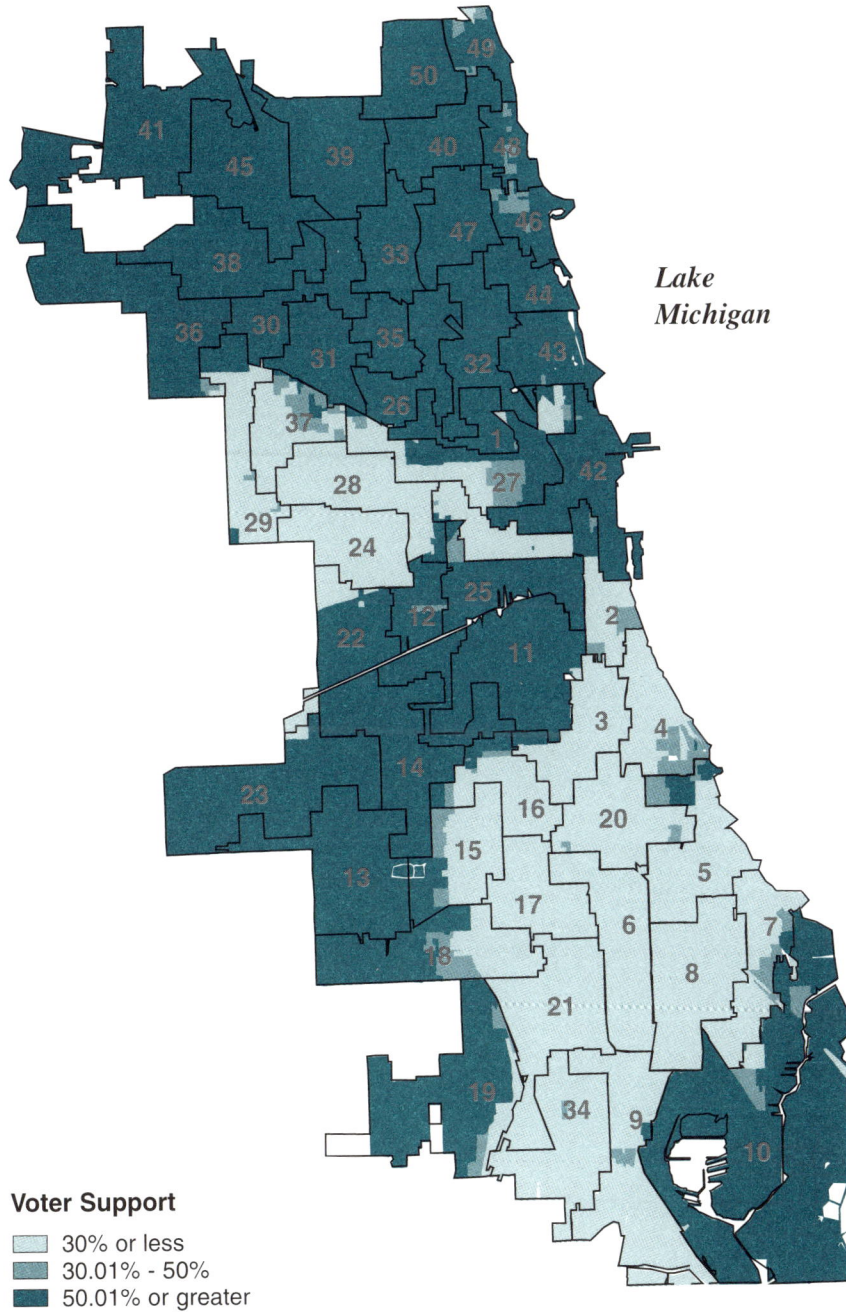

Results from Recent Elections

Mayor of Chicago, April 1995

Lake Michigan

Voter Support

30% or less
30.01% - 50%
50.01% or greater

Cook County Board President, November 1990

Since the 1930s, Chicago's Democrats have expected to win the presidency of the Cook County Board and to carry a majority of its members. Their expectations have only rarely been frustrated, and 1990 was not one of those occasions. The Democratic nominee, Richard Phelan, easily defeated his Republican opponent, carrying both suburban Cook County as well as the city of Chicago.

Phelan had not been the preferred candidate of the Democratic organization. The party's endorsement for the primary went to Ted Lechowicz, a Northwest Side ward committeeman, state senator, and county board member. Phelan was also challenged in the primary by Stanley Kusper, the incumbent county clerk, and by R. Eugene Pincham, a former judge and one of the county's leading trial attorneys. Pincham mobilized African-American support and carried the city in the primary, but Phelan overcame his deficit in the city and won the nomination by piling up a large suburban

Table 2.16

The 1990 Cook County Board Presidential Race

Ward Group[1]/Area	%Richard Phelan (D)	%Aldo DeAngelis (R)	%Barbara Norman (HW)	Total Votes
White Northwest Side	64.1	32.9	3.0	118,538
White South Side	71.1	22.7	6.1	125,580
Black South Side	47.4	4.6	48.0	172,467
Black West Side	54.3	4.1	41.6	44,071
Latino	73.6	13.8	12.6	22,246
North Lakeshore	62.2	28.2	9.6	85,618
Other White North Side	72.2	22.5	5.3	62,936
Mixed	55.5	22.8	21.7	31,962
Chicago Total	60.9	19.0	20.2	**663,418**
Suburban Cook County	50.0	4.8		617,564
Cook County Total	55.6	12.8		**1,280,982**

Note: D=Democrat, R=Republican, HW= Harold Washington Party

[1]For a deatailed explanation of these ward grouings, see pages 4-8 in the introduction to this atlas. Keep in mind, however, that figure 2.16a maps the city using the ward boundaries in effect at the time of the election.

vote. However, Phelan's attacks on Pincham during the primary battle left residual bitterness and encouraged the Harold Washington party to run its own candidate in the general election.

With an African American competing with Phelan for votes among the party's most reliable constituency, the Democratic nominee failed to carry a majority of the African-American vote. But he polled 70 percent of the Latino vote and two-thirds of the white vote, carrying the city by a wide margin over his Republican challenger, State Senator Aldo DeAngelis. A suburban resident himself, Phelan also surprised most political observers by polling a bare majority of the vote in suburban Cook County. In fact, 43.3 percent of the total vote cast for Phelan in the county came from its suburbs.

Results from Recent Elections

Cook County Board President, November 1990

The Race in the City: How Voters of Different Races/Ethnicities Supported the Candidates

Race/Ethnicity	Phelan	DeAngelis	Norman	Turnout[1]
White	67.4%	27.9%	4.5%	47.6%
Black	44.9%	2.5%	52.4%	27.4%
Latino	70.0%	0.0%	29.7%	6.2%
Total				36.6%

[1]Turnout is the percentage of the voting age population who cast ballots for a candidate for this office in this election.

Results from Recent Elections

Cook County Board President,
November 1990

Figure 2.16a
Chicago Support for Phelan

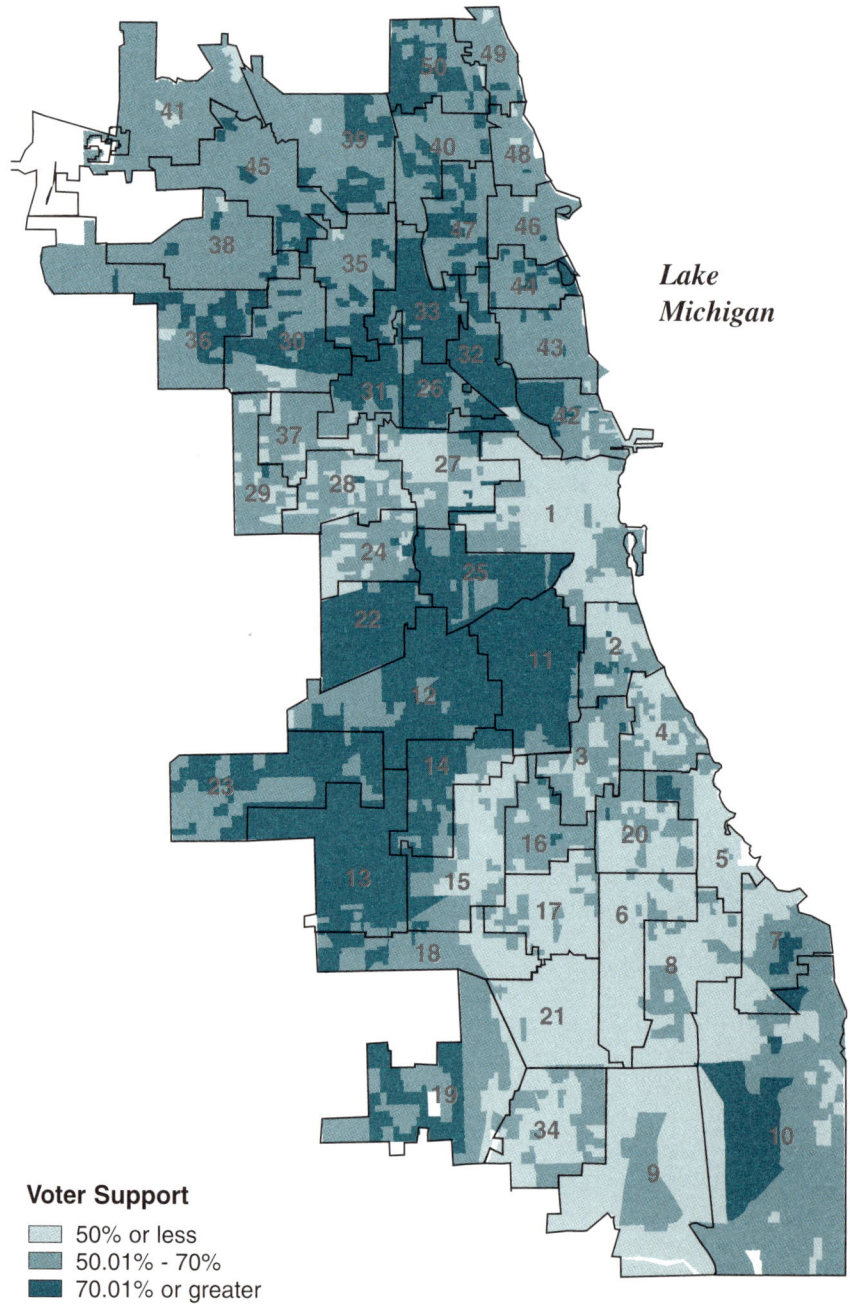

Lake Michigan

Voter Support

- 50% or less
- 50.01% - 70%
- 70.01% or greater

Figure 2.16b
Cook County Township Support for Phelan

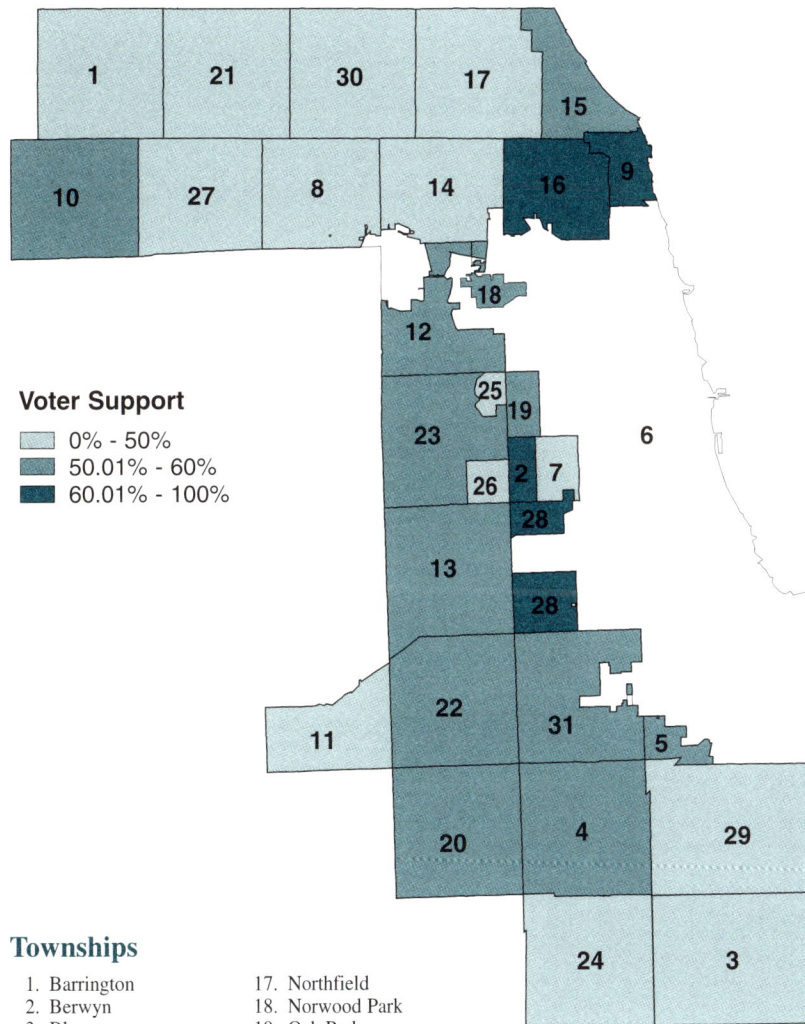

Voter Support

- 0% - 50%
- 50.01% - 60%
- 60.01% - 100%

Townships

1. Barrington	17. Northfield
2. Berwyn	18. Norwood Park
3. Bloom	19. Oak Park
4. Bremen	20. Orland Park
5. Calumet	21. Palatine
6. See figure a	22. Palos
7. Cicero	23. Proviso
8. Elk Grove	24. Rich
9. Evanston	25. River Forest
10. Hanover	26. Riverside
11. Lemont	27. Schaumburg
12. Leyden	28. Stickney
13. Lyons	29. Thornton
14. Maine	30. Wheeling
15. New Trier	31. Worth
16. Niles	

**Results from
Recent
Elections**

Cook County Board President,
November 1994

Cook County Board President, November 1994

In 1990 the Democratic candidate had won the presidency of the Cook County Board despite losing the African-American vote in Chicago to the Harold Washington party's candidate. This unusual development was balanced by the equally unusual feat of a Democrat's polling a majority in the county's suburbs. The result was a reasonably easy Democratic victory.

The 1994 election was not a replay of 1990. The Democratic candidate won again, but the patterns of voting support were quite different. In 1990 Richard Phelan had run as an outsider and a critic of the Democratic organization, which had not endorsed him for the nomination. In 1994 the Democratic nominee was John Stroger, a ward committeeman and long-time loyalist of the Democratic organization. Stroger was also an incumbent member of the county board, the chair of its important finance committee, and an African American who could be expected to surmount the division in that community's vote which had reduced Phelan's strength in 1990.

Table 2.17

The 1994 Cook County Board Presidential Race

Ward Group[1]/Area	%John Stroger (D)	%Joseph Morris (R)	%Aloysius Majerczyk (HW)	%Minor Candidate	Total Votes
White Northwest Side	57.4	37.6	4.0	1.0	85,044
White South Side	71.5	23.6	4.2	.7	86,669
Black South Side	91.2	3.2	4.9	.7	16,8274
Black West Side	88.4	5.2	5.5	1.0	44,806
Latino	75.4	18.6	4.6	1.4	34,277
North Lakeshore	70.6	26.0	2.5	.9	54,437
Other White North Side	68.5	28.1	2.3	1.1	67,844
Mixed	73.6	21.3	4.3	.7	27,708
Chicago Total	76.4	18.6	4.1	.9	**569,059**
Suburban Cook County	46.1	51.1	1.9	.7	582,110
Cook County Total	61.1	35.0	3.0	.8	**1,151,169**

Note: D=Democrat, R=Republican, HW=Harold Washington Party

[1]For a detailed explanation of these ward groupings, see pages 4-8 in the introduction to this atlas.

As a city resident and loyalist of the Democratic organization, Stroger lacked Phelan's appeal to suburban voters, and he didn't carry the suburbs as Phelan had four years earlier. But Stroger ran considerably stronger than Phelan had in Chicago, mainly due to solid support and higher turnout from African-American voters. As a result, Stroger's margin over his Republican challenger was 2,998 votes more than Phelan's had been over his Republican opponent.

In Chicago, Stroger ran behind Phelan's 1990 levels in the white wards on the North and Northwest Sides. And his citywide percentage among whites was 3.9 percentage points below Phelan's. Among the city's minority voters, however, Stroger was much stronger than Phelan had been. Without an African-American competitor, Stroger polled 92.7 percent of the African-American vote, much higher than Phelan's 44.9 percent. And he bettered Phelan's percentage among Latinos by 10.2 percentage points.

Results from Recent Elections

Cook County Board President, November 1994

The Race in the City: How Voters of Different Races/Ethnicities Supported the Candidates				
Race/Ethnicity	Stroger	Morris	Majerczyk	Turnout[1]
White	63.5%	32.3%	3.4%	41.2%
Black	92.7%	1.5%	4.7%	31.7%
Latino	80.2%	11.8%	5.2%	7.6%
Total				31.4%

[1]Turnout is the percentage of the voting age population who cast ballots for a candidate for this office in this election.

Results from Recent Elections

Cook County Board President,
November 1994

Figure 2.17a
Chicago Support for Stroger

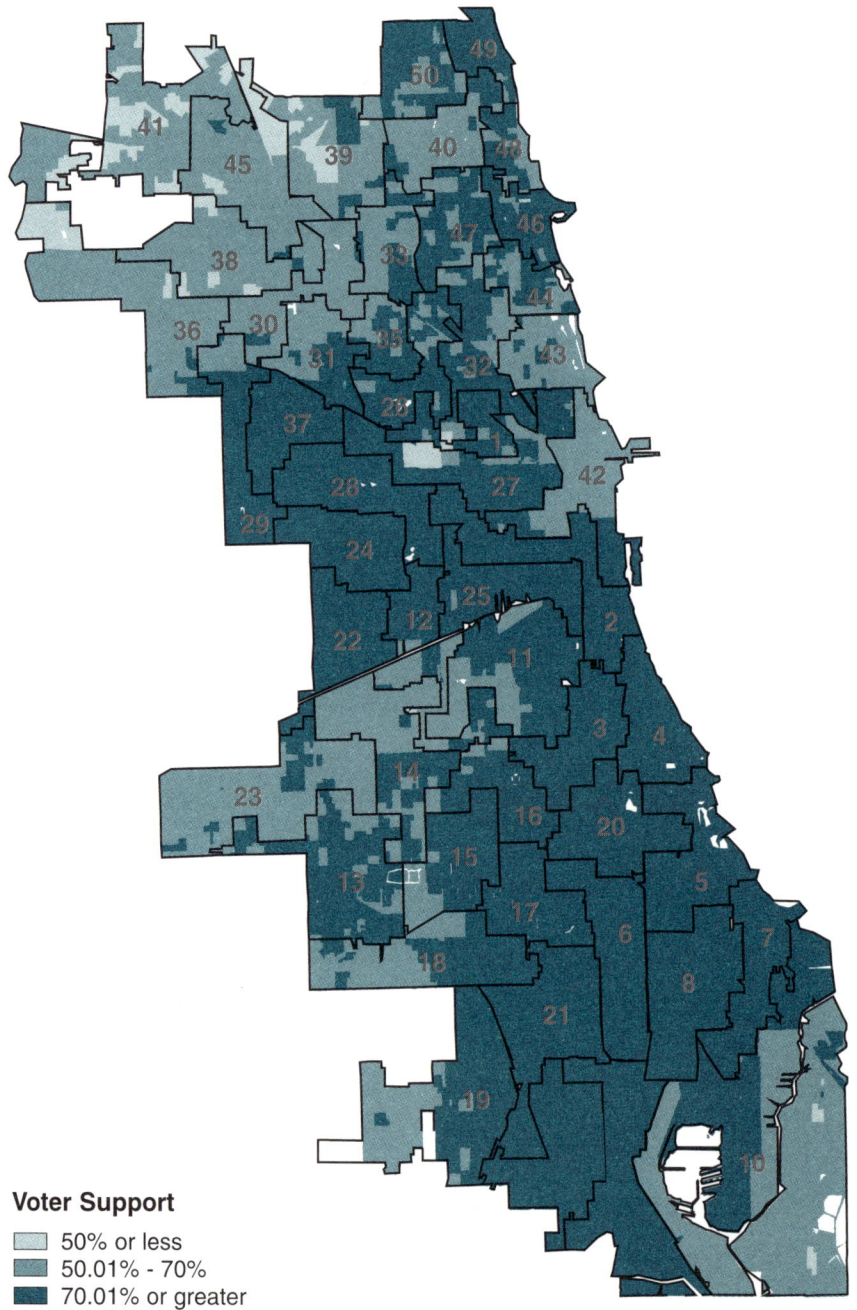

Voter Support
- 50% or less
- 50.01% - 70%
- 70.01% or greater

Figure 2.17b
Cook County Township Support for Stroger

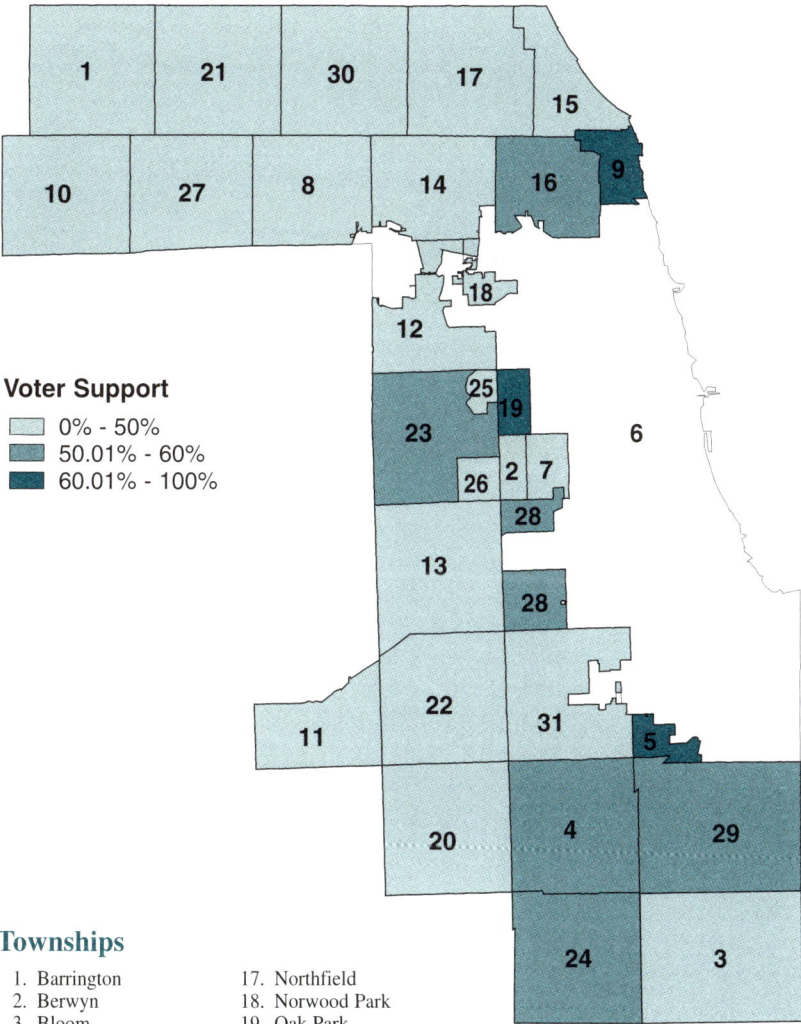

Voter Support

- 0% - 50%
- 50.01% - 60%
- 60.01% - 100%

Townships

1. Barrington	17. Northfield
2. Berwyn	18. Norwood Park
3. Bloom	19. Oak Park
4. Bremen	20. Orland Park
5. Calumet	21. Palatine
6. See figure a	22. Palos
7. Cicero	23. Proviso
8. Elk Grove	24. Rich
9. Evanston	25. River Forest
10. Hanover	26. Riverside
11. Lemont	27. Schaumburg
12. Leyden	28. Stickney
13. Lyons	29. Thornton
14. Maine	30. Wheeling
15. New Trier	31. Worth
16. Niles	

Cook County State's Attorney, November 1992

In the 1992 state's attorney's contest, Jack O'Malley handily defeated his Democratic opponent, Patrick O'Connor, 40th ward alderman. O'Malley polled 61.3 percent of the county vote and defeated O'Connor by 469,136 votes.

O'Malley had first been elected state's attorney in the special election of 1990, when he defeated Cecil Partee, an African American who had been appointed state's attorney following Richard M. Daley's election as mayor of Chicago. In his 1990 race, O'Malley had polled 53.0 percent of the county vote. He carried the suburbs of Cook County with 71.5 percent, while losing Chicago with 36.0 percent. However, while losing the citywide vote, O'Malley carried the predominantly white ethnic areas and the North Lakeshore wards. In fact, O'Malley won the citywide white vote, polling 55.5 percent to Partee's 41.1 percent in 1990. But O'Malley's support was barely visible among the city's minority voters: he garnered only 2.9 percent of the African-American vote and 1.5 percent of the Latino vote in 1990.

Table 2.18

The 1992 Cook County State's Attorney Race

Ward Group[1]/ Area	%Patrick O'Connor (D)	%Jack O'Malley (R)	Total Vote
White Northwest Side	31.2	68.8	140,212
White South Side	40.1	59.9	126,224
Black South Side	67.1	32.9	321,939
Black West Side	73.1	26.9	100,094
Latino	55.6	44.4	73,944
North Lakeshore	35.4	64.6	115,820
Other White North Side	39.2	60.8	127,065
Mixed	48.0	52.0	48,857
Chicago Total	51.1	48.9	**1,054,155**
Suburban Cook County	25.8	74.1	1,018,555
Cook County Total	38.6	61.3	**2,072,710**

Note: D=Democrat, R=Republican

[1]For a detailed explanation of these ward groupings, see pages 4-8 in the introduction to this atlas.

Two years later, running for his first full term as state's attorney, O'Malley expanded his earlier base of voting support. He polled over two-thirds of the white vote, winning all of the predominantly white ward groups in the city. He also attracted over a quarter of the African-American and Latino votes. Despite his expanded voting support, however, O'Malley still lost the city, although by only 23,425 votes, a 2.2 percentage-point margin. African Americans and Latinos, consistently the city's most reliable Democratic voters, delivered enough support to O'Connor to allow him to eke out a narrow citywide victory. But O'Malley swamped O'Connor in the suburbs, polling nearly three-quarters of the vote there, improving his impressive 71.5 percent vote share in 1990.

Figures 2.18a and 2.18b map the support for O'Connor. It makes for an interesting comparison to figures 2.19a and 2.19b, which map Richard Devine's returns in his successful 1996 bid to unseat O'Malley.

Results from Recent Elections

Cook County State's Attorney, November 1992

The Race in the City: How Voters of Different Races/Ethnicities Supported the Candidates

Race/Ethnicity	O'Connor	O'Malley	Turnout[1]
White	30.5%	69.4%	70.3%
Black	71.9%	28.0%	67.4%
Latino	72.1%	27.8%	21.0%
Total			58.2%

[1]Turnout is the percentage of the voting age population who cast ballots for a candidate for this office in this election.

Results from Recent Elections

Cook County State's Attorney, November 1992

Figure 2.18a
Chicago Support for O'Connor

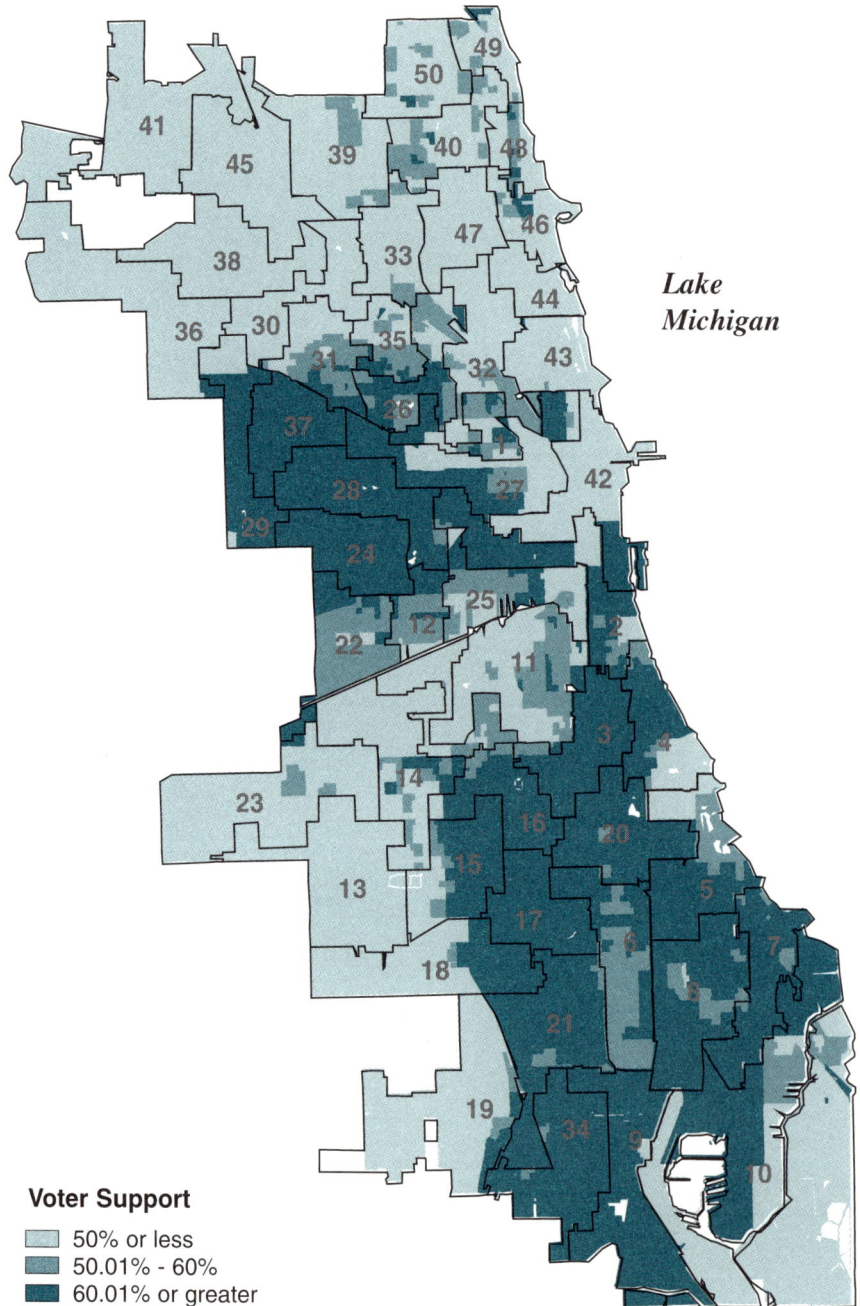

Lake Michigan

Voter Support

- 50% or less
- 50.01% - 60%
- 60.01% or greater

Figure 2.18b
Cook County Township Support for O'Connor

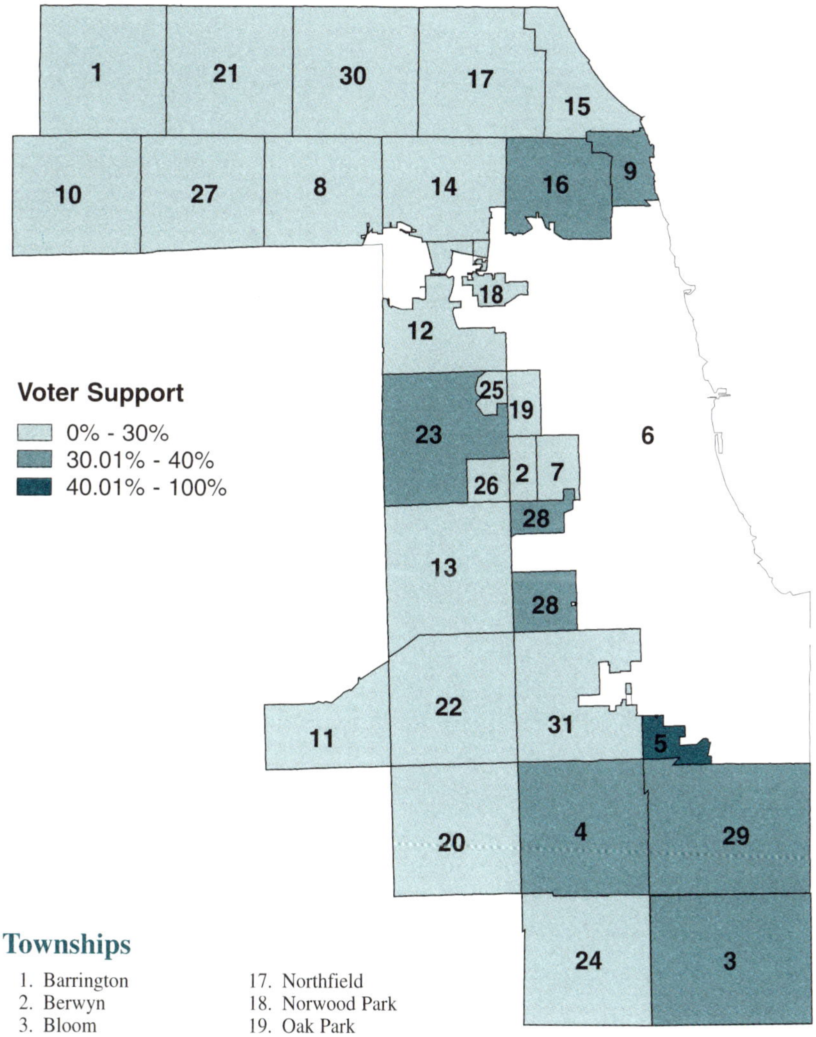

Voter Support

- ☐ 0% - 30%
- ▨ 30.01% - 40%
- ▰ 40.01% - 100%

Townships

1. Barrington	17. Northfield
2. Berwyn	18. Norwood Park
3. Bloom	19. Oak Park
4. Bremen	20. Orland Park
5. Calumet	21. Palatine
6. See figure a	22. Palos
7. Cicero	23. Proviso
8. Elk Grove	24. Rich
9. Evanston	25. River Forest
10. Hanover	26. Riverside
11. Lemont	27. Schaumburg
12. Leyden	28. Stickney
13. Lyons	29. Thornton
14. Maine	30. Wheeling
15. New Trier	31. Worth
16. Niles	

Results from Recent Elections

Cook County State's Attorney, November 1996

The major surprise of the 1996 election cycle was the defeat of the incumbent Republican state's attorney, Jack O'Malley. He had run well in 1990 and 1992, in the latter year capturing over a quarter of the votes of African Americans and Latinos and two-thirds of the white vote in Chicago. Preelection polls showed him well ahead of Richard Devine, Mayor Daley's choice for the Democratic nomination. And Devine's prospects were further damaged by the entry of two African-American candidates who were bound to attract votes from one of the city's most dependable Democratic voting groups. Accordingly, all of the preelection punditry assumed an easy victory for the incumbent Republican. O'Malley himself made a similar assumption, waging a limited campaign consisting mainly of a series of triumphalist efforts that simply assumed victory to be inevitable. But when the ballots were tallied, Devine had scored a stunning upset.

Compared with 1992, O'Malley's vote fell off everywhere. He polled 281,507 fewer votes in suburban Cook County than he had four years before, while Devine ran 56,100 votes better than Patrick O'Connor had. In the city, Devine ran 80,275 below O'Connor's 1992 mark, but O'Malley fell by an astounding 309,264 votes. As a result of O'Malley's enormous loss of

Table 2.19

The 1996 Cook County State's Attorney Race

Ward Group[1]/ Area	%Richard Devine (D)	%Jack O'Malley (R)	%Lawrence Redmond (HW)	%R. Eugene Pincham (J)	Total Votes
White Northwest Side	48.7	49.3	.5	1.5	115,120
White South Side	58.7	37.6	.6	3.0	105,001
Black South Side	57.3	6.6	4.1	32.0	254,868
Black West Side	61.1	8.4	3.6	26.9	75,976
Latino	69.9	23.2	1.9	5.0	61,179
North Lakeshore	55.8	37.0	1.7	5.5	89,212
Other White North Side	57.3	37.8	1.1	3.8	101,705
Mixed	55.9	28.2	1.9	14.1	38,920
Chicago Total	57.3	25.7	2.2	14.8	**841,981**
Suburban Cook County	38.3	56.9	.8	3.8	837,763
Cook County Total	47.8	41.2	1.5	9.3	**1,679,744**

Note: D=Democrat, R=Republican, HW=Harold Washington Party, J=Justice

[1]For a detailed explanation of these ward groupings, see pages 4-8 in the introduction to this atlas.

votes, Devine was able to get 47.8 percent of the county's total vote and win the election, even though he polled 24,225 fewer votes than O'Connor had in losing by a 22.7 percentage-point margin.

In the final analysis, Chicago's minorities delivered the victory to Devine. O'Malley carried the suburbs by 155,817 votes, an 18.6 percentage-point edge. And the city's white vote split closely, with Devine enjoying only a 4 percentage-point lead, not enough by itself to offset O'Malley's margin in the suburbs. But O'Malley's support among minorities virtually evaporated. He polled only 3.9 percent among blacks and 12.1 percent among Latinos, both well below his support levels in 1992. While Lawrence Redmond and R. Eugene Pincham attracted over a third of the African-American vote, Devine got the majority of it, along with 85.4 percent of the Latino vote. It was the margins Devine built up among Chicago's minority voters that enabled him to offset O'Malley's edge in suburban Cook.

Straight-ticket voting—the famous "Punch-10" campaign—played an important role in the city's minority wards. Of all the ballots cast in the seven Latino wards, 45.6 percent were straight Democratic votes, and so were 42.8 percent of the ballots in the five African-American West Side wards. Nine of the 14 black wards on the South Side went over 40 percent in straight Democratic ballots, and overall 39.3 percent of all the ballots cast in these wards were straight Democratic ones. Only four White wards—11, 13, 14, and 50—hit the 40 percent mark in straight Democratic ballots. Straight-party voting in the African-American wards was especially critical: it cut the pulling power of Redmond and Pincham and correspondingly increased the number of votes that went to Devine. Of all the votes that Devine received in the West Side wards, 77 percent came from straight-ticket votes, as did 74.3 percent of the votes he attracted in the Black South Side wards.

Results from Recent Elections

Cook County State's Attorney, November 1996

The Race in the City: How Voters of Different Races/Ethnicities Supported the Candidates				
Race/ Ethnicity	Devine	O'Malley	Minor Candidates	Turnout[1]
White	50.6	46.6	2.7	57.7
Black	58.5	3.9	37.5	48.7
Latino	85.4	12.1	2.4	28.9
Total				46.6

[1]Turnout is the percentage of the voting age population who cast ballots for a candidate for this office in this election.

Results from Recent Elections

Cook County State's Attorney, November 1996

Figure 2.19a
Chicago Support for Devine

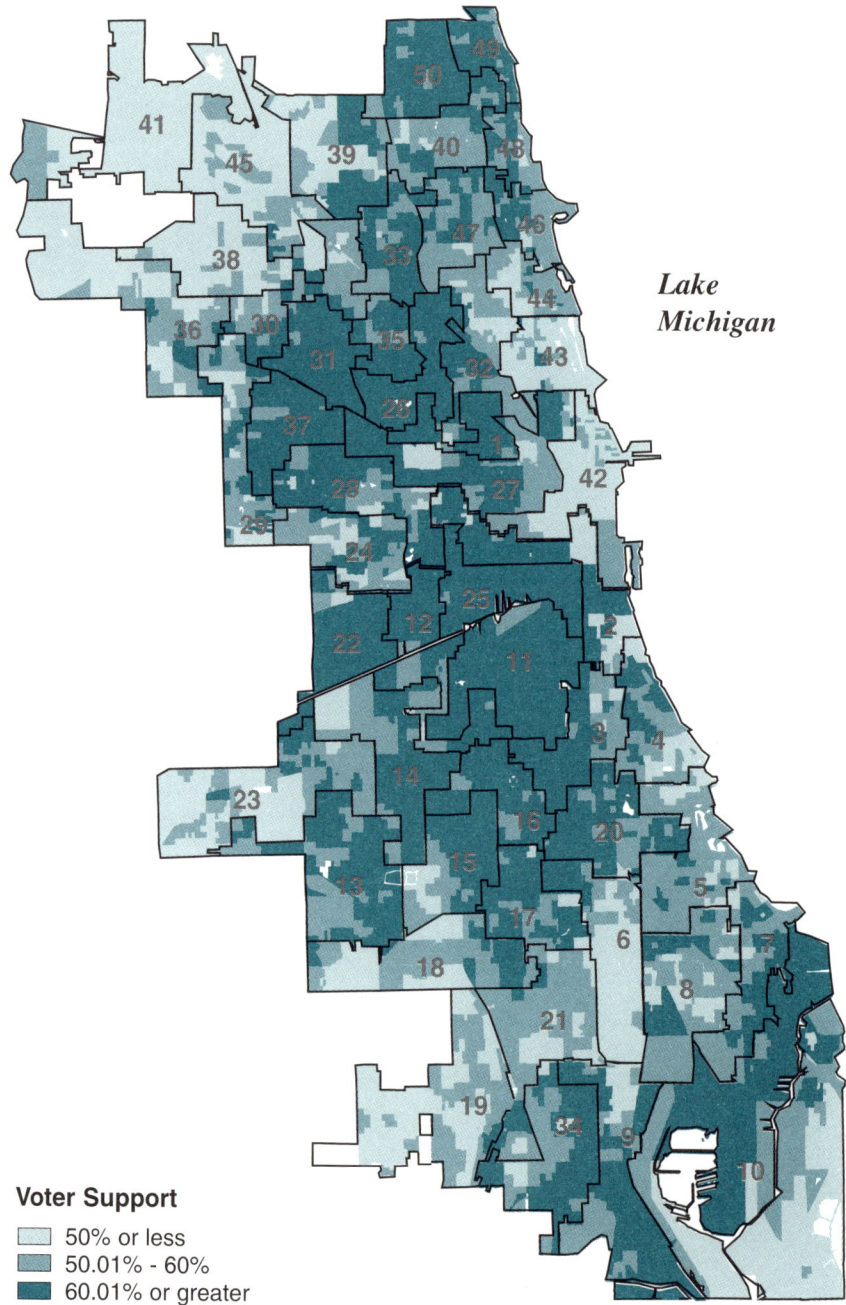

Lake Michigan

Voter Support
- 50% or less
- 50.01% - 60%
- 60.01% or greater

Figure 2.19b

Cook County Township Support for Devine

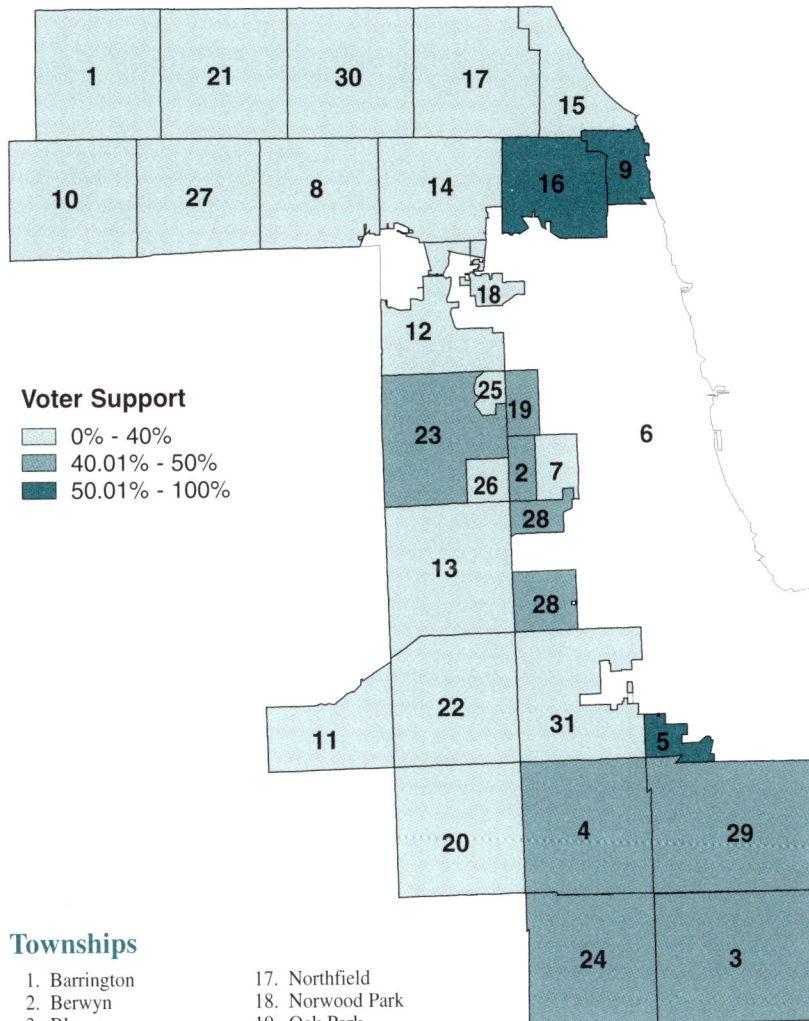

Voter Support

- ☐ 0% - 40%
- ▨ 40.01% - 50%
- ▉ 50.01% - 100%

Townships

1. Barrington	17. Northfield
2. Berwyn	18. Norwood Park
3. Bloom	19. Oak Park
4. Bremen	20. Orland Park
5. Calumet	21. Palatine
6. See figure a	22. Palos
7. Cicero	23. Proviso
8. Elk Grove	24. Rich
9. Evanston	25. River Forest
10. Hanover	26. Riverside
11. Lemont	27. Schaumburg
12. Leyden	28. Stickney
13. Lyons	29. Thornton
14. Maine	30. Wheeling
15. New Trier	31. Worth
16. Niles	

Results from Recent Elections

Chicago City Clerk: Democratic Primary, February 1991

Chicago City Clerk: Democratic Primary, February 1991

Although under investigation for appointing ghost payrollers in the city clerk's office, Walter Kozubowski was renominated by the city's Democratic voters. Kozubowski was part of the 14th ward organization of Edward Burke, chair of the city council's finance committee, and ran for renomination in 1991 as part of Mayor Daley's team. His opponents were Joseph Gardner, commissioner of the Metropolitan Water Reclamation District, and William Shaw, a state senator. Both Gardner and Shaw were African Americans.

With two opponents dividing the anti-organization vote, Kozubowski coasted to a comparatively easy victory. Solid support among white voters and a 60.7 percent turnout in the White South Side wards contributed to his triumph. The African-American vote split between Gardner and Shaw, with Gardner winning only a slim majority of it. (See figure 2.20 which highlights Gardner's support in the black sections of the city.) African-American turnout also lagged 12.2 percentage points behind white turnout citywide.

Table 2.20

The 1991 Chicago City Clerk Democratic Primary Race

Ward Group[1]	%Walter Kozubowski	%Joseph Gardner	%William Shaw	%Minor Candidate	Total Votes
White Northwest Side	79.0	16.3	3.3	1.4	112,591
White South Side	82.1	13.2	3.8	.9	128,128
Black South Side	11.0	54.0	31.9	3.1	138,094
Black West Side	13.0	43.7	39.7	3.6	35,755
Latino	59.7	27.9	9.2	3.2	21,417
North Lakeshore	54.0	35.7	7.9	2.5	60,135
Other White North Side	73.2	21.4	3.8	1.6	56,172
Mixed	55.1	31.2	11.8	1.9	29,529
Chicago Total	54.4	29.9	13.6	2.1	**581,821**

[1]For a detailed explanation of these ward groupings, see pages 4-8 in the introduction to this atlas. Keep in mind, however, that figure 2.20 maps the city using the ward boundaries in effect at the time of the election.

Even more telling for Gardner's chances, the Black South Side wards, where he was strongest, had a turnout of only 25.7 percent.

After the election, Kozubowski was indicted for ghost payrolling and entered a guilty plea. He was forced to resign.

The Race in the City: How Voters of Different Races/Ethnicities Supported the Candidates				
Race/ Ethnicity	Kozubowski	Gardner	Shaw	Turnout[1]
White	77.0%	18.9%	2.7%	38.2%
Black	7.2%	53.6%	35.4%	26.0%
Latino	78.8%	14.3%	4.0%	9.9%
Total				32.1%

[1]Turnout is the percentage of the voting population who cast ballots for a candidate for this office in this election.

Results from Recent Elections

Chicago City Clerk: Democratic Primary, February 1991

Figure 2.20
Support for Gardner

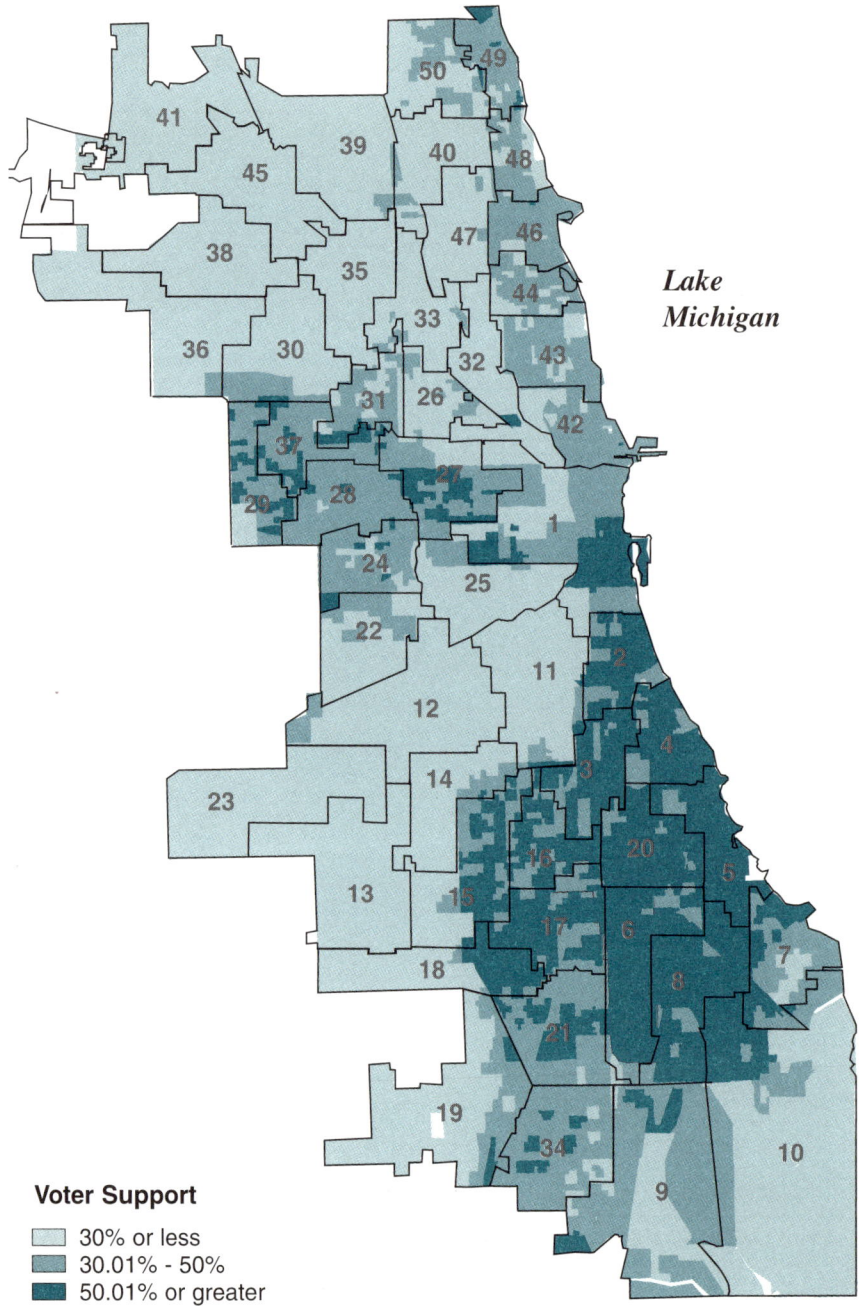

Lake Michigan

Voter Support
- 30% or less
- 30.01% - 50%
- 50.01% or greater

Chicago City Clerk: Democratic Primary, February 1995

The city clerk's race produced a crowded field of six contestants. From the outset, the reputed leader was James Laski, the 23rd ward alderman. Laski had had several disagreements with his ward committeeman, Congressman William Lipinski, and had spearheaded opposition in the city council to one of Mayor Daley's many tax hikes. Perhaps sensing that he might not be reslated for alderman and knowing that there was no incumbent running for reelection, Laski jumped into the contest for the clerk's job. So did State Senator Ricky Hendon, an African American from the West Side. Four other challengers also entered the fray, although none of them had previously run successful races for public office.

With his opposition split among five challengers, Laski won a reasonably easy victory, although polling less than a majority of the vote. His strength was in the white community, where he attracted 72.1 percent of the vote. And he was especially strong in the white ethnic areas on the Northwest and South Sides. Indeed, in the latter area he polled 80.7 percent of the vote and attracted a turnout of 35.7 percent, somewhat above the citywide white turnout rate for this election.

Table 2.21

The 1995 Chicago City Clerk Democratic Primary Race

Ward Group[1]	%James Laski	%Ricky Hendon	%Minor Candidates	Total Votes
White Northwest Side	63.0	6.0	31.0	68,965
White South Side	80.7	4.3	15.0	81,709
Black South Side	11.7	60.2	28.0	129,281
Black West Side	15.5	63.2	21.3	37,286
Latino	45.9	19.2	34.9	33,164
North Lakeshore	41.0	23.0	36.0	30,362
Other White North Side	57.4	12.5	30.0	44,342
Mixed	52.4	22.3	25.3	26,467
Chicago Total	43.7	29.6	26.7	**451,576**

[1]For a detailed explanation of these ward groupings, see pages 4-8 in the introduction to this atlas.

Results from Recent Elections

Chicago City Clerk: Democratic
Primary, February 1995

As figure 2.21 illustrates, Hendon polled majorities only in the African-American ward groups. And even there he had to share the vote with two of the other candidates who were African Americans. African-American turnout was also 7.8 percentage points below white turnout. The Latino vote was split, with Laski's 36.6 percent being the largest share given to any single candidate. Laski went on to take the general election.

The Race in the City: How Voters of Different Races/Ethnicities Supported the Candidates				
Race/Ethnicity	Laski	Hendon	Minor Candidates	Turnout[1]
White	72.1%	5.1%	22.6%	32.8%
Black	9.2%	64.2%	26.5%	25.0%
Latino	36.6%	17.7%	45.5%	9.1%
Total				24.9%

[1]Turnout is the percentage of the voting age population who cast ballots for a candidate for this office in this election.

Figure 2.21
Support for Hendon

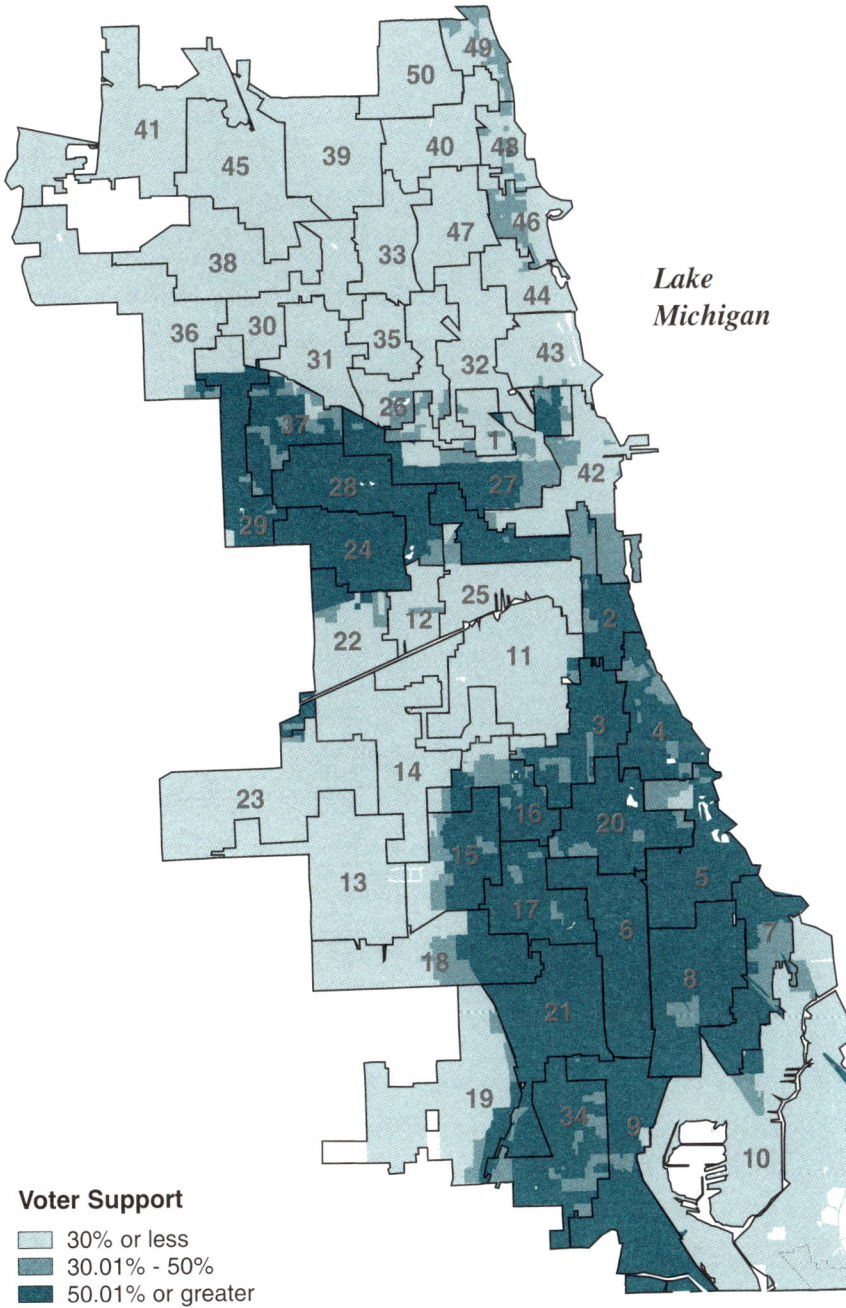

Lake Michigan

Voter Support

30% or less
30.01% - 50%
50.01% or greater

Chicago City Treasurer:
Democratic Primary, February 1991

Running in the Democratic primary as part of Mayor Daley's team, Miriam Santos had little difficulty defeating her two rivals, Edward Murray, a former city employee, and Mark Fairchild, a Larouche follower and frequent candidate for office. In doing so, Santos became the first Latina nominated for citywide office by the Democrats, and, with her victory in the general election, she became the first to win citywide office for her party.

Santos showed strength in virtually all parts of the city. She ran nearly as well in predominantly white areas as she did in Latino precincts, and she polled over three-quarters of the white vote citywide. Her support lagged

Table 2.22

The 1991 Chicago City Treasurer Democratic Primary Race

Ward Group*	%Miriam Santos	%Edward Murray	%Mark Fairchild	Total Votes
White Northwest Side	77.1	19.8	3.1	113,764
White South Side	77.3	20.1	2.5	128,390
Black South Side	51.7	37.7	10.7	130,220
Black West Side	45.9	42.6	11.4	35,229
Latino	78.7	17.2	4.0	23,600
North Lakeshore	78.3	17.4	4.3	63,438
Other White North Side	81.5	15.5	3.0	57,814
Mixed	64.5	30.4	5.1	29,192
Chicago Total	69.6	25.0	5.4	**581,647**

[1]For a detailed explanation of these ward groupings, see pages 4-8 in the introduction to this atlas. Keep in mind, however, that figure 2.22 maps the city using the ward boundaries in effect at the time of the election.

The Race in the City: How Voters of Different Races/Ethnicities Supported the Candidates

Race/Ethnicity	Santos	Murray	Fairchild	Turnout[1]
White	78.6%	18.9%	2.3%	39.3%
Black	46.9%	40.6%	12.4%	24.2%
Latino	87.7%	10.2%	1.9%	11.3%
Total				32.1%

[1]Turnout is the percentage of the voting age population who cast ballots for a candidate for this office in this election.

only in predominantly African-American areas. She failed to poll a citywide majority only among African Americans, but captured 40.6 percent of their vote. While her association with Daley gave her a boost among white voters, it apparently hurt her candidacy among African Americans.

Figure 2.22
Support for Santos

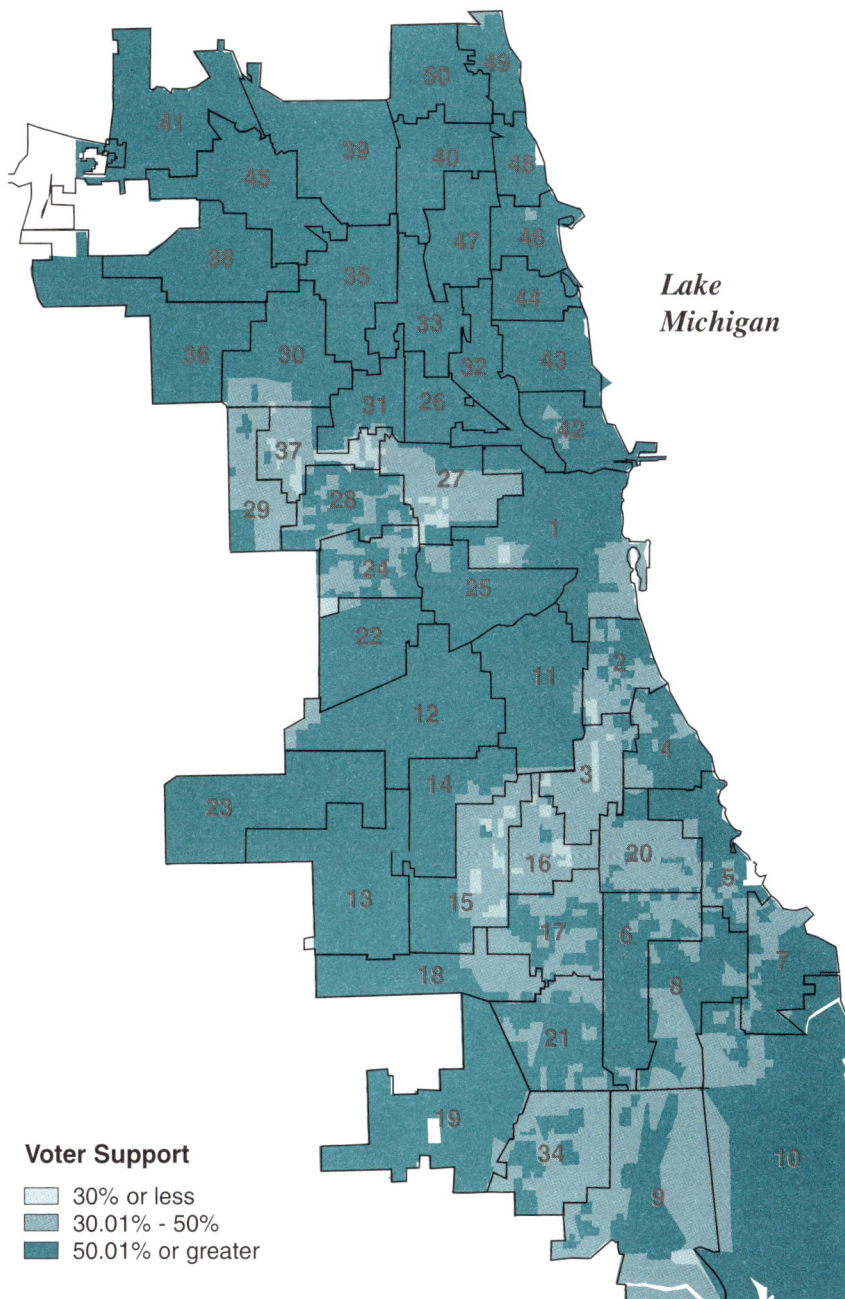

Lake Michigan

Voter Support
- 30% or less
- 30.01% - 50%
- 50.01% or greater

Results from Recent Elections

Chicago City Treasurer: Democratic Primary, February 1995

The 1995 race for the Democratic nomination for treasurer was expected to be a hard-fought and close contest. Those expectations were not realized, as Miriam Santos easily won renomination for the office she had first been elected to four years earlier.

In 1991 Santos had run as part of Mayor Daley's team. But she and the mayor had had highly publicized policy disputes since then and she ran for renomination without Daley's backing. Moreover, she was challenged by Larry Bloom, the 5th ward alderman, who brought to the contest high name recognition, a good-government image, and considerable strength among African Americans due to his earlier backing of Harold Washington during the contentious era of "council wars." But these assets weren't enough, as Bloom's candidacy quickly fizzled.

Santos handily won renomination, running almost as strongly as she had four years earlier when she had the mayor's active backing. She polled 66.8 percent of the city's vote, just 2.8 percentage points off her level in 1991. She defeated Bloom by 179,553 votes, a margin of victory that was smaller than the one she had enjoyed in 1991 (259,274 votes) but was still larger than Daley's edge over his nearest rival in the 1995 mayoral primary (173,210 votes).

Table 2.23

The 1995 Chicago City Treasurer Democratic Primary Race

Ward Group[1]	%Miriam Santos	%Larry Bloom	%Minor Candidate	Total Votes
White Northwest Side	74.0	23.3	2.7	75,954
White South Side	76.5	21.7	1.8	83,234
Black South Side	52.8	44.5	2.7	141,185
Black West Side	63.0	32.7	4.2	38,392
Latino	84.2	13.8	2.0	40,570
North Lakeshore	62.4	35.5	2.1	38,158
Other White North Side	67.8	30.2	2.0	52,137
Mixed	72.5	25.4	2.1	28,987
Chicago Total	66.8	30.8	2.5	**498,617**

[1]For a detailed explanation of these ward groupings, see pages 4-8 in the introduction to this atlas.

Citywide, Santos carried nearly three-quarters of the white Democratic vote, down only 6.2 percentage points from the 1991 primary. And she ran even more strongly in the white ethnic areas than she did in the North Lakeshore wards, a minor reversal of the 1991 primary pattern. Santos also polled 97.5 percent of the Latino vote—an increase of 9.8 percentage points from her earlier primary contest, and increased her support among African Americans by 7.4 percentage points, this time carrying a majority of that community's vote.

Results from Recent Elections

Chicago City Treasurer: Democratic Primary, February 1995

The Race in the City: How Voters of Different Races/Ethnicities Supported the Candidates			
Race/Ethnicity	Santos	Bloom	Turnout[1]
White	72.4%	25.5%	35.7%
Black	54.3%	42.6%	26.7%
Latino	97.5%	1.6%	12.2%
Total			27.5%

[1]Turnout is the percentage of the voting age population who cast ballots for a candidate for this office in this election.

Results from Recent Elections

Chicago City Treasurer:
Democratic Primary,
February 1995

Figure 2.23
Support for Santos

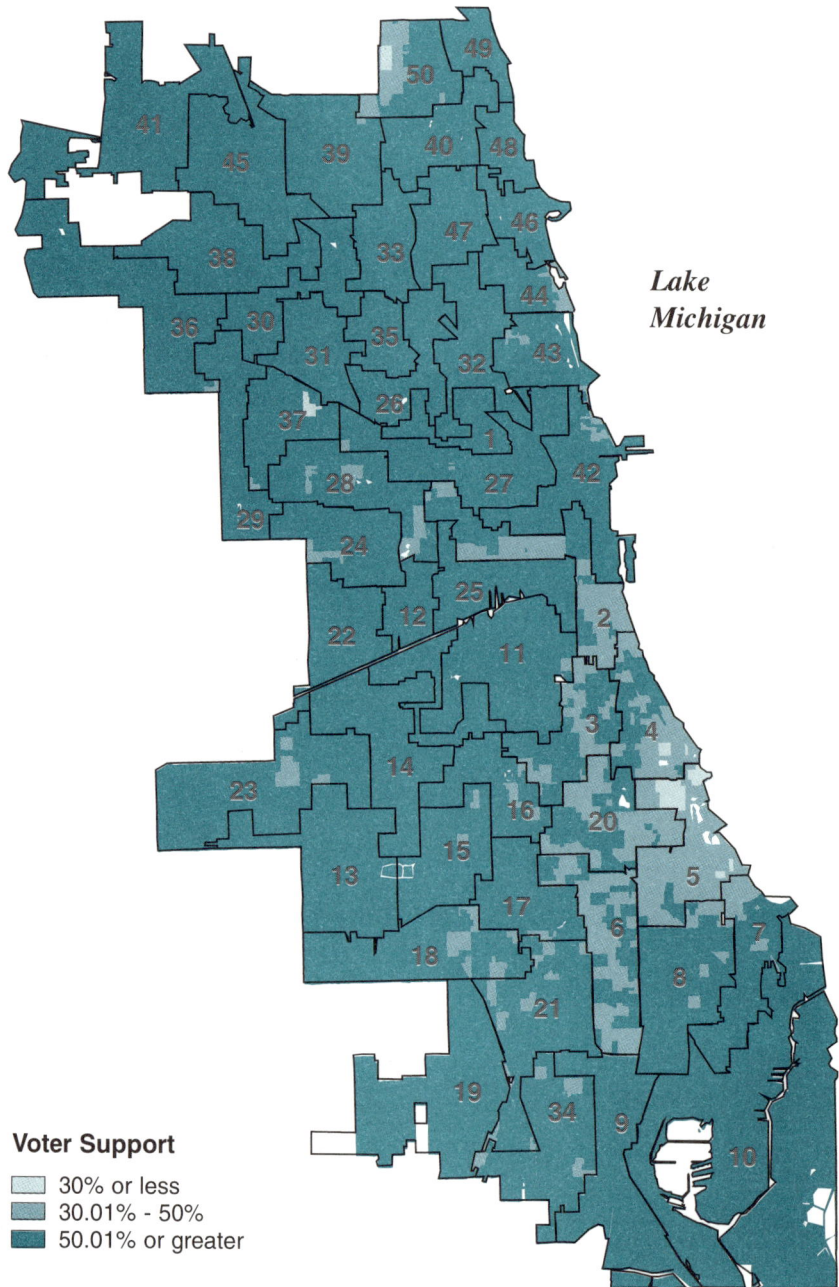

Lake
Michigan

Voter Support
- 30% or less
- 30.01% - 50%
- 50.01% or greater

Chapter 3: Republicans in Chicago

Virtually alone among the nation's major cities in the late 1990s, Chicago remains an unchallenged bastion of Democratic voting strength.

In the 1930s, the country's ten-largest cities, along with most of its medium-sized manufacturing centers, swung sharply to the Democrats, many breaking decades-long commitments to the Republicans in the process. The urban-industrial policies of the New Deal, especially its efforts to create jobs for the unemployed and its general tilt in favor of labor unions, cemented Democratic voting support among urban workers and their families. Throughout the 1940s and most of the 1950s, strong urban support for the Democrats was a prominent feature of U.S. elections. In no city in the country did local politicians do a better job of capitalizing on the popularity of Franklin Roosevelt and the New Deal than those in Chicago. Local politicians built a patronage-fueled organization that was envied—and eventually emulated—by other cities.

But while Chicago and other major cities were Democratic strongholds in the 1930s, 1940s, and 1950s, conditions began to change in the 1960s. First, many of those who had become New Deal Democrats in the 1930s were passing from the scene, being replaced by younger cohorts of voters who had not formed their political attachments in response to the Great Depression and the New Deal. Second, new issues became salient to voters during the 1960s, and one of these—race—had a special capacity to splinter the New Deal's voting coalition in cities. Since whites and blacks lived in close proximity in cities, the demands for integration in housing, education, and hiring threatened long-standing practices that discriminated against blacks. Facing loss of the preferential treatment that they had long benefitted from, whites struck back at the voting booth against politicians whom they perceived to be supportive of equal opportunities for blacks. Outside the South, the backlash vote in the 1966 and 1968 elections seriously reduced Democratic strength and produced Republican wins or near wins in most of the country's urban areas. The New Deal coalition was permanently fragmented, as integration issues split it along racial lines.

In the mid-1960s, in most of the country's large cities, Republicans benefitted from this backlash vote. In the process, they again became a political presence in urban America. They didn't always win city elections, although they elected mayors in New York City and Philadelphia, but they were able to mount viable challenges and run respectable campaigns. Moreover, cutting into the usual Democratic margins in urban areas enabled Republicans to win statewide contests in places like Massachusetts and Rhode Island, where defeat had almost become habit forming.

Republicans in Chicago

Chicago was the great exception to this pattern of political change in the 1960s. There was a backlash vote in Chicago, and it showed itself clearly in the 1966 elections. Then the white ethnic redoubts on the city's Northwest and Southwest Sides delivered large majorities of their votes to *Republican* candidates for both U.S. Senate and president of the Cook County board of commissioners. In the white precincts of Bogan, Gage Park, Marquette Park, and Cragin, sites of open-housing marches that summer, the Democratic losses ran as high as 10 to 15 percent. Even Democratic congressmen and state legislators who survived won by much smaller margins than usual.

But Republicans did not capitalize and build on their 1966 inroads. Nor have they subsequently developed enough grassroots support to mount a viable challenge to the Democratic Machine's long-standing hegemony. In any other big northern city, the conservative economic and social views of politicians like Richard M. Daley, Michael Madigan, and Edward Burke would make them Republicans, but in Chicago they remain Democrats. And while urban Republicans elsewhere have become electorally competitive, and even have been able to elect mayors in New York and Los Angeles, in Chicago they sometimes seem to be candidates for a political endangered-species list. In 1995 the Republican party's preferred candidate for the mayoral nomination lost the party's primary to Ray Wardingly, better known as "Spanky the Clown." And to many observers of the city's politics, having a professional clown at the head of the Republican city ticket was an apt metaphor for the party's forlorn condition.

Party Identification

Today, only slightly more than one-tenth of the city's residents call themselves Republicans, while over half classify themselves as Democrats (see table 3.1). The Republicans are outnumbered both by the Independents, who make up a substantial 21 percent of the identifiers, and even by those who say they have no party identification, who make up another 14 percent of the city's electorate.

Viewed geographically (see table 3.2), Republican identification is strongest in the North Side of the city (17 percent), which includes the Near North lakefront areas, and in the Northwest Side (also 17 percent). The Southwest Side, at 13 percent, is the third-ranking area of Republican identification. But in a city that regularly returns large Democratic majorities on election day, it is significant to notice that the percentage of residents who call themselves Democrats is below half in all areas except the West Side (56 percent) and the South Side (65 percent).

Table 3.1

Party Identification of Chicago Residents

Identification	Percent
Republican	11.2
Democrat	52.5
Independent	20.8
Other	1.7
None	13.8
Total	100.0

Source: Combined 1990-1995 MCIC Metro Surveys

From the point of view of Republican strategy, the figures on party identification present a significant, but not insurmountable, challenge to mounting a competitive election effort in the city. The key to doing that involves understanding four factors:

- the nature of core Republican support
- the values and interests of Independents
- the likelihood of attracting the "Nones"
- the issues Republicans can use to attract votes from Democrats.

Demographic Differences Between Chicago's Republicans and Democrats

Discussions of party loyalty in Chicago most often begin with race, and for good reason. As table 3.3 shows, whites and Asians are much more likely to call themselves Republicans than are blacks or Latinos. Among whites, about 20 percent are Republicans, and that level is generally consistent across the three largest white ethnic groups—Germans, Irish, and Poles. A majority of only two groups in the city say they are Democrats: 72 percent of the blacks, and 61 percent of the Puerto Ricans. But these survey responses may somewhat understate Democratic strength since a large majority of the Mexicans, who vote predominantly Democratic, say they have no party affiliation.

Viewed another way, about three-quarters (77 percent) of the self-identified Republicans in Chicago are white. Meanwhile, over half (52 percent) of the Democrats are black and only a minority of them (38 percent) are white.

But Democrats are weakest among the youngest group of voters, those 18 to 30 years of age (see table 3.4). This is the age cohort that is more likely than any other to say they are Republicans (15 percent). Apparently, the kinds of issues that attract voters to the

Republicans in Chicago

Table 3.2

Party Identification by Geographic Area

Area	Republican	Democrat	Independent, Other, None
North	17.3%	44.7%	38.0%
Northwest	16.9%	39.5%	43.7%
Southwest	13.1%	49.3%	37.7%
West	6.8%	56.2%	37.0%
South	5.2%	65.4%	29.5%

Source: Combined 1990-1995 MCIC Metro Surveys

Table 3.3

Party Identification by Race/Ethnic Group

Group	Republican	Democrat	Independent, Other, None
White	19.6%	42.3%	38.1%
Germans	21.3%	43.2%	35.6%
Irish	19.2%	48.0%	32.7%
Poles	15.3%	45.0%	39.7%
Asian	19.4%	23.0%	57.6%
Latino	6.7%	40.1%	53.2%
Puerto Rican	9.5%	61.0%	29.4%
Mexican	5.1%	29.0%	65.9%
Black	3.1%	71.8%	25.0%

Source: Combined 1990-1995 MCIC Metro Surveys

Republicans in Chicago

Republican cause, and the way they have been presented, have somewhat more appeal to the youngest age group in Chicago. All the older age groups are about 10 percent Republican and 55 percent Democratic. The somewhat greater appeal of the Republican party to the youngest age cohort means that the average age of Republican identifiers—40.7 years—is somewhat lower than the average age of Democrats—43.8 years.

Table 3.4

Party Identification by Age Groups

Age Group	Republican	Democrat	Independent, Other, None
18-30	14.5%	46.3%	39.1%
31-40	10.2%	54.2%	35.6%
41-50	10.7%	55.2%	34.0%
51-60	7.0%	54.5%	38.5%
61+	10.5%	57.6%	31.9%

Source: Combined 1990-1995 MCIC Metro Surveys

Table 3.5

Party Identification by Education Level

Education Level	Republican	Democrat	Independent, Other, None
College Graduates	18.2%	41.9%	39.9%
Some College	11.1%	53.1%	35.8%
High School Graduates	9.2%	56.8%	34.0%
Some High School	5.6%	64.9%	29.5%
0-8th Grade	6.8%	49.5%	43.8%

Source: Combined 1990-1995 MCIC Metro Surveys

Chicago Democrats and Republicans differ considerably both in education and household income levels. Table 3.5 shows that 18 percent of the college graduates in Chicago are Republicans, while 42 percent identify themselves as Democrats. At all other education levels, a majority of the respondents called themselves Democrats.

Of course, educational differences are related to differences in incomes and lifestyles. Table 3.6 shows that among those in households with annual incomes of $70,000 or more—approximately the top 8 percent of Chicago incomes—about 22 percent call themselves Republicans. The percent of Republican identifiers drops for each successively lower income level. The median family income for Chicago Republicans is $37,800 per year. It is $27,200 for Democrats.

The reason for the income difference is primarily because Republicans have more technical, more managerial, and/or higher-paying jobs. We draw this conclusion because the difference in family income is only marginally related to the number of employed workers in the household. About 27 percent of Republicans live in homes with two employed adults, as opposed to 21 percent of Democrats.

Perhaps the most significant family-structure and lifestyle difference that affects interests and opinions on policy measures is the fact that Republicans are substantially less likely than Democrats to have children at home. Table 3.7 shows that among families with two adults and no children, 14 percent are Republican; and among households with one adult and no children, 13 percent are Republican. The percentage of Republicans among households with children is much lower. One of the more remarkable findings in this set of demographic tables is the fact that, among households with one adult and children, only 5 percent are Republican and 65 percent are Democrat. Overall, 31 percent of Republicans live in a household with children under age 18, compared to 44 percent of Democrats.

Although Republicans are less likely to have children in the household, they are more likely to have stable marriages. Overall, 47 percent of Republicans are currently married, compared to 40 percent of Democrats. Among people who have ever been married, about 17 percent of Republicans have been divorced, compared to 23 percent among Democrats. On other "family value" characteristics, however, the differences are less clear-cut. For example, about 20 percent of both Republicans and Democrats report that they are not married, but they live in a "marriage-like" relationship.

Republicans in Chicago

Table 3.6

Party Identification by Annual Family Income

Income Level	Republican	Democrat	Independent, Other, None
$70,000 or more	21.7%	47.9%	30.5%
$40,000-$70,000	14.6%	47.4%	38.0%
$20,000-$40,000	10.6%	52.9%	36.5%
$20,000 or less	6.6%	60.6%	32.8%

Source: Combined 1990-1995 MCIC Metro Surveys

Table 3.7

Party Identification by Household/Family Structure

Family Type	Republican	Democrat	Independent, Other, None
Two adults, no child	13.6%	48.3%	38.1%
One adult, no child	13.0%	51.4%	35.7%
Two adults + child(ren)	10.6%	49.6%	39.8%
One adult + child(ren)	4.6%	65.4%	30.0%

Source: Combined 1990-1995 MCIC Metro Surveys

Differences in Public Policy Preferences Between Chicago's Republicans and Democrats

Each year Metro Chicago Information Center (MCIC) member organizations propose a wide range of questions measuring preferences, perceptions, and actions on a variety of public policy issues for the annual survey of the metropolitan area. MCIC's sample of questions reflects the diversity of its members and is not designed to pinpoint differences between Republicans and Democrats. Nevertheless, the results from the combined 1990-1995 MCIC surveys show some clear areas of distinction between Republicans and Democrats in Chicago and some areas of agreement that provide an interesting mirror on national trends.

The principal conclusions that emerge from the survey results are that compared to Democrats, Republicans are:

- more opposed to policies that aid the poor and programs that primarily benefit the poor

Republicans in Chicago

- more suspicious of judicial discretion, but in agreement on other specific recommendations for improving the effectiveness of the judicial system

- more opposed to using tax dollars to support abortions and family planning for the poor, but in agreement on the general principle of access to abortion and birth control

- in agreement on a wide array of issues including waste management, the environment, tuition vouchers, and user fees.

Table 3.8 shows the results for a variety of questions that involve the symbolism of "the poor." The first row of the table shows a 26 percent difference between Republicans (41 percent) and Democrats (15 percent) in agreement with the statement that "the state and local governments spend

Table 3.8

Chicago Partisans on Benefits to "The Poor"				
Statements	Percentage of Republicans Who Agree	Percentage of Independents Who Agree	Percentage of Democrats Who Agree	Republican/ Democrat Difference
State and Local Government:				
Spend too much on the poor	41%	23%	15%	26%
Wastes too much money	83%	86%	76%	7%
Workers are not motivated to do a good job	54%	60%	58%	-4%
Very Important to Spend State and Local Taxes on:				
Health	68%	79%	87%	-19%
Public Transportation	42%	56%	58%	-16%
Parks and Recreation	49%	58%	61%	-12%
Would Pay Higher State/ Local Taxes for:				
Better school buildings in poor areas	68%	76%	85%	-17%
Higher teacher pay in poor areas	64%	71%	76%	-12%
Subsidized Housing:				
Would vote for small increase in subsidized housing	59%	65%	78%	-19%
Any increase in subsidized housing would harm the community	52%	33%	39%	13%

Source: Combined 1990-1995 MCIC Metro Surveys

too much on the poor." The difference is not due to generally more negative views about government among Republicans than among Democrats. As table 3.8 also shows, on questions asking whether the government "wastes too much money" and whether government workers "are not motivated to do a good job," there is no difference between Republican and Democratic identifiers in Chicago.

Other results in table 3.8 show substantially less support among Republicans than among Democrats for a number of specific policies and programs that clearly target the poor or provide benefits that are more likely to be enjoyed by the poor. These include:

- the importance of spending tax dollars on health, public transit, and parks and recreation

- willingness to pay higher taxes to improve school buildings and raise teacher salaries in poor areas

- willingness to vote for a small increase in subsidized housing so that lower income workers can live near their community.

Table 3.9 presents the survey results on the judicial system. Republicans are 14 percent less likely than Democrats to favor judicial discretion in sentencing. But, they are equally likely to favor prison alternatives for nondangerous offenders and the use of tax dollars to build more prisons.

Republicans in Chicago

Table 3.9

Chicago Partisans on Judicial Discretion

Issue	Republicans	Independents	Democrats	Republican/ Democrat Difference
Favor judicial discretion in sentencing	23%	23%	37%	-14%
Favor spending more state and local taxes for prison construction	59%	58%	61%	-2%
Favor prison alternatives for nondangerous offenders	87%	91%	86%	1%

Source: Combined 1990-1995 MCIC Metro Surveys

Table 3.10 reviews the results on abortion and family-planning issues. A solid majority—with no significant difference between Republicans and Democrats—support a woman's right to an abortion when:

Republicans in Chicago

- the woman's life is endangered by the pregnancy;
- the woman is married and doesn't want more children; and,
- the family is poor and can't afford to have more children.

A near majority—with no significant difference between Republicans and Democrats—say that teens should be able to obtain an abortion without their parent's consent. A solid majority—again with no significant difference between Republicans and Democrats—support teen access to birth control.

The differences between Republicans and Democrats on family-planning issues are shown at the bottom of table 3.10. Republicans are much less likely than Democrats to agree that tax dollars should be used to pay either for abortions for low-income patients or for family-planning clinics (which are used primarily by low-income families). It is the issue of the use of government resources to benefit low-income residents that differentiates party identifiers on family-planning issues, not the principles of abortion or family planning.

Table 3.10

Chicago Partisans on Family Planning & Abortion and Tax Funding for Family Planning & Abortion

Issue	Republicans	Independents	Democrats	Republican/ Democrat Difference
Favor Abortion Access for:				
Cases where pregnancy is life threatening	87%	87%	90%	-3%
Married women	67%	63%	66%	1%
Low-income women who can t afford more children	67%	60%	65%	2%
Teens without parent's consent	48%	55%	48%	0%
Favor Teen Access to Birth Control	74%	80%	80%	-6%
Think State and Local Taxes Should Be Used for:				
Low-income abortion patients	45%	59%	60%	-15%
Family-planning clinics	59%	70%	69%	-10%

Source: Combined 1990-1995 MCIC Metro Surveys

On a very wide variety of other issues, there are no significant patterns of difference between Republicans and Democrats in Chicago. The results in table 3.11 show no difference in the priority for spending tax dollars on:

- the environment
- waste management

- recycling
- arts and cultural organizations
- tuition subsidies for religious schools
- tuition subsidies for private schools.

    Republicans are as likely as Democrats to agree on the need for a new runway at O'Hare Airport and on a wide range of taxes and user fees, including:

- higher taxes on alcohol to pay for treatment
- higher taxes on cigarettes to pay for health care costs associated with smoking
- a 10-cent deposit on soda cans and bottles
- higher gas taxes to fund mass transit and cleaner air.

Republicans in Chicago

Table 3.11

Chicago Partisans on a Wide Range of Policy Issues

Issue	Republicans	Independents	Democrats	Republican/ Democrat Difference
Think it is Very Important to Spend State/Local Taxes on:				
The environment	56%	63%	62%	-6%
Waste management	64%	67%	64%	0%
Recycling	53%	52%	50%	3%
Would Pay Higher State/Local Taxes for Arts and Culture	37%	40%	43%	-6%
Think State and Local Taxes Should be Used for:				
Help with tuition for religious schools	35%	35%	33%	2%
Help with tuition for private schools	34%	32%	31%	3%
Think O'Hare Should Build a New Runway	64%	57%	58%	6%
Other Taxes or User Fees:				
Favor a higher alcohol tax for treatment	76%	79%	82%	-6%
Favor a 10-cent deposit on soda cans/bottles	75%	80%	71%	4%
Favor higher cigarette taxes to pay health care costs	72%	75%	77%	-5%
Favor a higher gas tax to fund mass transit and promote cleaner air	46%	51%	50%	-4%
Favor garbage pickup charges based on amount of garbage	47%	45%	34%	13%

Source: Combined 1990-1995 MCIC Metro Surveys

Republicans in Chicago

The only tax/user fee issue where we find a difference is that Republicans are more likely to favor charging for garbage pickup based on the amount generated.

Voting Patterns

Chicago's Republican identifiers are not antigovernment ideologues. Theirs is not a generalized opposition to "big government" but a more narrowly targeted antipathy: they oppose those government policies and programs that tilt in favor of aiding the poor. This is so even when they support the principle underpinning the program (e.g., while supporting the right to abortion, they oppose spending tax money to give poor women access to this right). But on most other issues, even those that are cutting-edge ones at the national level, Chicago's Republicans and Democrats are virtually indistinguishable ideologically.

Unable to identify themselves with any issue or cluster of issues that could arouse and mobilize the city's electorate, Republicans have failed to mount a competitive challenge to the virtually hegemonic control exercised by the city's Democratic Machine. Republican candidates have come close to carrying the city in only a few elections since 1980, while usually the party's nominees have not even polled as much as a third of the vote (see table 3.12). Typically, Republicans have run poorest in mayoral elections, except for the unusual 1983 contest when the white Republican candidate garnered support from white Democrats deserting their party's African-American nominee. But in 1987, 1989, 1991, and 1995, Republican candidates weren't even able to poll in double digits, capturing an average of only 3.5 percent of the popular vote. And this miserable showing came in the face of deep fissures within the Democratic party—divisions that Republican leaders were unable to capitalize on.

However, Republicans have mounted stronger efforts in contests for other offices. They have done best since 1980 in races for Cook County State's Attorney. In local lore, this office is one that the Machine is anxious to control because it has prosecutorial jurisdiction over the misdeeds of local politicians. But, recent Republican state's attorneys Bernard Carey and Jack O'Malley have been careful not to pursue charges of corruption against Democratic officeholders. Instead, they have preferred to leave that large task to the federal attorney, whose office has become the *de facto* ethics commission for city officeholders notorious for ghost payrollers, no-bid contracts for friends and financial backers, and other corrupt practices. Nevertheless, the office's old reputation as the public's last, best hope for limiting local corruption still lingers, and Republicans apparently benefit from the legend. In addition, in both the 1990 special election and in 1992, O'Malley benefitted even more from running against weak Democrats. Cecil Partee, an African American who had been appointed to the office in 1989, ran weakly in the city's white strongholds in his 1990 bid to win the office in his own right.

Table 3.12

Chicago General Election Results, 1980-1996

(Arranged in order of the percentage of Republican strength)

Year	Office	Republican Percentage	Republican Votes	Democrat Percentage	Democrat Votes
1992	State's Attorney	48.8	515,365	51.1	538,790
1983	Mayor	48.1	619,608	51.9	667,929
1980	State's Attorney	38.1	422,140	61.9	685,286
1994	Governor	36.4	219,053	62.3	374,612
1990	State's Attorney	36.0	244,543	52.1	354,086
1984	U.S. President	34.4	409,114	64.9	770,612
1990	Governor	32.8	222,460	65.4	443,212
1986	Governor	32.2	250,166	56.8	441,962
1984	U.S. Senate	29.9	351,253	68.7	807,332
1988	U.S. President	29.7	315,961	69.2	734,676
1982	Governor	26.1	259,661	73.0	726,937
1980	U.S. President	26.0	302,935	67.4	785,100
1986	Cook County Board President	25.7	189,072	74.3	546,216
1996	State's Attorney	25.7	216,191	57.3	482,692
1988	State's Attorney	24.9	252,808	75.0	762,085
1984	State's Attorney	23.5	274,855	76.5	892,509
1992	U.S. Senate	23.2	250,091	74.8	806,478
1990	Cook County Board President	18.9	125,882	60.8	403,809
1990	U.S. Senate	18.7	127,416	81.2	551,918
1994	Cook County Board President	18.5	105,589	76.4	435,011
1992	U.S. President	18.1	198,827	72.0	790,162
1996	U.S. Senate	17.3	147,773	80.3	685,025
1996	U.S. President	15.3	132,688	79.7	690,641
1986	U.S. Senate	15.1	115,808	83.4	641,556
1987	Mayor	4.3	47,648	53.8	600,252
1991	Mayor	3.6	23,421	70.6	450,581
1989	Mayor	3.4	35,964	55.4	576,620
1995	Mayor	2.7	16,568	60.0	359,466

Republicans in Chicago

Table 3.12 (continued)

Summary Data	
Office	**Mean Republican Percentages**
State's Attorney	32.8
Governor	31.8
U.S. President	24.7
Cook County Board President	21.0
U.S. Senate	20.8
Mayor	12.4 (3.5 without 1983)

Two years later, Patrick O'Connor, a white alderman who had been part of the anti-Washington bloc on the city council during the 1983-87 Council Wars, drew only tepid support both from African-American voters and from some white ethnic strongholds, whose Democratic ward bosses preferred the cooperative and unthreatening O'Malley.

In these and the other state's attorney's contests, the Republicans nominated pragmatic, nonideological candidates. They have followed the same formula in selecting recent gubernatorial candidates. The wheeling and dealing James Thompson and the more phlegmatic Jim Edgar have both run reasonably well for Republicans in Chicago, polling nearly a third of the city's vote. Both have been able to augment the small Republican base by attracting votes from Independents and even Democratic crossovers, especially among African Americans in Edgar's close 1990 race against Neil Hartigan. To run this well, Thompson and Edgar have avoided hard-edged ideological postures, preferring instead to present themselves as competent and prudent managers of the state's bureaucracy. More so than Thompson, Edgar has also crafted a picture of himself as a frugal guardian of the state's finances, eschewing tax boosts except as a last resort to aid education, a stance that public opinion polls indicate to be both popular and safe politically.

When Republican nominees come across as ideologues they don't fare well among Chicago's voters. Republican U.S. Senate candidates Judy Koehler in 1986, Rich Williamson in 1992, and Al Salvi in 1996 were all too narrow ideologically to appeal to the city's Independents and wavering Democrats. So was Joe Morris, the right-winger who was the party's nominee for Cook County board president in 1994. Of these four, only Williamson was able to get as much as 20 percent of the city's vote, mainly because he benefitted from white crossovers against his African-American opponent, Carol Moseley-Braun. Of course, even a moderate image doesn't provide much of a boost when the campaign is obviously inept, as both Lynn

Martin and Aldo DeAngelis demonstrated in their 1990 and 1994 races, respectively, for the U.S. Senate and Cook County board president.

The only Republican presidential candidate to poll as much as a third of the city's vote was Ronald Reagan in his 1984 reelection bid. While Reagan was in many ways *the* most ideological of Republican candidates, his effort never became as identified with hard-edged ideological issues as, for example, did Al Salvi's bid for the U.S. Senate in 1996. Reagan also benefitted from the economic revival that the city, the state, and the country were experiencing in 1984. He further benefitted from running against Walter Mondale, who was identified with Jimmy Carter's ill-fated presidency and who had committed himself to a tax increase to reduce the soaring deficit that "Reaganomics" had inflicted upon the economy. But in 1992, when economic circumstances were less auspicious, George Bush, even though he had a more moderate image than Reagan, was unable to crack the 20 percent mark.

Table 3.13 gives us another view of Republican voting in Chicago in recent elections. This table measures Republican strength by summing the votes cast for party's candidates at the two most recent elections for each office and then calculates that as a percentage of total votes cast in the two contests. Looked at by ward groupings we've identified earlier in this atlas, the resulting percentage tells us where and among which groups Republican candidates ran best.

Republicans in Chicago

Table 3.13

Republican Voting in Chicago: Percentage of Support for the Two Most Recent Elections

Ward Group[1]	State's Attorney	Governor	U.S. Senate	Cook County Board President	U.S. President	City Treasurer	Mayor
White Northwest Side	60.0	53.5	43.9	34.8	34.7	14.7	5.5
White South Side	49.7	41.6	37.8	23.0	28.5	7.6	3.9
Black South Side	21.3	17.7	3.5	3.9	3.0	5.3	.9
Black West Side	18.9	15.7	5.2	4.6	4.5	5.5	1.2
Latino	34.7	33.3	18.7	16.6	15.7	9.6	2.7
North Lakeshore	52.5	40.4	24.2	27.3	22.8	11.9	4.5
Other White North Side	50.5	39.6	28.8	25.4	24.7	10.5	3.9
Mixed	41.4	39.6	26.6	22.1	19.2	9.6	3.2
Total	38.5	34.5	20.6	18.7	16.5	9.2	3.1

Note. The data in this table refers to the 1992 and 1996 races for state's attorney, U.S. Senate, and U.S. President; the 1990 and 1994 races for governor and Cook County board president; and the 1991 and 1995 races for city treasurer and mayor.

[1]See pages 4-8 for a detailed explanation and depiction of the ward groupings.

Republicans in Chicago

The pattern of support is unsurprising. Republicans consistently ran strongest in the white ethnic areas of the Northwest Side. They also usually did quite well among the white voters on the city's South Side, although there the continuing vitality of some of the Democratic ward organizations probably held down their vote. When Republican candidates have captured a third or more of the citywide vote, it was because they attracted a sizable vote from the North Lakeshore and Other White North Side wards, about a third of the Latino vote, and nearly a fifth of the African-American vote.

While centrist Republican candidates for some state and county offices have been able to run respectably in Chicago, the party's nominees have not been able even to mount reasonable, let alone serious, challenges for city offices, as the votes for city treasurer and mayor indicate. Since the early 1980s, the city's Democratic party has been openly split along racial lines, with African-American leaders often fielding their own slate of candidates in city and county races. Yet Republican leaders in Chicago haven't been able to use this split even as a springboard to electoral credibility, let alone to victory.

Why not? Why haven't Chicago's Republicans done a better job of making themselves competitive? Their efforts have been thwarted by the city's Democratic leaders who have effectively captured the Republican bases for fundraising and voting support.

The pro-business tilt of public policy decisions under the Daley I and Daley II administrations has more than satisfied the city's corporate and financial elite, usually the backbone of Republican fundraising and party-building efforts. Since usually Republican contributors fund the campaigns of city Democrats, potential Republican nominees know that they will have to fend for themselves. This has made it impossible for Republican leaders to recruit candidates with sufficient name recognition and credibility to challenge the Democrats for city offices, especially mayor.

Chicago's Democrats also captured the backlash vote in the mid-1960s, preventing local Republicans from building a voting base in the city's white ethnic neighborhoods. In other northern cities, Republicans began their rebound by attracting this backlash vote of white ethnics who were resisting efforts to end the discriminatory system that had for so long given whites preferences in housing, schools, and hiring. Then, in the 1970s and early 1980s, urban Republicans consolidated this support and broadened their appeal, recruiting votes among middle-income African Americans and newly arriving Asians and Latinos. What emerged was something of a "rainbow coalition," although one that was sharply skewed economically.

Chicago's Republicans were not able to replicate this approach to building a voting base. When the Democrats coopted the backlash vote, the party took on a retrograde character much like those in the states of the Deep South. To be sure, the rhetoric of Chicago's Democratic party leaders was (usually) less inflammatory than that of their counterparts in Alabama or Mississippi, but their actions were not much different. On all of the integration issues that were at the core of the civil rights movement of the 1960s, for example, the white leaders of Chicago's Democratic party sided with the white resisters.

Despite the importance of votes from African Americans for local and national Democratic candidates, Chicago's white Democratic leaders opted for their own, the white European immigrant-stock groups. In the later 1960s, Richard J. Daley's administration openly sided with the foes of integration. It opposed plans for even limited school desegregation, choosing instead to wage a long and losing battle in the courts. It resisted efforts to end the preferential hiring of whites in the police and fire departments, denying all along that discrimination had played any role in producing their nearly lily-white ranks. And it opposed efforts to desegregate public housing or to mitigate in any other way the city's notorious residential segregation.

On all of these fronts, the Daley I administration lost its legal battles. While the litigation dragged on, whites left the public schools, the changing neighborhoods, and eventually the city itself. Through it all, however, Richard J. Daley stood resolute in his opposition to meaningful integration. Ordered by the courts to desegregate public housing by building new sites in white neighborhoods, Daley simply saw to it that no new public housing was constructed. After entering into a consent decree that laid down rules for future hiring practices to integrate the fire department, the mayor's administration simply imposed a hiring freeze. By siding with the white resisters on these and other integration issues, the Daley I administration and the Democratic organization, which was practically synonymous in the public mind, positioned themselves as defenders of the values of the city's white European immigrant-stock groups, their last hope for continued white control.

The city's white voters responded to these racial policies. The Daley I organization acquired new voting strength in the working- and middle-class white ethnic wards, even those that had voted Republican in the elections of the mid-1960s. Recognizing the support that Daley's Democrats gave to a range of racist policies and practices that they favored, white voters in these wards gratefully delivered large majorities to his candidates. Even the conviction of key administration insiders for public corruption in the early 1970s failed to shake the gratitude and commitment of these white ethnic voters.

Daley's resort to this brand of racial politics had a different effect in the black wards. There, support for Daley's candidacy itself declined in every election after 1963, and, even more tellingly, African-American turnout in local elections dropped substantially. Daley's Democrats took no action to counter this decline. For example, the vaunted Democratic Machine has conducted no citywide registration or get-out-the-vote drives since the early 1960s, preferring instead to target its efforts and resources on the city's white wards. Demobilization of the African-American electorate was—and still remains—

Republicans
in Chicago

Republicans in Chicago

a vital part of the solution fashioned by the white leaders of the Democratic organization to maintain their control over the party and the city.

Of course, these developments left the local Republicans little room to maneuver. The backlash vote had no reason to desert Daley's Democrats, and the Republicans couldn't easily refashion themselves to appeal to the growing numbers of disgruntled African Americans. As a result, the racial conflict that has rent the unity of the Democratic electorate has thus far had no discernible effect on Chicago's partisan balance.

But what of the future? Crystal-ball gazing is always hazardous and especially so in this instance, since the "rules of the game" have been altered recently. In its 1995 session, the Republican-controlled state legislature provided for nonpartisan municipal elections in Chicago. This will produce an open primary for mayor, with the two leading contestants facing each other in a runoff if no one wins over 50 percent of the vote in the primary. To this point, other white aspirants have been restrained from challenging Daley in a Democratic primary, not wanting to be labeled "spoilers," the Chicago code term for candidates whose entry might split the white vote and allow an African American to win the nomination. The open primary with a runoff requirement changes this calculus and might encourage other white politicians to challenge the incumbent. In the short term, however, it is not clear that any of these challengers will be high visibility Republicans, since they would still face a very serious fundraising hurdle.

But there is potential for Republicans to develop more voting strength in contests for other offices. This will require building on the kind of diverse coalition that they have been able to pull together in some gubernatorial and county contests. This must involve appealing to younger voters in the North Lakeshore and Other White North Side wards—voters who are attracted to Republican economic programs but repulsed by the party's strident and reactionary positions on social questions. This approach will require more serious and sustained efforts to attract minority supporters, Latinos as well as African Americans. Appealing to the population groups that are growing and are restless with the glaringly subordinate position to which the Daley II machine consigns them offers more promise than banking the Republican party's future prospects on trying to compete with the Democrats for support from the aging and shrinking white populations on the city's Northwest and Southwest sides. By looking to the demographic future and crafting an appropriate agenda and message, Chicago's Republicans can again become a competitive force in the city's elections.

Chapter 4: White Ethnicity in Chicago Politics

For the longer term, the main problem seems likely to be one which has always been a key to urban politics—ethnicity. A resolution of conflicting aspirations between the traditional Irish machine leaders, the blacks, and the eastern Europeans (especially Poles) must be made if the machine is to survive....Indeed, for whites to continue to control the party, the Irish may well have to defer to the much more numerous Poles. But even that may avail little if the dynamic of black aspirations and demands continues, as it probably will.[1]

In chapter 2 we examined the results of recent elections by dividing Chicago along eight geographical and racial/ethnic boundaries, such as the White South Side and the Black South Side. Looking over the analyses in that chapter can lead to the impression that whites often vote as a bloc. In recent elections this may have been the case. However, whites in Chicago have not always voted so homogeneously. There was a time when the white vote was visibly more fractionalized along ethnic lines—especially between the city's Irish and Polish communities. In this chapter we'll look at the history of white ethnic politics in Chicago, and examine how the rise of a black political agenda seems—on the surface at least—to have united white voters in response to it. Then we'll examine voting patterns from some key Chicago political races of the past 30 years that reveal the residual effects of the traditional split between the city's Polish and Irish communities.

Race and Chicago's Political Systems

During this century, Chicago's electoral politics may be divided into two periods in which politics were organized in response to two different political cleavages. In the first of these periods, which lasted through the 1970s, whites contended for power among themselves, and the dominant political factions—whether Democrats or Republicans, North- or Southsiders, Irish or Polish—were predominantly white. This cleavage was replaced by a second one that took its present form in the early 1980s and is based on contention between whites, African Americans, and Latinos. The emergence of African Americans and Latinos as contenders for political power in Chicago was a product of their growth in population and occurred relatively recently. In 1990, African Americans exceeded whites in population in Chicago for the first time, and Chicago's Latino population had climbed to over 500,000 (19.6 percent).

White Ethnicity in Chicago Politics

Until the 1960s, whites had not been challenged to consider themselves as having a unity of interest as voters. The traditional split between North- and Southside whites broke down in the late 1960s, with 1966 being a turning-point election that shocked the Chicago Democratic Machine and led to changes in public policy postures and actions. After 1966, North- and Southside whites voted the same way in local elections. The glue that bound them together was race. Whites united and became highly mobilized to oppose African-American demands for integration. Therein lay the first distinctive white political agenda.

Prior to Anton Cermak's election as mayor in 1931, white Republicans contested citywide offices against white Democrats. Mayoral politics from 1931 through the 1960s was defined in terms of support or opposition to the Democratic Machine and, for the most part, African-American voters supported Machine candidates. Voters' identities were rooted in their religious or union affiliation, ethnic group, and in their neighborhood. For first or second generation immigrants, identity as Irish, Polish, or Italian was far more relevant than identification as a "white." Most would not have known what a white political agenda was. A common political interest of whites had not yet been created in opposition to blacks.

This is not to paint a rosy picture of race relations in Chicago prior to the 1960s. As Massey and Denton have demonstrated, whites went to great lengths to segregate themselves from blacks.[2] Blacks were far more heavily concentrated on the South- and West Side neighborhoods than were Irish, Polish, or Italians in their neighborhoods. Blacks and whites were rivals for jobs in Packingtown, and these antagonisms exploded in the 1919 riot on Chicago's South Side. However grudgingly white people of different ethnic backgrounds accepted one another in the neighborhood or the workplace, it was far more readily than they accepted blacks. Yet because of the strong control exerted over black voters by the Machine and the lack of acceptance of blacks by each white ethnic group, political issues to which blacks might take unique ownership failed to surface. So white political unity was unnecessary.

Historically, Chicago's whites have been less politically cohesive than they have appeared since the 1970s. Despite maintaining unprecedented control over the Chicago and Cook County Democratic parties and over the local public policy agenda, Richard J. Daley did receive major challenges in mayoral elections. These came from Democrat-turned-Republican Benjamin Adamowski in 1963 and maverick Democrat William Singer in 1975. While neither Adamowski nor Singer won, each hoped to pry apart the disparate elements of the Democratic coalition that were held together by Daley's political skills.

Jane Byrne's victory over Michael Bilandic in the 1979 mayoral election ended the heyday of the Chicago Democratic Machine. To many, Byrne took on the aura of a reformer. But the famous snowstorms turned the election into a referendum on "competence" with each candidate interpreting competence as a question of who would best maintain the Daley legacy.

That the two candidates crossed so many of Chicago's traditional political lines made the outcome of the election unpredictable. Bilandic was a Croatian who, by virtue of his insider ties to the Democratic Machine, expected to receive his strongest electoral support from South Side Irish neighborhoods. Byrne, who was Irish, grew up on Chicago's Northwest Side. Additionally, Byrne excited lakefront progressives because she appeared to be challenging the Machine's "politics as usual" and because she was a woman. In part because she appeared to be such an unknown quantity politically, Byrne gained the support of African-American voters who had become increasingly restive under the Machine since Congressman Ralph Metcalfe's split with the mayor and organization Democrats but had identified no mayoral candidate who stood a sufficient chance of winning. Additionally, African Americans had been further insulted by the failure of whites to support Wilson Frost as acting mayor upon the death of Richard J. Daley and by the closing of the CTA stations on the West Side during the snowstorms of the winter of 1979 so that whites might commute more easily to and from the Loop. Thus, in the last mayoral election in Chicago that featured two viable white candidates and no African-American candidate, whites in Chicago deeply divided across cleavages that were usually kept hidden but were now evident.

The potential for a black political agenda to form around the issue of open housing led to the emergence of a self-conscious "white" political identity that has since generally overshadowed regional and ethnic rivalries among whites in citywide elections. In turn, the presence of a united white political front that continued to exclude blacks from positions of political power during the 1960s and 1970s led to an independent and politically cohesive African-American electorate.

Whites had not turned out at such high rates nor voted so cohesively until the 1983 candidacy of Harold Washington upset their traditional political view of Chicago. Between the 1983 primary in February and the general election in April, a large majority of white Chicagoans concluded that being white transcended partisan political identification and concerns over public policy. The vast majority of white voters, most of whom had been lifelong Democrats, suddenly voted *en masse* for a white Republican, Bernard Epton, in the general election. That Harold Washington had the opportunity to run successfully in the Democratic primary by facing two white candidates, Byrne and Richard M. Daley, was the result of a miscalculation of both the strength and cohesion of the black vote based on blacks' history of deference to white leadership and low support for previous black mayoral candidates.

White Ethnicity in Chicago Politics

White Ethnicity in Chicago Politics

The Remnant of White Ethnic Politics

In recent years, the most difficult distinction to document among whites has been the persisting political division between white ethnics. Like many large American cities, Chicago has experienced a process of ethnic succession politically. In the early years of this century, Irish politicians supplanted native elites. This was followed by the political accommodation of newly arriving Eastern Europeans as Irish leadership exchanged slated candidacies for Machine support. In Chicago, this has meant reserving the city clerkship for a Pole (e.g., John Marcin, Walter Kozubowski, and James Laski). In the most recent two decades in Chicago and in other major cities, white ethnic coalitions have then either yielded to or shared power with African Americans and Latinos. But Chicago's Democratic Machine remains "a static hierarchy ruled by the Irish, managed at the intermediate levels by loyal but restive European ethnics, such as the Poles, Germans, and other eastern Europeans."[3]

Irish politicians controlled the Democratic party by the first decade of the twentieth century. Irish politicians took hold of major offices in Chicago and Cook County in the 1930s with the demise of Republicans and have maintained that control ever since. In 1931, Anton Cermak defeated Republican Bill Thompson for mayor, effectively ending two-party competition within city government and giving birth to the Democratic Machine. Although Cermak was of Czechoslovakian ancestry, he had ascended to the top of a political organization dominated by the Irish. Irish politicians controlled the mayor's office for the next 50 years as Cermak was succeeded by Edward J. Kelly from 1933 to 1947, Martin H. Kennelly from 1947 to 1955, and Richard J. Daley from 1955 through 1976.

At the local level, Chicagoans have generally tried to elect members of their own ethnic group to the city council, the state legislature, and to Congress. Most Chicago wards are easily characterized by the ethnicity of their elected officials, which corresponds to the predominant racial/ethnic group in the ward.

The city's major power brokers of recent years have maintained their political bases within ethnic communities. Irish political leadership such as Illinois House Speaker Michael Madigan, County Assessor Thomas Hynes, and Sheriff James Sheehan come from the Irish Southwest Side. Congressmen William Lipinski, Dan Rostenkowski, and Roman Pucinski were each elected from heavily Polish communities.

Second to the Irish as a political force among whites has been the Poles. Chicago has long held the mythic reputation as being the second largest Polish city in the world behind only Warsaw, and Poles have historically been Chicago's largest white ethnic group.[4] Yet many Poles feel that they have never been represented in city government and in citywide office in proportion to the significance of their group.[5] The city clerkship has probably never fully satisfied Polish political aspirations.[6] However, both Diane Pinderhughes and Edward Kantowicz point out that infighting within the Polish community during much of the first half of the century prevented Poles from realizing their full political potential. According to Kantowicz, their large numbers created the impression that political power could be attained, which led Irish leadership to view Poles as a potential threat.[7] However, Polish voting was never sufficient to win citywide elective office. The heart of the regular Democratic Machine remained the Irish-black coalition.

Over the century, a historical process has taken place that has resulted in a gradual erosion of the power of white ethnicity to determine political interests. Chicago's Polish community originally settled in five highly concentrated areas of the city. First generation immigrants held in common a desire to form communities where there would be sufficient concentrations of Polish population to support Polish-speaking parishes, stores that would carry Polish food, and social clubs. They wanted neighbors that would speak Polish. In 1930, only blacks lived in Chicago in greater concentration.[8] With the second and third generations came less connection to Poland and less dependence on Polish language institutions. The Polish community also changed economically as successor generations moved beyond the meat-packing and steel industries upon which first generation immigrants had depended. These changes, combined with increasing personal wealth, resulted in both a decrease in concentration of persons of Polish ancestry and dispersal to the perimeter neighborhoods of Chicago and the suburbs.[9]

Although the impact of ethnic ancestry has diminished, it has not disappeared. Analysis of citywide elections in which a clearly identifiable Polish candidate ran against other white candidates demonstrates the continued force of ethnicity. Benjamin Adamowski's 1955 run for mayor in the Democratic primary resulted in his winning three wards, the heavily Polish 32nd, 33rd, and 35th along the Milwaukee Avenue corridor, and the 12th, encompassing portions of the Back of the Yards. Adamowski provided an additional challenge in 1963 running as a Republican and garnering 44 percent of the vote, largely from wards with strong Polish neighborhoods in the city's Northwest and Southwest Sides.

Most of the remainder of this chapter will examine the results of elections of the past 30 years in order to trace the hidden Irish and Polish voting factors that still reside in pockets of the city. The modern dispersion of white ethnics across Chicago has made it increasingly difficult to identify voting patterns of white ethnic groups. In only a few of the census tracts across the city do those of Polish or Irish ancestry constitute as much as half of the population. In order to tease out information on the voting behavior of Chicago's Irish and Polish voters, we have identified census tracts over 50 percent Polish and precincts with coterminous or close to coterminous boundaries. Similarly, we identified census tracts that are predominantly

White Ethnicity in Chicago Politics

White Ethnicity in Chicago Politics

**Figure 4.1
Chicago's Irish
Wards (1994)**

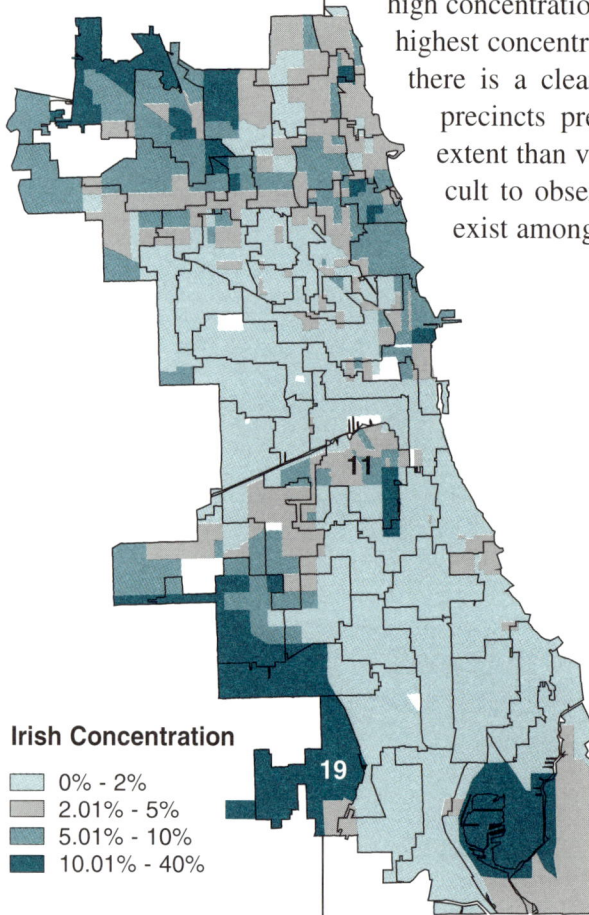

Irish (over 10 percent) and precincts with coterminous or close to coterminous boundaries. By analyzing precincts, we have, for purposes of this discussion, been able to identify the "Irish" and "Polish" wards of the city as they were at the time of each election we analyze.[10] For example, the Irish and Polish wards of the city using 1990 census data and the ward boundaries as fixed in 1994 would map out as shown in figures 4.1 and 4.2.

The tables that accompany our discussions of key races use census data from the census immediately preceding or following the election under consideration and use the ward number designations in effect at the time of the election. The tables compare election returns for precincts and wards with high concentrations of Polish persons to those precincts and wards with the highest concentrations of Irish persons. In each of the elections presented, there is a clear and consistent pattern of voters in Polish wards and precincts preferring candidates with Polish surnames to a stronger extent than voters in Irish wards and precincts. Thus, while often difficult to observe, it is clear that ethnic political divisions continue to exist among whites in Chicago.

**Figure 4.2
Chicago's Polish
Wards (1994)**

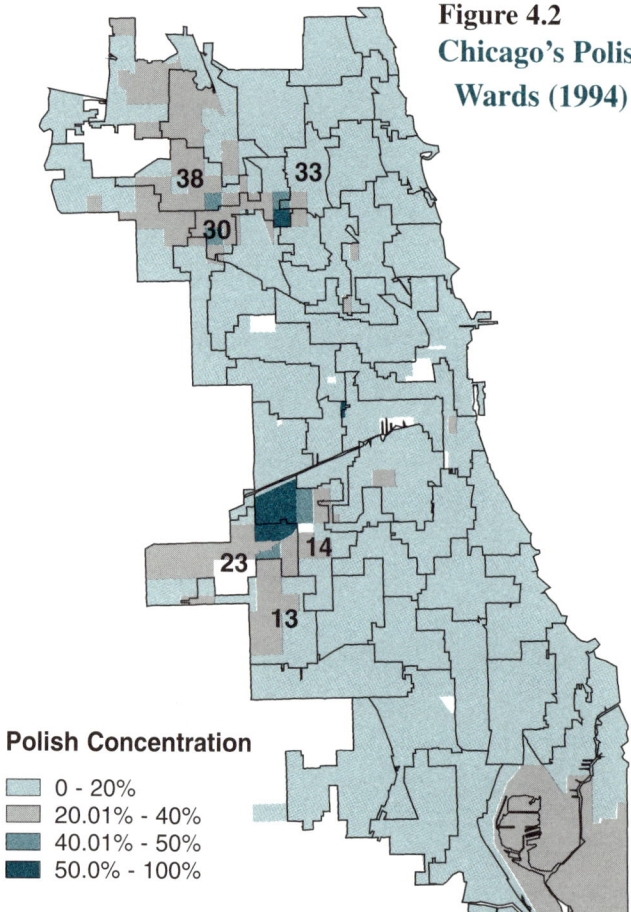

Irish Concentration

- 0% - 2%
- 2.01% - 5%
- 5.01% - 10%
- 10.01% - 40%

Polish Concentration

- 0 - 20%
- 20.01% - 40%
- 40.01% - 50%
- 50.0% - 100%

The 1972 General Elections

The 1972 general elections included elections for the U.S. Senate and for Illinois secretary of state that involved Polish candidates, and in the case of secretary of state, a Polish candidate (Kucharski) running against an Irish candidate (Howlett).

In the predominantly Irish 11th and 19th wards, Howlett outpolled Kucharski by 65 percent to 35 percent. However in the seven wards with highly concentrated Polish precincts, Kucharski, even though a Republican, actually beat Howlett 51 percent to 49 percent.

As table 4.1 shows, within the wards with high Polish concentrations, Kucharski ran even better in individual precincts that were over 50 percent Polish, averaging from around 50 percent to almost 60 percent of the vote. Likewise, Howlett ran stronger in the city's strongest Irish precincts than he

White Ethnicity in Chicago Politics

The 1972 General Elections

Table 4.1

The 1972 General Election for Secretary of State

	Percentage of Support in the Ethnic Precincts			Percentage of Support in the Remainder of the Ward			
Irish Wards	**Howlett**	**Kucharski**	**Others**	**Howlett**	**Kucharski**	**Others**	**Irish Factor[1]**
11	85.8	13.9	0.3	74.0	25.7	0.3	11.8
19	57.8	42.0	0.2	55.6	44.1	0.3	2.2
Irish Total	60.5	39.3	0.2	58.3	41.4	0.3	2.2
Polish Wards							**Polish Factor[2]**
11	65.7	33.9	0.4	75.3	24.3	0.3	9.6
12	44.1	55.5	0.5	48.9	50.6	0.5	4.9
13	41.3	58.1	0.5	46.2	53.5	0.3	4.6
23	41.3	58.4	0.3	43.7	55.8	0.5	2.6
35	43.4	56.1	0.5	46.7	52.9	0.5	3.2
36	47.3	52.2	0.5	48.7	50.7	0.5	1.5
37	40.2	59.5	0.3	67.5	31.9	0.6	27.6
Polish Total	44.1	55.4	0.4	48.9	50.7	0.5	4.7

[1]The Irish factor is the difference between the percentage of support Howlett had in the Irish precincts of the Irish wards and the percentage of support he had in the remaining precincts in those wards.

[2]The Polish factor is the difference between the percentage of support Kucharski had in the Polish precincts of the Polish wards and the percentage of support he had in the remaining precincts in those wards.

White Ethnicity in Chicago Politics

The 1972 General Elections

Table 4.2

did in the strongest Irish wards, by almost 12 percent in the 11th Ward and 2.2 percent in the 19th Ward.

Table 4.2 reveals that the race for U.S. Senator followed a similar pattern. In the city's Polish wards, Pucinski ran ahead of Percy. Pucinski ran consistently better in the concentrated Polish precincts than in the Polish wards, ranging from 2.5 percent better in the 12th Ward to 16.2 percent better in the 37th Ward.

The 1972 General Election for U.S. Senator

	Percentage of Support in the Ethnic Precincts			Percentage of Support in the Remainder of the Ward			
	Pucinski	Percy	Others	Pucinski	Percy	Others	
Irish Wards							
11	77.1	22.4	0.5	70.8	28.8	0.4	
19	45.4	54.3	0.3	40.9	58.8	0.3	
Irish Total	48.5	51.2	0.3	45.4	54.2	0.3	
Polish Wards							**Polish Factor[1]**
11	76.5	23.3	0.2	71.0	28.6	0.4	5.5
12	60.2	39.4	0.4	57.7	41.9	0.4	2.5
13	56.9	42.7	0.4	51.2	48.5	0.3	5.7
23	58.3	41.3	0.3	52.0	47.6	0.4	6.3
35	61.0	38.6	0.4	52.3	47.2	0.5	8.7
36	66.2	33.5	0.3	56.2	43.4	0.4	10.0
37	68.8	30.8	0.3	52.6	46.9	0.6	16.2
Polish Total	61.1	38.6	0.4	54.8	44.8	0.4	6.3

[1]The Polish factor is the difference between the percentage of support Pucinski had in the Polish precincts of the Polish wards and the percentage of support he had in the remaining precincts in those wards.

Pucinski also ran better in the concentrated Irish precincts than in the remainder of the wards that contained them. This may be attributable to the strength of the regular Democratic organization in those Irish precincts, given that Percy was neither a Democrat nor Irish.

The consistency of these results across the wards with Polish precincts in both elections attests to the importance of ethnicity in informing voting by white ethnics in the early 1970s.

The 1975 Mayoral Democratic Primary

Although there was no Polish candidate in the election, the 1975 mayoral primary is important because it was the last major electoral challenge to Mayor Richard J. Daley. Analysis of strongly Democratic, ethnic wards and precincts show some of the seeds of discontent that Jane Byrne managed to exploit four years later in her successful challenge to the Machine.

As expected, the mayor ran extremely well in the highly Irish and Democratic 11th and 19th Wards, although Singer did poll over 20 percent in the 19th. However, Daley ran 13 percent worse in the wards with high Polish concentrations. What opposition there was did not have a definite shape, however, as Hanrahan—no doubt viewed as an even more conservative alternative—received over 8 percent of the vote in Polish wards, and

White Ethnicity in Chicago Politics

The 1975 Mayoral Democratic Primary

Table 4.3

The 1975 Democratic Mayoral Primary

	Percentage of Support in the Ethnic Precincts				Percentage of Support in the Remainder of the Ward				
	Singer	Daley	Newhouse	Hanrahan	Singer	Daley	Newhouse	Hanrahan	Irish Factor[1]
Irish Wards									
11	4.2	91.0	3.3	1.5	7.4	86.7	4.4	1.6	4.3
19	17.7	73.1	3.0	6.1	25.3	63.9	5.0	5.8	9.2
Irish Total	15.8	75.8	3.0	5.4	19.6	71.2	4.8	4.4	4.6
Polish Wards									Nonethnic Factor[2]
11	8.6	84.0	4.9	2.4	7.0	87.2	4.2	1.5	3.2
12	17.5	70.4	3.5	8.5	16.9	71.7	4.5	6.9	1.3
13	17.9	70.9	3.4	7.8	15.4	73.6	3.8	7.2	2.7
23	20.5	66.0	3.1	10.5	20.8	67.4	3.0	8.9	1.4
35	26.0	62.5	3.0	8.4	35.0	53.6	2.7	8.7	-8.9
36	21.7	63.9	3.6	10.9	22.1	63.9	3.1	10.9	0
37	23.7	62.7	4.0	9.6	24.0	61.2	8.9	5.9	-1.5
Polish Total	19.4	68.5	3.4	8.7	19.3	69.5	3.8	7.4	1.0

[1]The Irish factor is the difference in the percentage of support Daley had in the Irish precincts of the Irish wards and the percentage of support he had in the remaining precincts in those wards.

[2]In this case we are examining the slight "nonappeal" for Daley based on his non-Polish ethnicity. The nonethnic factor is the difference between the percentage of support Daley had in the non-Polish precincts of the Polish wards and percentage of support he had in the Polish precincts in the Polish wards. In those instances where the Polish precincts of the Polish wards supported Daley more than the non-Polish precincts of the ward, the nonethnic factor is expressed as a negative number.

White Ethnicity in Chicago Politics

The 1975 Mayoral Democratic Primary

William Singer, the independent alternative, received almost 22 percent. While the pattern was not strong, Daley's opponents received greater support in Polish precincts than in the remainder of the wards in which those precincts were located. In fact, as table 4.3 shows, Daley's "nonethnic factor" is slightly in evidence in those wards. In the Irish precincts of the Irish wards, he grabbed 4.6 percent more support than he had in the remainder of the precincts in those wards. However, in the Polish precincts in the Polish wards his nonethnic factor was 1, meaning he won 1 percent less support than he had in the remaining precincts of those wards.

The 1977 Special Mayoral Democratic Primary

The 1977 mayoral primary included Mayor Michael Bilandic, who although Croatian, inherited the Irish-led regular Democratic organization. His main opposition was from Alderman Roman Pucinski, the most prominent of the city's Polish political leaders.

Bilandic, campaigning under Daley's mantle, won almost 77 percent of the vote in the Irish 11th and 19th Wards, but ran 26 percent lower in the wards with the greatest Polish concentrations. Despite the presence of strong regular Democratic organizations in those wards, Pucinski garnered 43 percent of the vote. Because of his close links to the deceased Daley, Bilandic ran slightly better (1.9 percent higher) in precincts with heavy Irish concentrations than in the remainder of those wards (see table 4.4).

White Ethnicity in Chicago Politics

The 1977 Special Mayoral Democratic Primary

Table 4.4

The 1977 Democratic Mayoral Primary

	Percentage of Support in the Ethnic Precincts				Percentage of Support in the Remainder of the Ward				
	Pucinski	Bilandic	Hanrahan	Others	Pucinski	Bilandic	Hanrahan	Others	Organ. Factor[1]
Irish Wards									
11	4.9	92.6	2.0	0.4	10.2	86.2	1.6	2.0	6.4
19	23.6	66.5	8.5	1.4	24.5	59.5	7.3	8.7	7.0
Irish Total	20.6	70.8	7.5	1.2	19.5	68.9	5.3	6.3	1.9
									Polish Factor[2]
Polish Wards									
11	19.4	77.7	2.1	0.8	9.2	87.3	1.6	1.9	10.2
12	48.0	45.8	3.9	2.4	35.1	57.3	5.1	2.6	12.9
13	44.0	50.2	4.9	0.9	28.6	64.4	5.7	1.3	15.4
23	48.1	46.2	4.1	1.3	35.9	57.2	5.5	1.4	12.2
35	70.7	25.8	2.4	1.1	62.0	30.6	5.6	1.8	8.7
36	60.1	36.2	2.4	1.3	44.8	46.9	6.6	1.8	15.3
37	72.8	23.3	2.3	1.7	23.4	52.2	5.8	18.5	49.4
Polish Total	51.0	43.8	3.6	1.5	35.9	56.8	5.2	2.1	15.1

[1]The organization factor is the difference in the percentage of support Bilandic had in the traditionally organization-loyal Irish precincts in the Irish wards and the percentage of support he had in the remaining precincts in those wards.

[2]The Polish factor is the difference between the percentage of support Pucinski had in the Polish precincts of the Polish wards and the percentage of support he had in the remaining precincts in those wards.

White Ethnicity in Chicago Politics

The 1977 Special Mayoral Democratic Primary

The presence of Polish voters has never been felt more strongly in recent elections. As table 4.4 shows, Pucinski's support in the heaviest Polish precincts was higher than his support in the remainder of the precincts in the Polish wards by a range from 8.7 percent in the Polish precincts of ward 35 to over 49 percent in the Polish precincts of ward 37: a clear demonstration of the Polish voters' preference for Pucinski over Bilandic.

The 1979 Mayoral Democratic Primary

The 1979 primary was the first of a series of elections difficult to analyze from an ethnic perspective because of the confounding of support for the regular Democratic organization, the perceived lack of strength of the organization candidate, and the presence of an Irish candidate (Byrne) who came out of an ethnically mixed community. Thus Bilandic pulled 86 percent of the vote in the strongly Democratic and traditionally Irish 11th Ward, but the Irish Byrne garnered 44 percent of the vote in the Irish 19th Ward.

Overall, Byrne ran 19 percent better in the Polish wards than in the Irish wards, although she failed to win a majority in either, due to her challenger status and the investment of the regular Democrats in the incumbent Bilandic. In fact, table 4.5 shows that both the Irish and Polish precincts had less support for Byrne than did non-Irish or Polish voters in wards 11, 23, 35, and 37.

White Ethnicity in Chicago Politics

The 1979 Mayoral Democratic Primary

Table 4.5

The 1979 Democratic Mayoral Primary

	Percentage of Support in the Ethnic Precincts		Percentage of Support in the Remainder of the Ward		
	Bilandic	**Byrne**	**Bilandic**	**Byrne**	**Irish Factor[1]**
Irish Wards					
11	87.5	12.5	86.1	13.9	-1.4
19	60.1	39.9	50.6	49.4	-9.5
Irish Total	64.1	35.9	60.6	39.4	-3.5
					Nonethnic Factor[2]
Polish Wards					
11	82.3	17.7	86.4	13.6	-4.1
12	53.8	46.2	57.5	42.5	-3.7
13	56.0	44.0	62.6	37.4	-6.6
23	57.8	42.2	56.6	43.4	1.2
35	43.2	56.8	35.1	64.9	8.1
36	54.4	45.6	55.2	44.8	-0.8
37	51.1	48.9	44.2	55.8	6.9
Polish Total	54.6	45.4	57.5	42.5	-2.9

[1]The Irish factor is the difference in the percentage of support Byrne had in the Irish precincts of the Irish wards and the percentage of support she had in the remaining precincts in those wards.

[2]In this case we are examining the "nonappeal" for Byrne based on her non-Polish ethnicity. The nonethnic factor is the difference between the percentage of support Byrne had in the non-Polish precincts of the non-Polish wards and the support she had in the Polish precincts in the Polish wards. In those instances where the Polish precincts of the Polish wards supported Byrne more than the non-Polish precincts of the ward, the nonethnic factor is expressed as a negative number.

White Ethnicity in Chicago Politics

The 1979 Mayoral Democratic Primary

The 1979 primary was the last mayoral election to be contested by two strong white candidates and no strong African American. With Washington's victory in the 1983 primary, no subsequent mayoral contest included meaningful competition between white candidates. The continuing presence of ethnic voting preference can, however, still be seen in elections for other offices, such as presidency of the Cook County Board.

The 1990 Cook County Board President Democratic Primary

The two dominant candidates in the 1990 election were a prominent Irish suburban attorney, Richard Phelan, and a Polish state legislator and County Board member, Ted Lechowicz. True to form, Phelan, despite weak ties to the regular Democratic organization or the city, ran from 5.9 to 12.7 percent better in precincts with high concentrations of Irish than in the remainder of the wards containing those precincts (see the Irish factor calculation in table 4.6). Clearly his Irish identity separated him from other candidates for many voters.

The persistence of Polish ethnic voting can be seen again in the comparison of the vote for Lechowicz in the homogenous Polish precincts as opposed to the wards in which the precincts are located. In every ward containing precincts with high concentrations of Polish persons, Lechowicz ran better in the Polish precincts than in the rest of the ward. In the 30th, 35th, and 38th Wards, Lechowicz's Polish support exceeded his support in the remainder of the ward by over 10 percent.

White Ethnicity in Chicago Politics

The 1990 Cook County Board President Democratic Primary

Table 4.6

The 1990 Democratic Primary for Cook County Board President

	Percentage of Support in the Ethnic Precincts				Percentage of Support in the Remainder of the Ward				
	Phelan	Kusper	Lechowicz	Pincham	Phelan	Kusper	Lechowicz	Pincham	Irish Factor[1]
Irish Wards									
11	39.9	7.0	52.2	0.9	34.0	8.8	47.3	10.0	5.9
19	60.0	6.4	28.9	4.7	47.3	6.1	20.4	26.2	12.7
Irish Total	57.6	6.5	31.7	4.3	45.3	6.4	24.4	23.8	12.3
Polish Wards									Polish Factor[2]
12	52.0	22.2	24.7	1.2	53.4	14.5	22.3	9.8	2.4
13	32.4	6.5	59.9	1.2	38.1	7.1	53.2	1.6	6.7
23	58.7	9.4	30.6	1.2	65.1	8.7	24.9	1.4	5.7
30	20.5	7.3	70.3	1.9	24.4	5.6	56.1	13.9	14.2
35	36.9	10.3	50.6	2.2	46.2	9.0	39.0	5.8	11.6
38	38.8	9.4	50.6	1.2	50.1	9.5	38.3	2.1	12.3
Polish Total	43.7	11.0	43.9	1.4	50.5	8.7	37.3	3.6	6.6

[1] The Irish factor is the difference in the percentage of support Phelan had in the Irish precincts of the Irish wards and the percentage of support he had in the remaining precincts in those wards.

[2] The Polish factor is the difference in the percentage of support Lechowicz had in the Polish precincts of the Polish wards and the percentage of support he had in the remaining precincts in those wards.

White Ethnicity in Chicago Politics

The 1994 Cook County Board President Democratic Primary

The 1994 Cook County Board President Democratic Primary

The 1994 Cook County Board Democratic primary presented a new anomaly, a long-time regular Democratic party loyalist John Stroger, an African American, carrying the Irish 11th and 19th Wards against two white candidates. Aided by the mayor's endorsement, Stroger won 60 percent of the vote in the 11th and 19th Wards, running as well in the homogenous Irish precincts as in the remainder of the two wards.

The strength of Polish ethnicity remained on view through the candidacy of Aurelia Pucinski, daughter of Roman Pucinski. Pucinski's lead over runner-up Maria Pappas in the Polish-concentration wards was probably as much due to her identification as a Northwest Sider as to her Polish ethnicity. However, again the comparison of homogenous Polish precincts to the wards in which they are located shows a consistent 6-point preference for Pucinski in the Polish precincts, a preference that reached almost 12 percent in the 30th Ward and over 14 percent in the 38th Ward (see table 4.7).

Table 4.7

The 1994 Democratic Primary for Cook County Board President

	Percentage of Support in the Ethnic Precincts			Percentage of Support in the Remainder of the Ward			
	Pappas	**Stroger**	**Pucinski**	**Pappas**	**Stroger**	**Pucinski**	
Irish Wards							
11	13.9	69.9	16.3	17.7	60.7	21.6	
19	19.4	56.9	23.7	18.5	61.7	19.8	
Irish Total	18.8	58.3	22.9	18.4	61.6	20.0	
Polish Wards							**Polish Factor[1]**
13	16.0	9.0	75.0	18.2	12.1	69.7	5.3
14	24.8	14.2	61.1	24.1	18.0	57.9	3.2
23	25.1	12.2	62.7	29.3	16.5	54.2	8.5
30	24.5	15.7	59.8	31.3	20.6	48.1	11.7
33	26.7	16.6	56.7	30.3	21.6	48.0	8.7
38	23.6	18.9	57.5	31.8	24.9	43.3	14.2
Polish Total	22.7	13.1	64.2	25.4	16.3	58.3	5.9

[1]The Polish factor is the difference in the percentage of support Pucinski had in the Polish precincts of the Polish wards and the percentage of support she had in the remaining precincts in those wards.

Conclusion

Political alignments and fronts often arise as a response to specific political and social challenges. Just as Harold Washington's political leadership masked rivalry between various political factions within the African-American community that became evident upon his death, the data presented in this chapter demonstrate the persistence of ethnic identification beneath a seemingly unified white political front.

Continued patterns of discrimination in employment, housing, and other areas of life create a unified interest among African Americans and other racial/ethnic groups. At times, it is necessary for government to take affirmative actions that address the need for an inclusive political system. These actions are appropriately defined along these racial/ethnic lines.

However, this broad social organization along racial lines does not have to result in political gridlock in which the "winners take all" and the losing groups are excluded from power. As Chicago moves into a new period where there will be roughly equal populations of whites, African Americans, and Latinos, it is increasingly important that all three groups be adequately represented among our elected officials and that no elected office become the province of a single racial or ethnic group. Ironically, it is through retreat from the broad categories of white, African American, and Latino that were defined in the first civil rights era, that a more plural political culture could develop constituted by component groupings found within these three. Such a system might be defined by more diverse and shifting coalitions of smaller interest groups defined by neighborhood, language group, class, or heritage.

White Ethnicity in Chicago Politics

Notes

[1] John M. Allswang, *Bosses, Machines and Urban Voters: An American Symbiosis,* (Port Washington, NY: Kennikat Press, 1977):148.

[2] See Douglas Massey and Nancy Denton, *American Apartheid: Segregation and the Making of the Underclass,* (Cambridge, MA: Harvard University Press, 1993).

[3] Dianne M. Pinderhughes, *Race and Ethnicity in Chicago Politics: A Reexamination of Pluralist Theory.* (Urbana and Chicago, IL: University of Illinois Press, 1987): 9.

[4] Joseph Zikmund II, "Mayoral Voting and Ethnic Politics in the Daley-Bilandic-Byrne Era" in *After Daley: Chicago Politics in Transition,* edited by Samuel K. Gove and Louis H. Masotti. (Urbana, IL: University of Illinois Press, 1982).

[5] Joseph Zikmund II, "Mayoral Voting and Ethnic Politics in the Daley-Bilandic-Byrne Era" in *After Daley: Chicago Politics in Transition,* edited by Samuel K. Gove and Louis H. Masotti. (Urbana, IL: University of Illinois Press, 1982); Edward R. Kantowicz, *Polish- American Politics in Chicago, 1988-1940.* (Chicago, IL: University of Chicago Press, 1975).

White Ethnicity in Chicago Politics

[6]Milton Rakove. *Don't Make No Waves, Don't Back No Losers: An Insider's Analysis of the Daley Machine.* (Bloomington, IN: Indiana University Press, 1975).

[7]Edward R. Kantowicz, *Polish-American Politics in Chicago, 1940-1988.* (Chicago, IL: University of Chicago Press, 1975).

[8]Thomas Lee Philpott, *In the Slum and the Ghetto: Neighborhood Deterioration and Middle Class Reform, Chicago, 1880-1930,* edited by Dianne M. Pinderhughes. (New York, N.Y.: Oxford University Press, 1978).

[9]Dominic A. Pacyga, "Polish America in Transition: Social Change and the Chicago Polonia, 1945 to 1980," in *Polish American Studies* 44, no. 1 (Spring 1987): 38-55.

[10]For the purpose of the analyses in this chapter, ethnic precincts are those in a census tract in which at least half of persons responding to U.S. Census questions regarding ethnicity responded that being Irish or Polish was either all or part of their ancestry. For analyses of elections in the 1970s, we used census data from 1980. (Thus, the 1980 census tracts of ward 11 contained precincts that qualified it, for our purposes, as both an Irish and Polish ward in the 1970s.) For analyses of elections in the 1990s, we used census data from 1990. In instances where precinct and tract boundaries were not coterminous, a precinct was included when, upon inspection of precinct and tract maps, it appeared that at least half of persons resident in the precinct lived within the ethnic census tract.

Chapter 5: Chicago's Registration Numbers: Facts or Fantasies?

Phantom voters once again may have replaced ghost payrollers as the leading ethereal contribution to Chicago's political culture. In the "bad old days" of the 1950s and 1960s, lakefront liberals, organized into a variety of good government associations, routinely protested that the registration rolls were inflated to give the city's vaunted Democratic Machine opportunities to steal elections. By voting the phantoms—many of whom had long since gone to their eternal rewards—precinct captains and ward committeemen were able to pile up high vote totals for the Machine's slated candidates. This boosted the captain's standing with the committeeman, as well as the latter's stature with the Machine's leaders. On election nights, some precincts were notoriously "tardy" in reporting their returns; but when their count was completed they somehow always managed to produce a large enough majority to boost the preferred candidates to victory. According to contemporary critics—and the courts on several occasions—these sorts of practices were key to the Machine's hegemonic control over the city.

But these "bad old days" are long gone. The city supposedly has entered a new political era, marked by clean elections, a downsized governmental apparatus, and a mayoral administration in which efficiency and businesslike practices have supplanted patronage. And the lakefront liberals, now preoccupied with saving landmark buildings and "greening" the upper-income areas of the city, have become involved with questions purportedly more vital than the purity of election administration. Content with the mayor's support for their preservationist causes, good government groups have responded with deafening silence to any signs of a restoration of machinelike dominance over the political process. Besides, this dominance now works to their advantage since the administration typically supports the policies to which they have given priority.

Measuring the Size of Chicago's Electorate

Despite the current silence of the city's good government groups, any examination of the relevant registration figures raises questions about their validity. Before proceeding to that examination, however, it is necessary to discuss how to measure the size of Chicago's electorate. This is not a tangential exercise but one that is central to understanding the registration rate. Since the latter is calculated by dividing the number of people registered by

Chicago's Registration Numbers

the number of people in the electorate, how the denominator is measured directly affects the result.

The decennial census of April 1, 1990, when the count was taken, reported that Chicago had living within its boundaries 2,061,090 people who were 18 years of age or older. This constituted the city's voting age population (VAP). But this number included some who, despite being of the appropriate age, were still not eligible to register or to vote. The factor that disqualified the largest number was that some people of voting age were not citizens: citywide there were 250,242 people who were in this category. Subtracting these noncitizens from the total voting age population leaves a remainder of 1,810,848, which is the size of Chicago's *eligible* voting age population. The eligible VAP will be used as the denominator in calculating the turnout rate for the city as a whole and for its wards and precincts.[1]

When the 1990 census numbers became available in the spring of 1991, it was immediately apparent that there was a problem—either with the census, the registration numbers, or both. Comparing the precinct-level registration numbers with the census figures showed that there were 402 precincts in the city in which more than 100 percent of the eligible VAP was registered for the March 1990 primary election. This amounted to 13.6 percent of all of the city's precincts. Moreover, 59.9 percent of these overenrolled precincts were in the predominantly African-American wards of the city, where the census showed the total population to be declining. In contrast, only 8.9 percent were in the North Lakeshore wards, where the population had been growing. Finally, since so little time had elapsed between the close of registration for the primary and the taking of the census—less than two months—the discrepancy couldn't be attributed to interim population shifts.

Of course, some portion of the discrepancy is no doubt due to the undercount of population by the census. To the extent that voting age population is missed by census enumerators, the size of the denominator for the turnout calculation is understated and the resulting percentage is inflated accordingly. However, while there clearly was an undercount, the Census Bureau's estimates were that the white VAP in Chicago was undercounted by 2.25 percent and the African-American VAP by 2.44 percent. Adjusting the size of the city's eligible VAP for the undercounts of these (and other) groups simply doesn't have that great an effect. For example, the registration rate for Chicago's March 1990 primary was 78.0 percent, using the size of its eligible VAP as the denominator. If that denominator is adjusted for the undercount, the size of the eligible VAP grows slightly and the registration rate falls somewhat—but only to 76.4 percent. This is a drop of only 1.6 percentage points citywide and hardly enough to account for the large number and high percentage of precincts in which registration was over 100 percent.

If invoking the undercount can't entirely explain the anomalies, then we are left with questioning the credibility of the registration numbers themselves. By early 1995 reputable sources were doing just that. The *Chicago Reporter* published a penetrating analysis of the registration numbers in its February issue.[2] This examination showed that the registration rate for Chicago's 1995 municipal primary was extremely high, and especially so for African Americans: 92.7 percent compared to 78.6 percent of eligible whites. Moreover, 10 of the 12 wards in the city with registration rates over 90 percent were African-American wards. Figure 5.1 shows the registration rates in the city's wards as they stood as of April 1995.

Two months later, the *Chicago Sun-Times* pursued the story. In a lengthy piece published on the Sunday prior to the municipal general election, *Sun-Times* reporters drew attention to the large number of people who were registered more than once, had moved from the addresses at which they originally registered, or were dead.[3] This investigation revealed over 47,000 duplicate names on Chicago's registration lists, which represented better than 3 percent of the city's registered voters. These duplicates were heavily concentrated in the African-American and Latino wards: 8.5 percent of the registrants in the seven Latino wards were duplicates, as were 5.3 percent in the Black South Side wards and 7.4 percent in the Black West Side wards. In contrast, only 2.9 percent of the registrations were duplicates in the White Northwest Side wards and 2.6 percent in the White South Side wards. But a door-to-door survey in one white ward on the Northwest Side, the 35th, showed that only 48 percent of the registrants still lived where election board records said they did. Finally, a check of names against the Social Security Administration's list of the dead showed 1,400 deceased persons still enrolled to vote at Chicago elections, and some of these had been ghosts for as long as five years.

Ghostbusting: The 1995 Cleanup of Voter Registration Records

How had the city's registration rolls become so polluted? Two factors seemed to be involved. First, after the 1991 municipal election, the City of Chicago's Board of Election Commissioners dropped door-to-door canvass-

Chicago's Registration Numbers

**Figure 5.1
Chicago Registration Rates, April 1995**

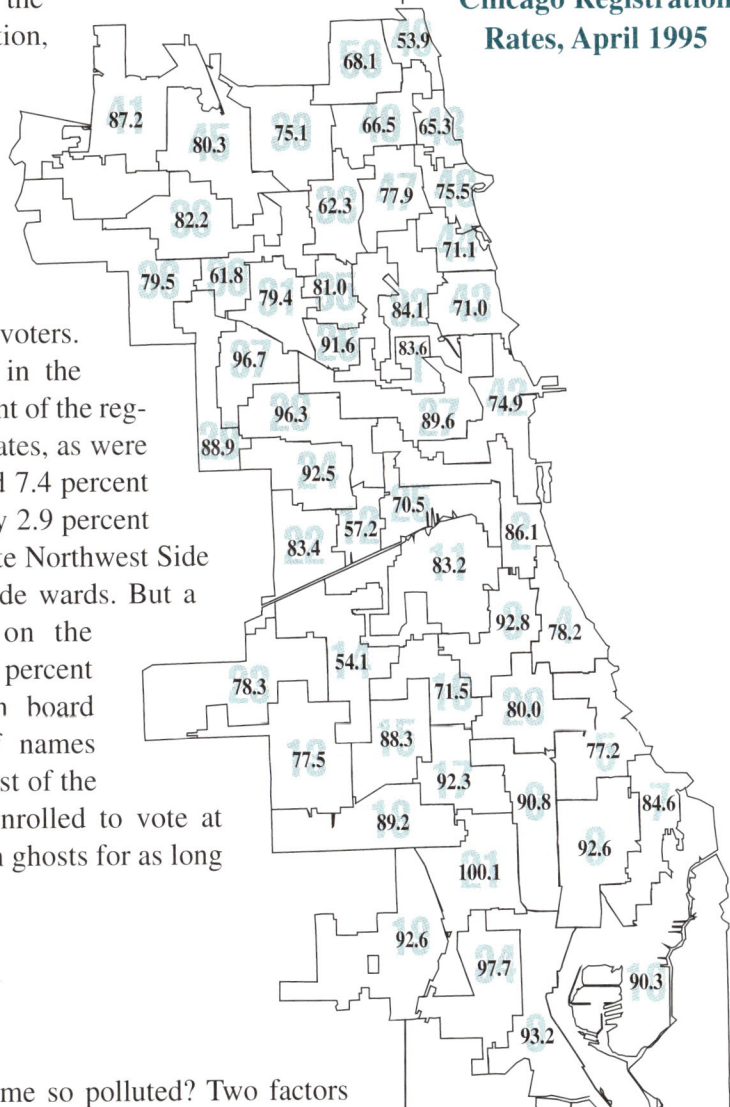

Chicago's Registration Numbers

ing as a means of updating its registration rolls. The board instead relied entirely on a mail canvass, in which the city sent voter cards to registered voters and assumed the information to be correct unless the card was returned corrected or as undeliverable. The board's confidence in mail canvassing overlooked the fact that Chicago regularly has been rated last in the nation for dependable mail service. As board spokespersons related, the cards often got lost in the mail or were delivered by mail carriers even if the voter no longer lived at the address. And current residents at an address often threw away cards directed to former residents rather than returning them to the board. Second, and even more incredible, the board routinely adds new registrations to its rolls without first checking to determine whether the person is already registered at another address.

Together these two factors probably accounted for most of the registration overcount. That the board does not routinely check and eliminate a previous registration when a person signs up from a new address is a guaranteed way to create a large problem of duplicate registrations. That over 3 percent of the Chicago's total registrations were duplicates in the spring of 1995 attests to how effective this practice was in polluting the registration lists. Moreover, a glance at the registration rate for general elections since 1980 (see table 1.4 on page 12) shows that after declining in the late 1980s it took a sharp upturn in 1990 and has remained unusually high since then. This citywide upturn has been due mainly to a boost in the registration rate for African Americans. Indeed, since 1991 the African-American registration rate has been higher than the white rate at every election, although prior to that point it had exceeded the white rate only in 1982 and 1983, both resulting from an extraordinary voter registration effort among blacks in preparation for the 1983 mayoral election. It is certainly significant that this upturn in the registration rate, especially the registration rate among African Americans, coincided with the board's decision to rely exclusively on mail canvassing to keep its lists clean.

In the face of these revelations and criticism from the Daley administration and some of its aldermanic supporters, the City of Chicago's Board of Election Commissioners announced in early September 1995 that it would undertake an unprecedented canvass aimed at cleaning the registration rolls. The board said it would spend $400,000 to conduct a door-to-door canvass in combination with a follow-up verification by mail to eliminate duplicate and dead registrants. This would be the first time that these two techniques had been used in combination.[4]

The board's historic canvass began on September 9, 1995, and ended on December 19. During the process, a total of 169,945 registered voters were challenged by the door-to-door canvass and another 27,904 were challenged in the mail verification. The board also reported that approximately 47,000 duplicate registrations—the number that the *Sun-Times* had reported—were removed from its lists. The board even conducted a special canvass of the city's 104 nursing homes, which produced a 36.1 percent drop in their registrations. As a result of its aggressive canvassing effort, the city's registration rolls on December 29, 1995, listed 203,530 fewer names than they had for the April 1995 municipal elections, and every single ward in the city experienced a net loss of registered voters in the process.[5]

The board was understandably proud of its accomplishment. "This canvass probably represents the most thorough and comprehensive verification of voters in any jurisdiction in the nation," Board Chairman Michael J. Hamblet said. "Maintaining accurate and up to date voter registration records is important to our efforts to eliminate vote fraud, since it removes the possibility of anyone voting in the name of a person who has died or left the jurisdiction."[6]

To assess the current status of Chicago's registration numbers, we need to look more closely at what the board's historic 1995 canvass accomplished and then at what has occurred since then. The information presented in table 5.1 allows us to begin to develop the needed perspective.[7]

Chicago's Registration Numbers

Table 5.1

Chicago Registration: From the 1995 Canvass to November 1996

Ward Group[1]	Registration as of April 1995	Registration as of December 1995	Net Loss from April to December 1995	Registration as of November 1996	Net Gain from December 1995 to November 1996
White Northwest Side	182,345	162,549	-19,796	175,325	12,776
White South Side	145,888	133,781	-12,107	144,063	10,282
Black South Side	470,132	406,682	-63,450	457,055	50,373
Black West Side	167,576	139,078	-28,498	153,084	14,006
Latino	136,205	109,532	-26,673	126,331	16,799
North Lakeshore	139,535	115,101	-24,434	146,341	31,240
Other White North Side	158,854	138,242	-20,612	162,506	24,264
Mixed	68,254	60,294	-7,960	64,090	3,796
City Total	**1,468,789**	**1,265,259**	**-203,530**	**1,428,795**	**163,536**

[1]See pages 4-8 for a detailed explanation and depiction of these ward groups.

The high number of registrations cut from the rolls through the canvass proved the validity of the earlier complaints by critics. Citywide, the canvass produced a net reduction of 13.8 percent in the number of April 1995 registrations, but the cuts were not spread evenly throughout the city. The largest net loss occurred in the Black South Side wards, with the Black West Side

Chicago's Registration Numbers

and Latino wards coming in a distant second and third, respectively. The two sets of African-American wards together experienced a net loss of 91,948 registrations, or 45.1 percent of the total citywide reduction. Since the Latino wards contributed another 13.1 percent, the three minority ward groups together accounted for 58.2 percent of the total net loss, although only 52.6 percent of the total April 1995 registrations had been in these ward groups. The White Northwest and White South Side wards, bastions of voting support for the Daley administration, had a net reduction of 31,903 registrations, or 15.6 percent of the city's total net change, although these two ward groups had accounted for 22.3 percent of the city's April 1995 registrations. Whatever its intent, the effect of the canvass was to increase the relative political importance of two areas of very strong support for the incumbent administration.

Rushing to put out the administration's spin on these disparities in the impact of the canvass, one columnist claimed that political motivation could not have been involved since the canvass had "purged the largest percentage of voters in Latino and northern lakefront wards that have voted overwhelmingly for Daley."[8] That observation is correct but wholly misleading, since elections pivot on absolute numbers not proportionate changes, as political analysts know, or ought to know. And the total net loss of registrations in the Latino and North Lakeshore wards was only 51,107—well below the number cut off the lists in the African-American wards.

Nevertheless, there are two reasons to refrain from imputing nefarious intent to the Board of Election Commissioners. First, the pattern exhibited by the deletions was what should have been expected given knowledge of the correlates of political participation. Analyzed at the precinct level, the deletion rate for the canvass correlated at a statistically significant level with median income ($r = -.286$, indicating that high percentages of deletions were associated with low values of median income), with the proportion of the adult population in the 18 to 24 cohort ($r = .275$), and with percent of adults who had not finished high school ($r = .151$). These were higher than the correlations with the Latino ($r = .117$) and black ($r = .082$) percentages of the eligible voting age population.[9]

Second, the pattern of the deletions was also consistent both with independent analyses of the registration numbers and with what is generally known about the vitality of political organizations in the various wards of the city. Since the April 1995 registration numbers were unbelievably high in the African-American wards and precincts, it was not surprising that they took large hits from the canvass. It was equally unsurprising that the white ethnic redoubts on the Northwest and South Sides lost so few registrations due to the canvass. The Democratic Machine's apparatus is still strong—and still fueled by patronage—in many of these wards, and their precinct captains work hard to keep the rolls clean. In contrast, since most of the

African-American wards get very little, if any, patronage, their ward organizations have become notoriously weak, with many precincts not even having captains to check on the registration rolls. Unreliable registration numbers in most of the African-American wards are the products of their weak ward organizations, and this organizational deficiency results from the fact that these wards have effectively been cut out of patronage and otherwise lack the resources to develop effective mechanisms to keep their registration lists current and clean.[10]

Some Ghosts Just Don't Die: The Swelling of the Voter Registration Rolls Since 1995

Table 5.2 adds another dimension of information both to our assessment of the canvass and to what happened subsequently. It presents the registration rates for the city's ward groups in April and December 1995 and November 1996.

Table 5.2

First, notice the extraordinarily high registration rates in both of the black ward groups in April 1995. In areas marked by large concentrations of persons with very low incomes and low levels of education, it bends credulity beyond the breaking point to suppose that nearly 9 out of every 10 eligible enrollees were actually registered. Second, even though these two black ward groups took the largest "hit" during the fall 1995 canvass,

Chicago's Registration Rates: April 1995 to November 1996

Ward Group[1]	April 1995	December 1995	November 1996
White Northwest Side	78.1%	69.7%	75.1%
White South Side	77.7%	71.2%	76.7%
Black South Side	87.6%	75.8%	85.2%
Black West Side	92.8%	77.0%	84.7%
Latino	78.6%	63.2%	72.9%
North Lakeshore	67.8%	55.9%	71.1%
Other White North Side	72.7%	63.2%	74.4%
Mixed	89.7%	79.2%	84.2%
Chicago Total	81.1%	69.8%	78.9%

[1]See pages 4-8 for a detailed explanation and depiction of these ward groups.

their registation rates in December 1995 were still higher than those of all but one of the other ward groups. Notably, their registration rates were higher than those in the economically better-off White Northwest and South Side wards and considerably above that of the affluent North Lakeshore wards. Finally, notice that new registrations in 1996 have boosted the rate in all of the city's ward groups.

The citywide registration total for November 1996 was just 39,994 below the April 1995 total, a mere 2.2 percentage points off the level that all serious observers said at the time was grossly inflated by bogus registrations. In the North Lakeshore and Other White North ward groups, the November

Chicago's Registration Numbers

1996 registration totals and rates actually exceeded those of April 1995, and the White South Side wards were within 2,000 registrations of their April 1995 level. The net new registrations in the Latino wards allowed them to recover 62.9 percent of their loss due to the canvass. The two African-American ward groups gained 64,379 net new registrations, recouping 70 percent of their loss due to the canvass and producing registration rates that were again the highest in the city. Four of the five wards in Chicago that had registration rates of 90 percent or more in November 1996 were African-American wards, and only two of the 19 African-American wards had registration rates below 80 percent.

What level of credibility should we assign to these November 1996 registration numbers? In particular, how plausible is it to suppose that the black ward groups actually have the highest rates of registration in Chicago?

To develop a response to these questions, let's begin by recapping what is known about the correlates of participation in the political process. What characteristics of individuals lead to high rates of participation? All of the studies of this topic since the 1950s have isolated a common set of important characteristics: income, education, and age. The higher the income and the better the education level, the higher the participation rate. The relationship with age is not always strictly linear, but consistently the age cohort under 25 has shown much lower levels of participation than the other age groups. These relationships also generally pertain to all of the country's major ethnic and racial groups. That is, among African Americans and Latinos, those with higher incomes and better education and who are over 25 years of age generally have higher rates of political participation than others.

While these characteristics are predictive of participation, they are not determinative. Other factors in the political environment may operate to produce participation rates higher (or lower) than some given set of social characteristics might predict. Good political organizations, especially frequent personal contacts by political workers, have been shown to boost registration and turnout rates among people whose income and education levels would otherwise have predicted very low participation. And ethnic and racial minority groups often respond with extremely high rates of participation and cohesiveness when they perceive the political situation to involve an assault on them as a group, as African Americans did in 1982 and 1983 in Chicago.

As we have seen, the deletions made during the canvass followed predictable social contours, but the December 1995 and the November 1996 registration patterns do not. Table 5.2 shows that even after the canvass the African-American ward groups had registration rates that were among the highest in the city. But these are wards whose aggregate social characteristics (see table 5.3) predict low political participation.

Compared to the white ward groups, the African-American ones have lower median incomes, higher percentages of adults with less than high school educations, lower percentages of college graduates, and higher percentages of people who are of the age group that is least likely to be politically active. Moreover, persistent and concentrated poverty has a depressive impact on political participation over and above that of individual poverty, and much of Chicago's African-American community is scarred by such characteristics. Yet the official numbers show that in November 1996 the registration rates of the wards containing these areas exceeded those of each of the four white ward groups. That is a glaring anomaly, one totally inconsistent with everything that is known about the social correlates of political participation and one wholly at odds with current patterns in other major U.S. cities.[11]

Could other factors be operating that explain Chicago's unique registration patterns? Robust ward organizations could produce such a difference, but most of the city's African-American wards lack such organizations. And their political leaders also lack access to the financial resources necessary to develop surrogate organizations that could track registrations and keep the lists reasonably current. A high level of politically focused group consciousness could also work to boost political participation above what the social profile of a community would otherwise predict. This is what happened in 1982 and 1983, when black leaders succeeded in creating a movement fervor that swept through the black community, energized church, civic, and social organizations, and through their activities produced extraordinarily high levels of registration and turnout. No one could plausibly argue that anything even remotely resembling this type of fervor exists now, or has at any time in the recent past. Yet if the official registration numbers are to be believed, the citywide registration rate for African Americans in November 1996 was 1.9 percentage points *higher* than it had been for the great crusade that produced Harold Washington's election as mayor in April 1983.

Chicago's Registration Numbers

Table 5.3

Social Characteristics of Chicago's Ward Groups

Ward Group[1]	Median Income	Less Than High School	College Graduate or More	18-24 Age Cohort
White Northwest Side	$40,989	28.0%	18.9%	9.1%
White South Side	$38,279	31.7%	13.8%	9.4%
Black South Side	$24,145	34.0%	15.4%	11.4%
Black West Side	$20,726	45.9%	7.5%	12.4%
Latino	$22,905	55.7%	7.6%	13.0%
North Lakeshore	$44,744	15.2%	47.5%	12.8%
Other White North Side	$39,984	21.3%	38.1%	10.3%
Mixed	$34,973	33.8%	8.9%	10.3%
Citywide	$33,343	31.1%	22.7%	11.3%

[1]See pages 4-8 for a detailed explanation and depiction of these ward groups.

Chicago's Registration Numbers

Figure 5.2
Chicago Registration Rates, November 1996

Despite the election board's historic canvass, it is hard to escape the conclusion that the city's registration rolls in November 1996 (see figure 5.2) were almost as badly polluted as they had been in April 1995. A major source of the problem remains the board's practice of adding new registrations without first determining whether the persons signing up are already registered from other addresses. Since about 40 percent of Chicagoans change their residences in a five-year period, this practice will invariably produce lists that contain large numbers of duplicate registrations. The task of keeping the lists current and clean devolves to the ward organizations; and if they lack the resources to do the job, it simply doesn't get done. Since most of the African-American wards have weak ward organizations, it is easy to see how their rolls become inflated by duplicate and otherwise invalid registrations.

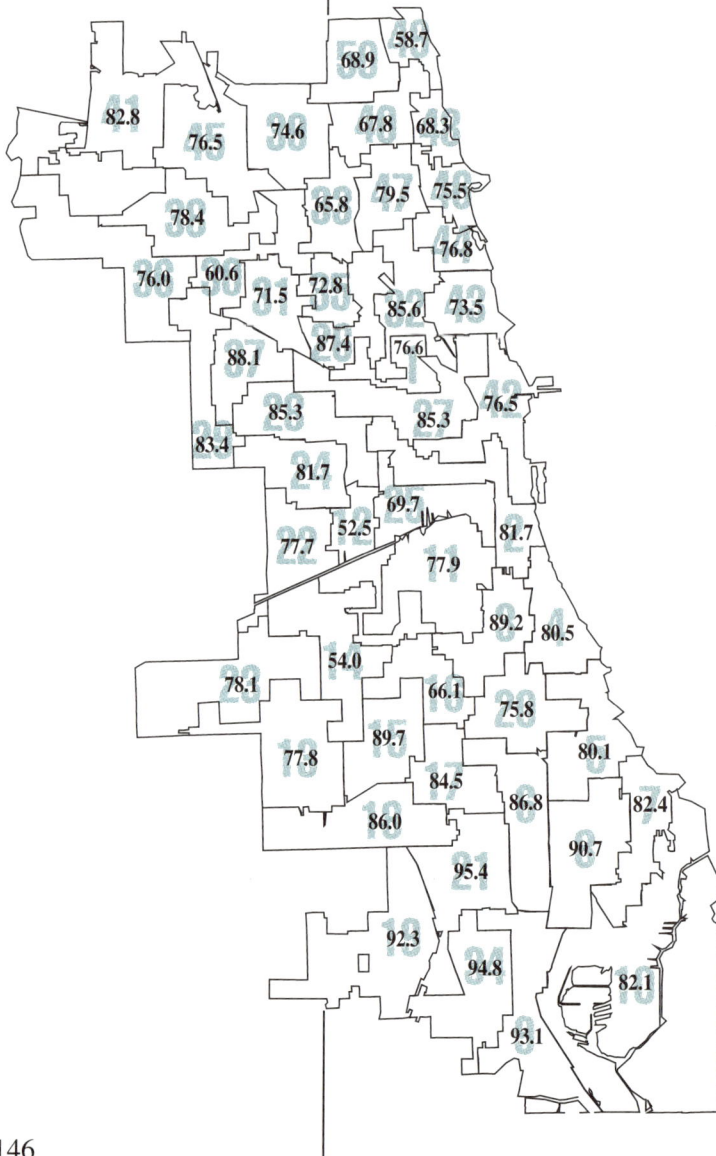

Notes

[1] Developing this chapter's estimates of the size of the eligible VAP at the ward and precinct levels required using the Public Use Microdata Sample (PUMS) from the 1990 census. A unique citizenship rate was calculated for each major ethnic/racial group in each of the city's 19 PUMS areas; wards and precincts were then assigned to the PUMS area in which they fit; and then the appropriate citizenship rates were applied to the groups within the wards and precincts. The result is a better and more defensible estimate than would have resulted from applying the same city-wide rates to groups in all parts of the city.

[2] Burney Simpson, "Voter Registration: Too Good to Be True," *The Chicago Reporter* 24 (February 1995): 1, 6-8, and 11.

[3] Tom Brune and Deborah Nelson, "Voter Lists Invite Fraud," *Chicago Sun-Times,* 2 April 1995. Also see the post-election follow-up piece: Deborah Nelson and Tom Brune, "Dead Voters Create Havoc with City's Rolls," *Chicago Sun-Times,* 16 April 1995.

[4] Fran Spielman, "City Canvass Aims for Clean Slate of Voters," *Chicago Sun-Times*, 7 September 1995.

[5] City of Chicago, Board of Election Commissioners press release of 4 January 1996. The 203,530 figure was the net loss; altogether the board claimed to have cut more than 248,000 unqualified names from its lists.

[6] Board of Election Commissioners press release, 4 January 1996. Also see Fran Spielman, "City Voters Vanish," *Chicago Sun-Times,* 6 January 1996; and Nancy Ryan, "Elections board spirits away city's ghost voters," *Chicago Tribune,* 6 January 1996.

[7] The registration numbers for April and December 1995 and the net change figure were developed from the ward totals given in a one-page summary that accompanied the BEC press release, 4 January 1996. The registration figures for November 1996 were also obtained from the Board of Election Commissioners.

[8] Steve Neal, "City Boots 250,000 From Voter Rolls," *Chicago Sun-Times,* 31 January 1996.

[9] In a more complex multiple regression analysis, the demographic variables remained statistically significant predictors of the deletion rate, while the racial and ethic ones faded to statistical insignificance. The deletion rate was simply the number of registrations dropped divided by the size of the eligible voting age population in the precinct.

[10] The two African-American wards with the closest ties to the Daley administration, and therefore continuing access to patronage, were also the ones that experienced the smallest absolute and proportionate reductions due to the canvass. The 8th Ward lost a net of 3,468 registrations, or 8.8 percent of its April 1995 base; and the 34th Ward lost 2,812 registrations, or 7.4 percent of its earlier base. The other 12 Black South Side wards as a group experienced a net reduction of 14.5 percent in their April 1995 registrations.

[11] Analyzed at the precinct level, Chicago's registration rates for December 1995 and November 1996 fail to show any statistically significant associations with income, education, and age measures that are strong predictors of political participation elsewhere.

Chicago's Registration Numbers

Chapter 6: Financing Chicago Elections

Chicago politicians raise and spend considerable amounts of money on city elections. For the 1995 city elections (the period from July 1, 1994, to June 30, 1995), contributors made over $8.5 million available to candidates for the Chicago City Council, of which 138 candidates spent almost $6 million. Mayor Daley raised $3.4 million during the election year, bringing his total amount available for the election to over $7.4 million. The mayor accounted for 93.2 percent of all the funds reported by all mayoral candidates for the 1995 election.

The figures presented in this chapter map the sources of contributions from businesses and from individuals to candidates for the city council and to the mayor's reelection campaign.[1] As the maps show, wide variance exists in contribution levels across the city. Although the correlation is not perfect, there is a strong tendency toward higher levels of political contributions coming from communities with higher income levels. As in 1991, the largest individual contributions to aldermanic candidates came from neighborhoods on the Near North Side (see figure 6.1). The zip code with the highest level of contributions, $142,532, is located there. Additional significant levels of contributions came from the North Lakefront and Southeast Sides. Among African-American communities, the largest contribution levels came from the Hyde Park and South Shore areas, and parts of the 7th, 8th, and 9th wards.

The level of contributions from businesses to city council candidates corresponds closely to the presence of businesses in communities. Because businesses tend to support incumbents (and most wards had one), and because most contributions to city council campaigns are from within wards, there is less variation in business contributions across the city than in levels of individual contributions. The most distinctive aspect of figure 6.2 is the concentration of business contributions in the West and Northwest Sides of the city and the relative lack of business contributions on the South Side. Zip code 60610 on the Near North Side had the highest level of

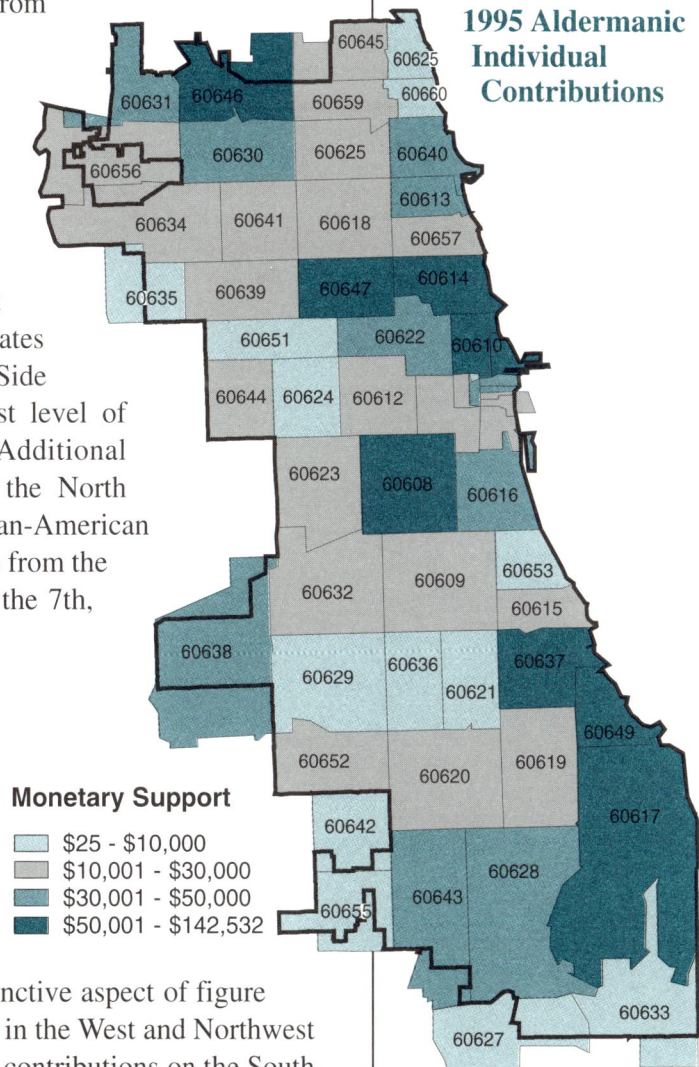

Figure 6.1

1995 Aldermanic Individual Contributions

Monetary Support

- $25 - $10,000
- $10,001 - $30,000
- $30,001 - $50,000
- $50,001 - $142,532

Financing Chicago Elections

Aldermanic Contributions

Figure 6.2

1995 Aldermanic Business Contributions

contributions to city council campaigns, $109,072. The relative lack of businesses located in neighborhoods with high concentrations of African Americans represents a significant barrier to fundraising for black candidates.

Figures 6.3 and 6.4 map the pattern of contributions to the mayor's reelection campaign. Perhaps most striking in the map of individual contributions is the broad base of financial support the mayor garnered across the city. The mayor received particularly high levels of support from individuals living in the high income Near North Side, such as zip code 60610 which generated over $197,000, but the mayor also received significant contributions from areas located on the Northwest, North Lakefront, and South Sides of the city. Zip codes yielding the largest volume of business contributions to the mayor were downtown, in the Near North and Near West parts of the city. The mayor also received sizeable contributions from businesses in industrial zones extending through the Southwest parts of the city.

Notes

[1] Campaign finance data for this chapter were accumulated from reports filed by candidates with the State Board of Elections. Candidate filings include the source of contributions, the contributor's address, date of contribution, and the contribution amount. Data analyzed here include itemized contributions to candidates exceeding $150. (Candidates are not required to report contributions under $150.) Data analyzed here are from candidate filings covering the period July 1, 1994, through June 30, 1995. Comprehensive analysis of contributions to candidates for the 1995 election can be found in *The Price of Democracy: Financing Chicago's 1995 City Elections* by Anthony Gierzynski, Paul Kleppner, and James Lewis, published by the Chicago Urban League and the Office for Social Policy Research, Northern Illinois University.

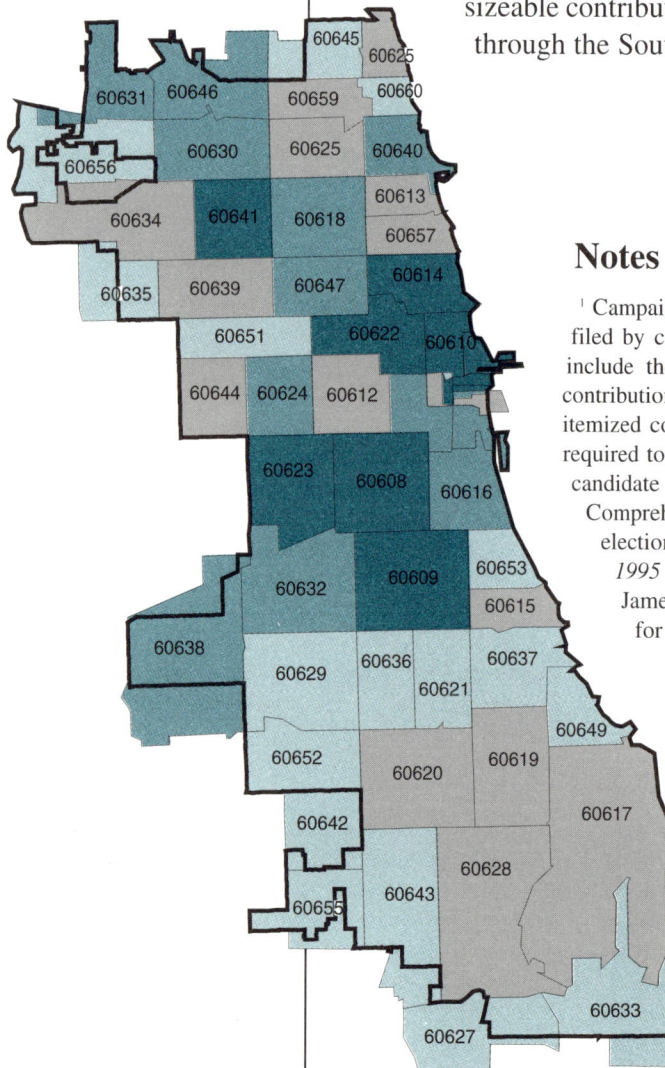

Monetary Support
- $0 - $10,000
- $10,001 - $30,000
- $30,001 - $50,000
- $50,001 - $109,072

Figure 6.3

**1995 Mayoral
Individual Contributions**

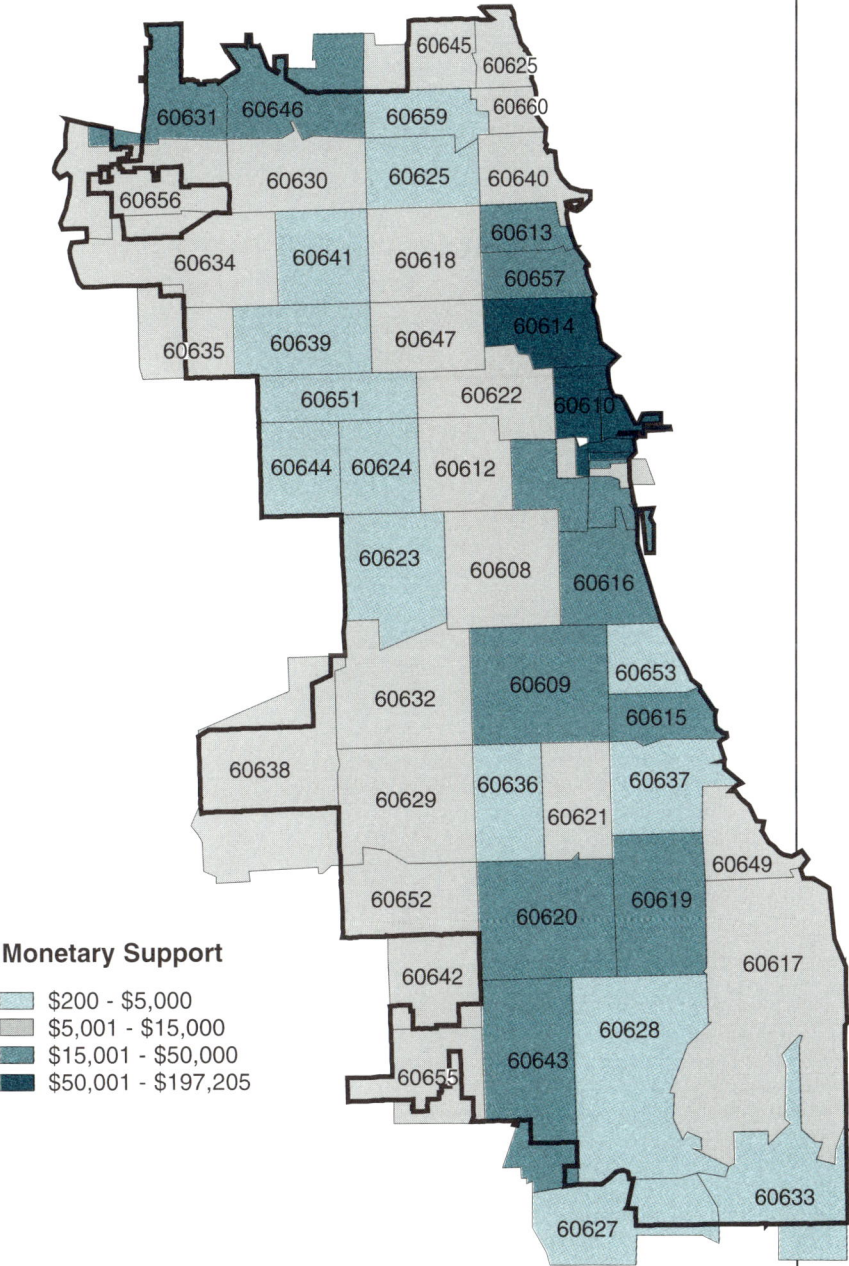

60645
60625
60631 60646 60659 60660
60630 60625 60640
60656
60613
60634 60641 60618 60657
60614
60635 60639 60647
60610
60651 60622
60644 60624 60612
60623 60608 60616
60609 60653
60632 60615
60638 60636 60637
60629 60621
60652 60649
60620 60619
60642 60617
60628
60655 60643
60633
60627

Monetary Support

- $200 - $5,000
- $5,001 - $15,000
- $15,001 - $50,000
- $50,001 - $197,205

Financing Chicago Elections

Mayoral Contributions

Figure 6.4

1995 Mayoral Business Contributions

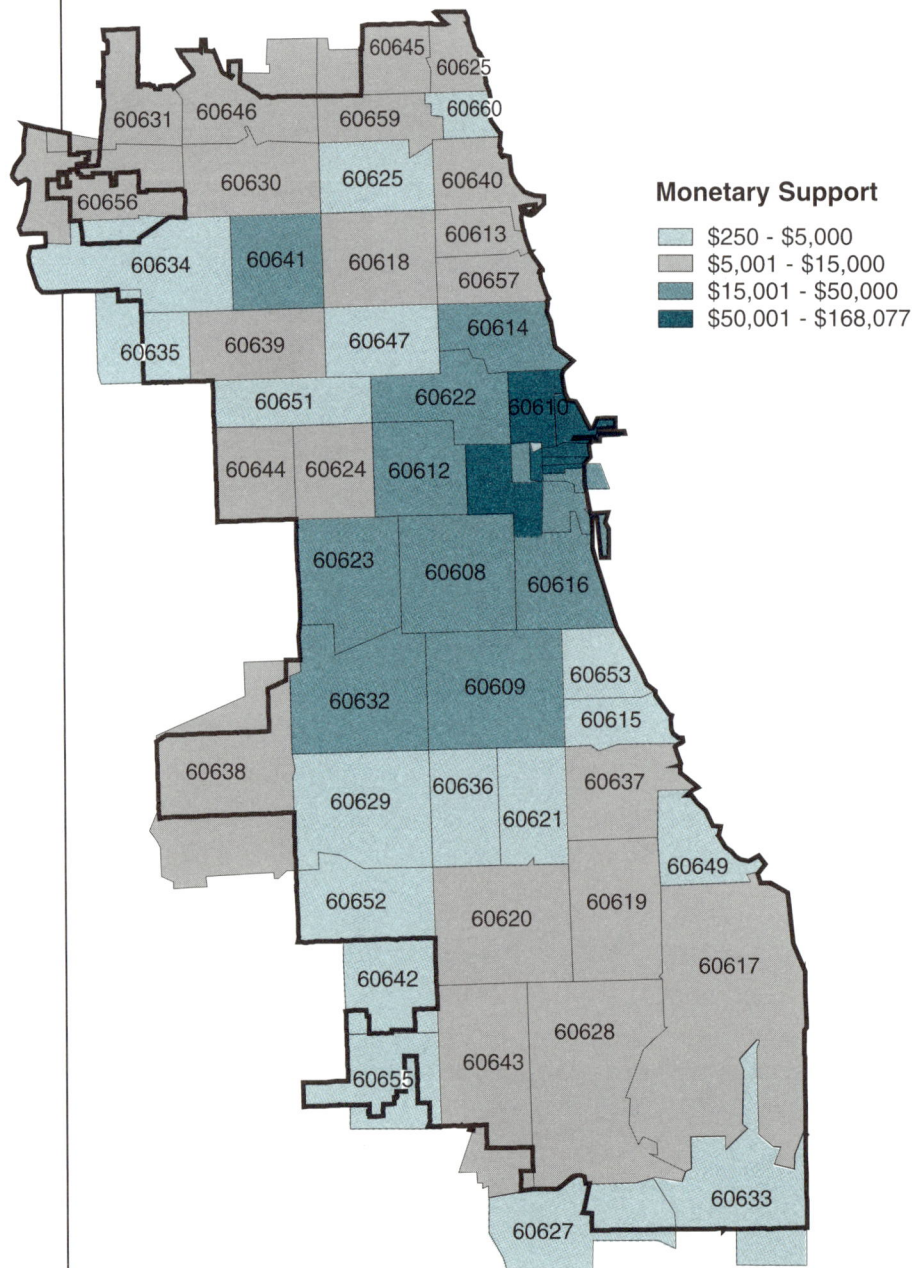

Monetary Support

- $250 - $5,000
- $5,001 - $15,000
- $15,001 - $50,000
- $50,001 - $168,077

60645
60625
60631
60646
60659
60660
60656
60630
60625
60640
60613
60634
60641
60618
60657
60635
60639
60647
60614
60651
60622
60610
60644
60624
60612
60623
60608
60616
60632
60609
60653
60615
60638
60629
60636
60637
60621
60649
60652
60620
60619
60617
60642
60628
60655
60643
60633
60627

Chapter 7: Partisan Alignments in the Illinois State Legislature

Partisan Alignments in the Illinois State Legislature

According to Article IV, Section 3 of the 1970 Constitution of the State of Illinois, in the year following the taking of a new U.S. census, the General Assembly must redraw the legislative district maps in order to ensure that the population of legislative districts remains equal. Redrawing these legislative boundary lines affords members of the General Assembly the opportunity to manipulate the shape of districts so as to maximize opportunities for either Democratic or Republican candidates to win elections. Although it is impossible to predict the outcomes of elections in some districts, each of the political parties spends hundreds of thousands of dollars following the census in an attempt to ensure that they are able to draw a map that is most likely to produce electoral outcomes favorable to them.

Every 10 years, in the legislative session following a new census Democrats and Republicans draw their maps and work to pass them through the legislature. The goal is to get a plan to the governor's desk for his signature. If one party were able to control both houses of the General Assembly and the governor's office in a redistricting year, a new legislative map would sail through the process unscathed, and the party in control, in theory anyway, would set itself up to retain control of the General Assembly for a decade.

In 1991, Democrats controlled both chambers of the Illinois legislature, but the governor was Republican. The Democrats' map passed the General Assembly, but it was vetoed by the governor. In this case, the state constitution calls for the formation of an eight-member Legislative Redistricting Commission, no more than four of whose members can be of the same political party. When this commission predictably failed to agree on a single map in 1991, a ninth commission member was randomly selected from the names of one Democrat and one Republican submitted to the secretary of state, also a procedure prescribed by the constitution. In September, 1991, Republican Al Jourdan's name was drawn as the ninth member. His vote provided a 5 to 4 majority for adoption of the Republican map proposal.

Partisan Alignments in the Illinois State Legislature

Partisan Alignments in the Illinois House of Representatives in the 1990s

With the new map in place, Republicans were expected to win majorities in both houses of the legislature in the 1992 elections. They did win in the state senate, but were unable to win a majority in the lower house. In the Illinois House elections in 1992, a surprising number of Democratic incumbents held onto their seats, in many cases in reconfigured districts now encompassing territory many Democratic legislators would not, themselves, have chosen to represent. The poor showings of President Bush and Richard Williamson, the Republican candidate in the U.S. Senate race, provided no coattails for lower-ballot Republican candidates and may have depressed Republican turnout, which dragged some Republican candidates to defeat. Two years later, Republicans won control of both chambers of the legislature in their historic 1994 landslide. In 1996, Republicans retained control of the state senate but were unable to keep control of the state house as local officeholders were again hitched to weak Republican presidential and senate candidates, and appeared in some areas of the state to be unresponsive to popular demands for greater state financial support for local schools.

Democrats began the 1990 census and redistricting cycle with what appeared to be a nearly impregnable majority in the Illinois House of Representatives: a margin of 72 Democrats to 46 Republicans. This margin had been sustained in large part by the legislative map drawn a decade before that maximized opportunities for the election of Democrats to the state legislature.

The Republican-leaning 1991 legislative map was supposed to maximize the opportunity for Republican candidates to win state legislative seats. The map finally passed by the Legislative Redistricting Commission used conventional legislative redistricting principles—such as packing Democratic voters into a few districts, placing Democratic incumbents into the same district thereby forcing them to run against one another, and splitting urban bastions of Democratic support—to give the Republicans an advantage. Republicans also benefitted from substantial population gains in the Chicago suburbs and a corresponding loss of population in heavily Democratic Chicago.

Analysis of the underlying party affiliation of voters in the new districts appeared in 1991 to confirm that the mapmakers had accomplished their aims. Analyzing the results of elections for trustees of the University of Illinois has long been an established means of assessing the underlying partisanship of a district. Because candidates for University of Illinois trustee are at the bottom of the ballot, are relatively unknown to most voters, and are generally not popularly associated with divisive issues, it is believed, and has been accepted by courts, that the vote for these offices tends to represent the underlying partisanship of voters.

Table 7.1

Democratic, Republican, and Swing Districts of the Illinois House of Representatives as Predicted by the 1990 Election of University of Illinois Trustees

	Percent the 1990 University of Illinois Trustee Election Index Indicated as Democrat	Number
Republican Districts	< 20%	0
	20% to 30%	4
	30% to 40%	25
	40% to 45%	20
Swing Districts	45% to 50%	15
	50% to 55%	5
Democratic Districts	55% to 60%	13
	60% to 65%	9
	65% to 70%	5
	70% to 80%	7
	> 80%	15

As table 7.1 shows, analysis of the 1990 trustee election results for the 1990 elections revealed a map that could swing to either Democrats or Republicans. Forty-nine districts appeared to be strongly Democrat, 49 appeared to be strongly Republican, and 20 could swing either way. Figures 7.1a and 7.1b at the end of this chapter show the anticipated partisan representation of the Illinois House districts based on the 1990 trustee index.

Next, we'll examine the 1992, 1994, and 1996 Illinois House races in more detail to show whether the outcomes of these elections indeed favored the Republicans, as their research and mapmaking predicted they would. Then, we'll examine the 1992, 1994, and 1996 Illinois Senate races to see if they bear out a predicted Republican advantage.

The 1992 Illinois House Elections

With the adoption of their map, Republicans were expected to make substantial inroads into the then-existing Democratic majority. How deep those inroads would be was subject to outcomes of elections in the "swing" districts. It was, therefore, something of a surprise that Republicans gained only five seats in the 1992 election, the first held under the new map.

Partisan Alignments in the Illinois State Legislature

In understanding the outcome of the 1992 election, and future outcomes of Illinois legislative elections, it is important to recognize two key factors. First, the party of many of the legislators who won in 1992 deviated from the partisanship of the legislator's district as projected from the 1990 trustee votes. Second, the partisanship of several districts as indicated by trustee votes appeared to shift toward the Democrats between 1990 and 1992.

Analysis shows, however, that the 1992 Democratic majority was living on borrowed time. According to the 1990 trustee projections used to assess the likely partisan results of the 1992 election, 19 districts deviated from expected partisanship in the 1992 election (see table 7.2). In 17 of these,

Table 7.2

1992 "Surprise" Winners in the Illinois House and the Shifting Partisanship of Districts as Indicated by Election of University of Illinois Trustees

Dist.	1990 Partisanship as Indicated by Trustee Election	1992 Partisanship as Indicated by Trustee Election	1992 Illinois House Election Party (Winner)
11	54% Republican	57% Democrat	Democrat (Erwin)
13	57% Republican	51% Republican	Democrat (Capparelli)
35	61% Republican	56% Republican	Democrat (Steczo)
37	61% Republican	54% Republican	Democrat (Sheehy)
47	55% Republican	50% Democrat	Democrat (McAfee)
58	65% Republican	51% Republican	Democrat (Schoenberg)
60	58% Republican	51% Republican	Democrat (Gash)
68	59% Republican	59% Republican	Democrat (Giolitto)
69	52% Republican	53% Republican	Democrat (Rotello)
73	53% Republican	51% Republican	Democrat (Wessels)
80	58% Republican	54% Democrat	Democrat (Ostenburg)
85	51% Republican	52% Democrat	Democrat (Novak)
95	52% Republican	52% Republican	Democrat (Edley)
97	52% Democrat	52% Democrat	Republican (Ryder)
99	54% Republican	55% Republican	Democrat (Moseley)
100	53% Republican	51% Republican	Democrat (Curran)
102	50% Republican	51% Republican	Republican (Noland)
103	59% Republican	57% Republican	Democrat (Prussing)
110	52% Democrat	50% Democrat	Republican (Stephens)

Democrats won elections they might have lost and in only 2 districts did Republicans win unexpectedly. In many instances, the deviation was marginal in that these were swing districts where trustee data indicated only a slim Republican majority. However, in a number of districts, the trustee count shifted toward the Democrats between the 1990 and 1992 elections.

The 1994 Illinois House Elections

The 1994 elections resulted in a partisan upheaval in the Illinois House of Representatives of historic proportions. The Democrats' 67 to 51 advantage was erased and Republicans emerged with a 63 to 55 advantage. This sweep by Republicans in Illinois partially reflected the Republican victories nationwide that delivered the U.S. House of Representatives to them for the first time since 1954. The Republican electoral victory in Illinois brought the partisan identification of state legislators into alignment with the partisan underpinnings of the 1991 state legislative map.

The 1994 elections aligned the partisanship of a number of state representatives to the trustee partisanship that would have been predicted based on the 1990 and 1992 trustee counts. Of the 19 district partisan deviations that had occurred in 1992, 11 were corrected in the 1994 election. In each of these 11 instances, a Republican took a seat held by a Democrat in 1992.

Additional seats changed parties when, in the 115th District, Republican Mike Bost won in a strong Democratic southern Illinois district, Republican John Jones scored an upset in the Democratic 107th, and Republican Flora Ciarlo won in the 80th, which had gone from a Republican seat (48 percent Democrat according to the 1990 trustee index) to a Democratic seat (54 percent Democrat according to the 1992 trustee index).

Only in the 13th (Capparelli-D), 58th (Schoenberg-D), 60th (Gash-D), 97th (Ryder-R), and 110th (Stephens-R) districts did the partisanship of the representative deviate from both the 1990 and 1992 projections. In each of these cases, the deviation was by two percent or less, indicating a swing district. In each case, the winner was an incumbent legislator.

The 1996 Illinois House Elections

In 1996 partisan control of the lower house reversed again, with Democrats attaining a majority by two, 60 seats to 58 seats. This narrow advantage was the result of Democrats retaking six districts carried by Republicans in 1994. Five of these six districts had Republican University of Illinois trustee majorities in 1990 and 1992.

Democrats scored upsets in districts 35, 36, 37, and 79, south of Chicago where Crotty, Brosnahan, McCarthy, and Giglio each won in districts

Partisan Alignments in the Illinois State Legislature

projected Republican by the 1990 and 1992 University of Illinois trustee indicator. In district 80, Democrat George Scully defeated Republican Ciarlo in a district that had shifted from Republican to Democrat from 1990 to 1992. In district 75, Democrat Mary O'Brien won in a projected Republican district (47 percent Republican according to the 1992 trustee indicator).

With the completion of the 1996 elections, legislative partisanship of 15 districts deviates from the 1990 projections based on University of Illinois trustee data from 1990. In 5 of these districts, Republicans hold seats in ostensibly Democratic districts, while in 10 districts the reverse is true (see table 7.3). Figures 7.2a and 7.2b at the end of this chapter show the partisan representation of the Illinois House after the 1996 election.

Table 7.3

1996 Illinois House Districts Whose Legislative Partisanship Deviates from the Projections Based on the 1990 University of Illinois Trustee Data

Dist.	Representative	Party	1990 Projected Percentage of Partisan Support (Based on Trustee Elections)	
11	Erwin	Democrat	53.6%	Republican
13	Capparelli	Democrat	57.1%	Republican
35	Crotty	Democrat	61.3%	Republican
36	Brosnahan	Democrat	55.3%	Republican
37	McCarthy	Democrat	61.4%	Republican
58	Schoenberg	Democrat	64.6%	Republican
60	Gash	Democrat	57.7%	Republican
75	O'Brien	Democrat	52.9%	Republican
79	Giglio	Democrat	61.8%	Republican
85	Novak	Democrat	51.0%	Republican
97	Ryder	Republican	51.9%	Democrat
102	Noland	Republican	50.4%	Democrat
107	Jones	Republican	55.9%	Democrat
110	Stephens	Republican	51.5%	Democrat
115	Bost	Republican	59.5%	Democrat

Partisan Predictability of Illinois House Races in the 1990s

As this data and analyses of the house races show, the partisan outcomes of legislative districts can be predicted accurately, but not perfectly. Of the 118 lower house districts, the 1990 University of Illinois trustee data correctly predicted the party of the winning state legislator 103 times, including those districts that might properly be classified as swing districts (where each party was close to 50 percent of the voters' support). Of the 15 districts that, as of 1996, continue to deviate, five had partisan trustee majorities in 1990 of 52.9 percent or less. Of the remaining 10 districts, discrepancies between predictions and actual election results can be accounted for in a variety of ways.

- Although the 11th District was ostensibly Republican in 1990, it is located in the heart of downtown Chicago and Republican affiliation can be misleading in local elections where grassroots Democratic organizations remain strong.

- In the 58th District, on Cook County's north lakefront, incumbent Democrat Jeff Schoenberg has adopted moderate positions, making himself acceptable to moderate Republicans who have presented only token opposition in three elections.

- In several districts, the 1990 Republican strength has clearly eroded during the 1990s. In districts 35, 36, 37, and 79, concern over financing public schools has created an environment enabling Democrats to be elected to the state legislature in districts where large numbers of voters regularly support Republicans.

Partisan Alignments in the Illinois Senate in the 1990s

Analysis of the 1990 University of Illinois trustee election results revealed that the 1991 redistricted map was drawn to almost certainly deliver a Republican majority in the upper chamber. As table 7.4 shows, 26 districts appeared to be strongly Republican, 22 appeared to be strongly Democrat, and 11 were swing districts. To gain a majority of 30 senate seats, Republicans needed to win only 4 of the 11 swing districts.

Partisan Alignments in the Illinois State Legislature

Table 7.4

Democratic, Republican, and Swing Districts of the Illinois Senate as Predicted by the 1990 Election of University of Illinois Trustees

	Percent the 1990 University of Illinois Trustee Election Index Indicated as Democrat	Number
Republican Districts	< 20%	0
	20% to 30%	1
	30% to 40%	11
	40% to 45%	14
Swing Districts	45% to 50%	5
	50% to 55%	6
Democratic Districts	55% to 60%	5
	60% to 65%	4
	65% to 70%	1
	70% to 80%	7
	> 80%	5

Partisan Alignments in the Illinois State Legislature

Figures 7.3a and 7.3b at the end of this chapter show the anticipated partisan representation of the districts based on the 1990 trustee index.

The 1992 Illinois Senate Elections

The 1991 legislative map quickly delivered a majority to Republicans in the Illinois Senate that they have not as yet relinquished. Entering the 1992 elections, Democrats enjoyed a 31 to 28 advantage in the Illinois Senate. The Republicans achieved a net gain of 4 seats in the election to hold a majority of 32 to 27.

The 1990 trustee data was remarkably accurate in projecting outcomes of the 1992 elections. In only 3 instances out of 59 did the outcome of the senate race differ from what would have been expected on the basis of the 1990 trustee data. In district 58, incumbent Republican Ralph Dunn retained his seat despite running in a district with a 55.8 percent Democratic trustee count. In district 55, incumbent Republican Frank Watson retained his seat in a swing district with a 53.5 percent Democrat trustee count. In district 29, Grace Mary Stern upset incumbent Republican Roger Keats in a district projected to be strongly Republican (66 percent Republican according to the 1990 trustee index).

The 1994 Illinois Senate Elections

The 1994 election provided little change in the Illinois Senate. In only one case, the 29th District north of Chicago, did a seat change partisan hands as Republican Kathleen Parker upset incumbent Democrat Grace Mary Stern in what is ordinarily a strongly Republican region. This increased the Republican majority in the Illinois Senate to 32 to 27, and left only 2 districts deviating from projections based on 1990 trustee data.

The 1996 Illinois Senate Elections

The 1996 election resulted in Democrats regaining two senate seats. In the 30th District, Democrat Terry Link won an open seat after the retirement of long-time incumbent Republican David Barkhausen in a district that trustee data suggested had become increasingly—although not overwhelmingly—Democratic. In the 40th District, Democrat Debbie Halvorson defeated long-time incumbent Republican Aldo DeAngelis. Trustee data indicated that the district had moved from a strong Republican district in 1990 to a swing Democratic district by 1992. Democrats defeated Republicans in two component legislative districts, 79 and 80, in the 1996 election. Following the 1996 elections, Republicans retained a majority of 31 to 28. Figures 7.4a and 7.4b show the partisan representation of the Illinois Senate districts after the 1996 election.

Figure 7.1a

Anticipated Partisan Alignment of Illinois House Districts —1991

(Based on Board of Trustees Data)

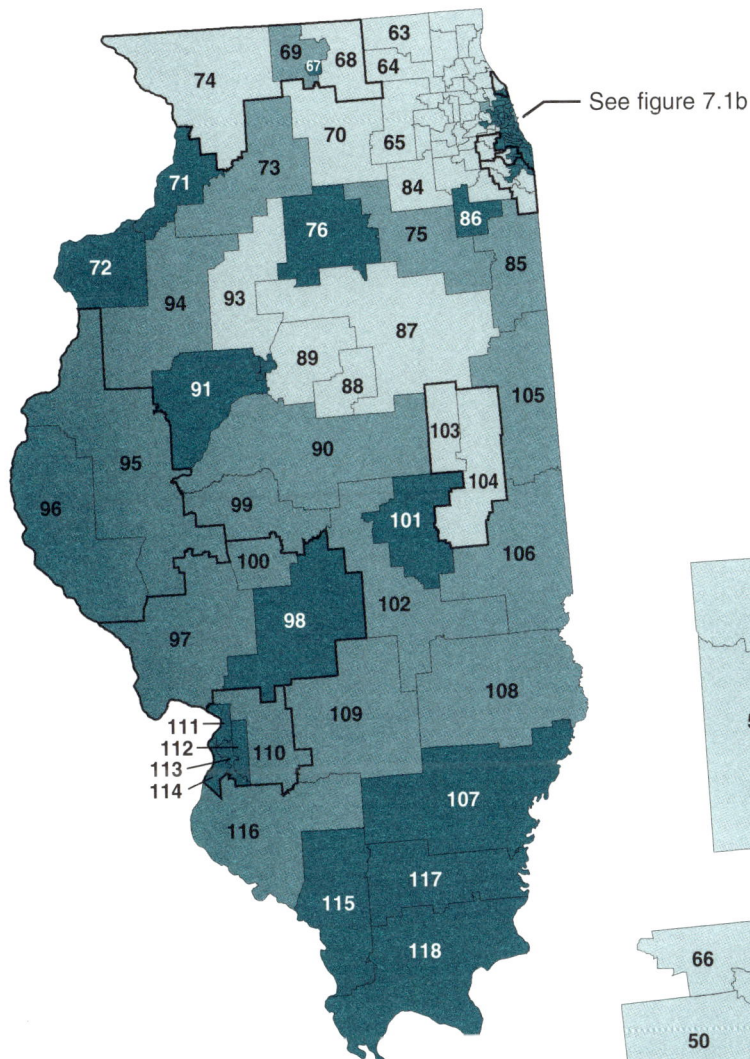

See figure 7.1b

Figure 7.1b

Anticipated Partisan Alignment of Illinois House Districts — 1991

(continued)

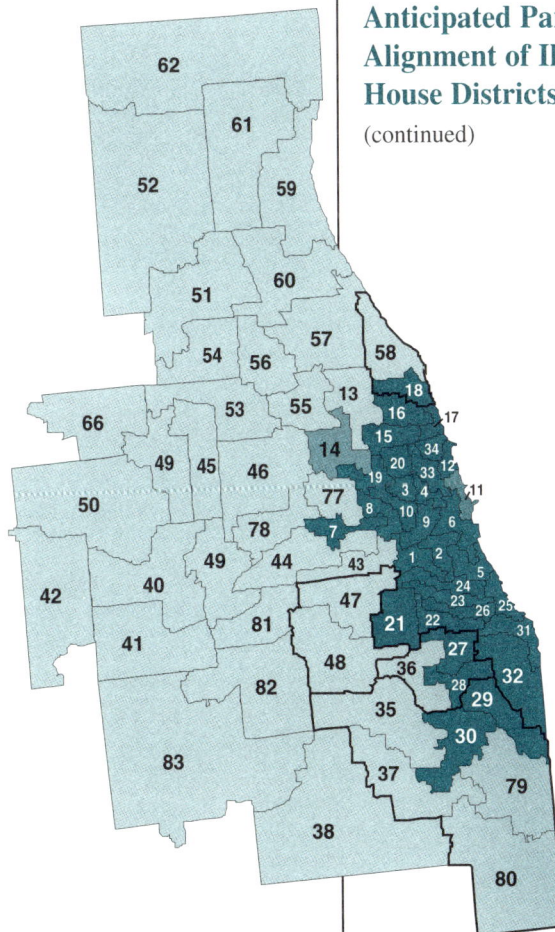

Democrats Per District

0% - 45%	Republican District
45.01% - 55%	Swing District
55.01% - 100%	Democrat District

Partisan Alignments in the Illinois State Legislature

Illinois House Districts

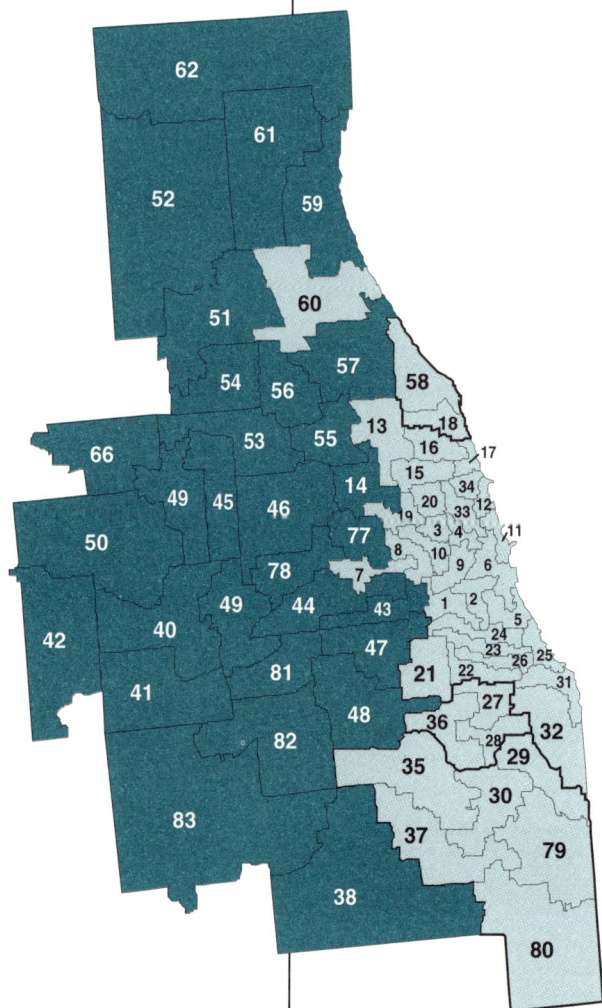

Figure 7.2a

Actual Partisan Representation of Illinois House Districts — 1996

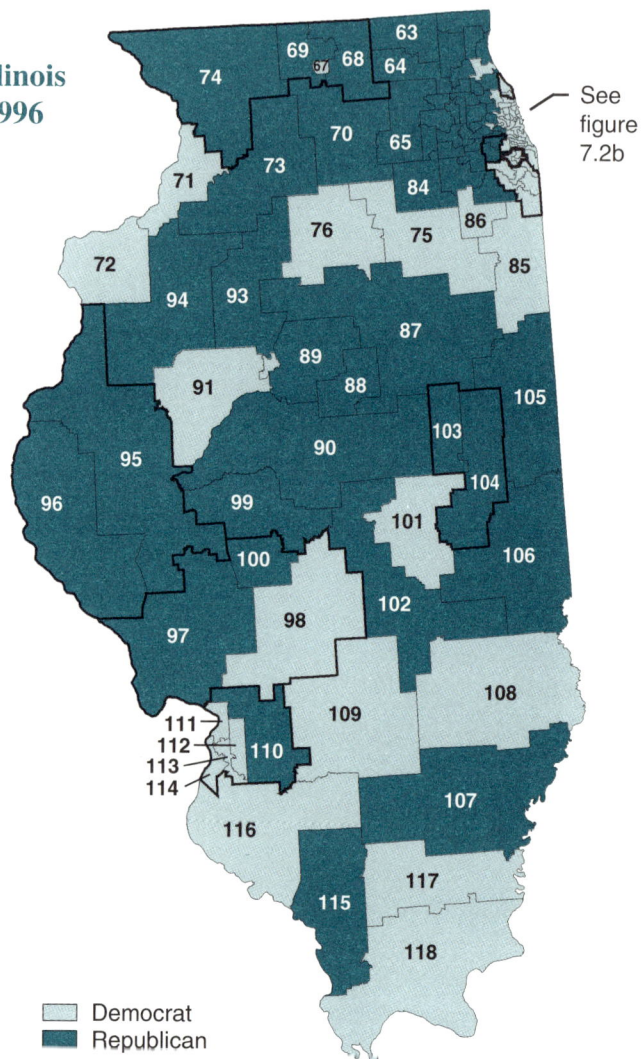

Democrat
Republican

See figure 7.2b

Figure 7.2b

Actual Partisan Representation of Illinois House Districts — 1996

(continued)

Figure 7.3a

Anticipated Partisan Alignment of Illinois Senate Districts — 1991

(Based on Board of Trustees Data)

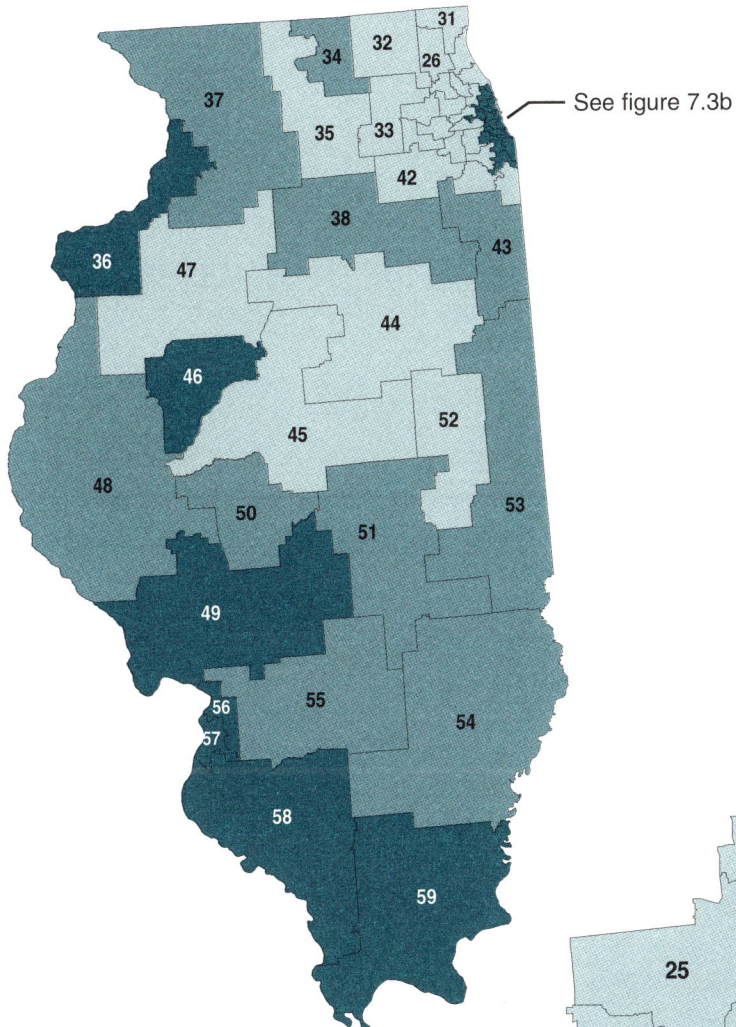

See figure 7.3b

Figure 7.3b

Anticipated Partisan Alignment of Illinois Senate Districts — 1991

(continued)

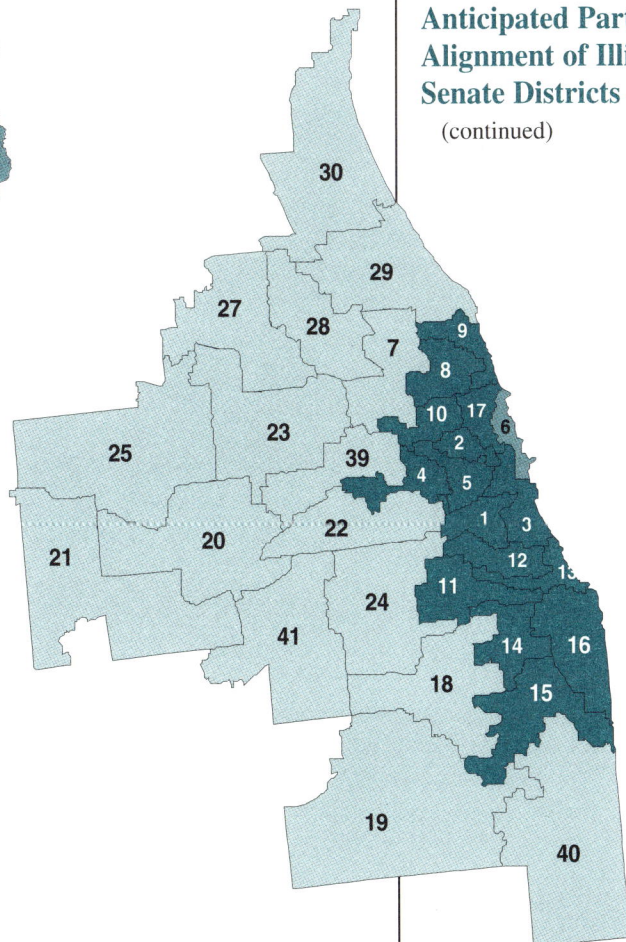

Democrats Per District

0% - 45%	Republican District
45.01% - 55%	Swing District
55.01% - 100%	Democrat District

Partisan Alignments in the Illinois State Legislature

Illinois Senate Districts

Figure 7.4a

Actual Partisan Representation of Illinois Senate Districts — 1996

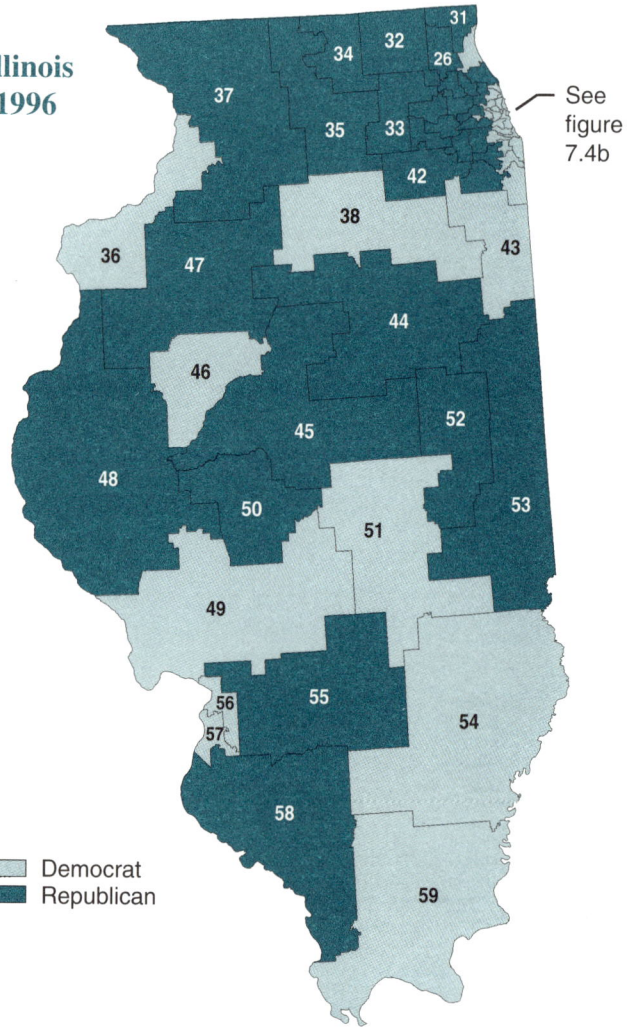

Democrat
Republican

Figure 7.4b

Actual Partisan Representation of Illinois Senate Districts — 1996

(continued)

About the Authors

Paul Kleppner is Director of the Office for Social Policy Research at Northern Illinois University in DeKalb. He holds a PhD in Recent U.S. History and Political Sociology with a concentration on electoral behavior and statistical methodology from the University of Pittsburgh. He has written five books and numerous articles dealing with voting behavior, especially the behavior of ethnic, religious, and racial groups.

James H. Lewis is Vice President of Research and Planning at the Chicago Urban League. He holds a PhD in American History from Northwestern University. Lewis served as a participant in the legislative remap process—city, county, and federal. He is co-author of *The Price of Democracy: Financing Chicago's 1995 City Elections* (1996).

D. Garth Taylor is Executive Director of the Metro Chicago Information Center. For the past 25 years he has been a researcher, writer, pollster, commentator, and occasional practitioner in Chicago politics. He is a master of state-of-the-art techniques for analyzing and presenting information about elections. Taylor is the author of award-winning research on politics and urban life.